PATHWAYS

Reading, Writing, and Critical Thinking 1

Mari Vargo Laurie Blass

Australia • Brazil • Japan • Korea • Mexico • Singapore • Spain • United Kingdom • United States

Pathways 1
Reading, Writing, and Critical Thinking
Mari Vargo and Laurie Blass

Publisher: Andrew Robinson

Executive Editor: Sean Bermingham

Senior Development Editor: Bill Preston

Assistant Editor: Vivian Chua

Contributing Editors: Sylvia Bloch,
  Ingrid Wisniewska

Director of Global Marketing: Ian Martin

Marketing Manager: Emily Stewart

Director of Content and Media Production:
  Michael Burggren

Senior Content Project Manager: Daisy Sosa

Manufacturing Buyer: Marybeth Hennebury

Associate Manager, Operations:
  Leila Hishmeh

Cover Design: Page 2 LLC

Cover Image: Julien Gille/iStockphoto

Interior Design: Page 2, LLC

Composition: Page 2, LLC

© 2013 National Geographic Learning, a part of Cengage Learning

ALL RIGHTS RESERVED. No part of this work covered by the copyright herein may be reproduced, transmitted, stored or used in any form or by any means graphic, electronic, or mechanical, including but not limited to photocopying, recording, scanning, digitizing, taping, Web distribution, information networks, or information storage and retrieval systems, except as permitted under Section 107 or 108 of the 1976 United States Copyright Act, without the prior written permission of the publisher.

> For permission to use material from this text or product,
> submit all requests online at **cengage.com/permissions**
> Further permissions questions can be emailed to
> **permissionrequest@cengage.com**

International Student Edition:

ISBN-13: 978-1-133-31286-4

ISBN-10: 1-133-31286-1

U.S. Edition:

ISBN-13: 978-1-133-31711-1

ISBN: 1-133-31711-1

National Geographic Learning
20 Channel Center Street
Boston, MA 02210
USA

Cengage Learning is a leading provider of customized learning solutions with office locations around the globe, including Singapore, the United Kingdom, Australia, Mexico, Brazil, and Japan. Locate your local office at:
ngl.cengage.com

Cengage Learning products are represented in Canada by Nelson Education, Ltd.

Visit National Geographic Learning online at **ngl.cengage.com**

Visit our corporate website at **www.cengage.com**

Printed in the United States of America
1 2 3 4 5 6 7 8 15 14 13 12

Contents

	Scope and Sequence	vi
	Explore a Unit	x
1	Life in a Day	1
2	Learning Experiences	21
3	Family Ties	41
4	The Trouble with Trash	61
5	The World in Our Kitchen	81
6	Future Living	101
7	Exploration and Discovery	121
8	Musicians with a Message	141
9	Behavior	161
10	The Power of Image	181
	Video Scripts	203
	Independent Student Handbook	209
	Vocabulary and Skills Index	218

PLACES TO EXPLORE IN

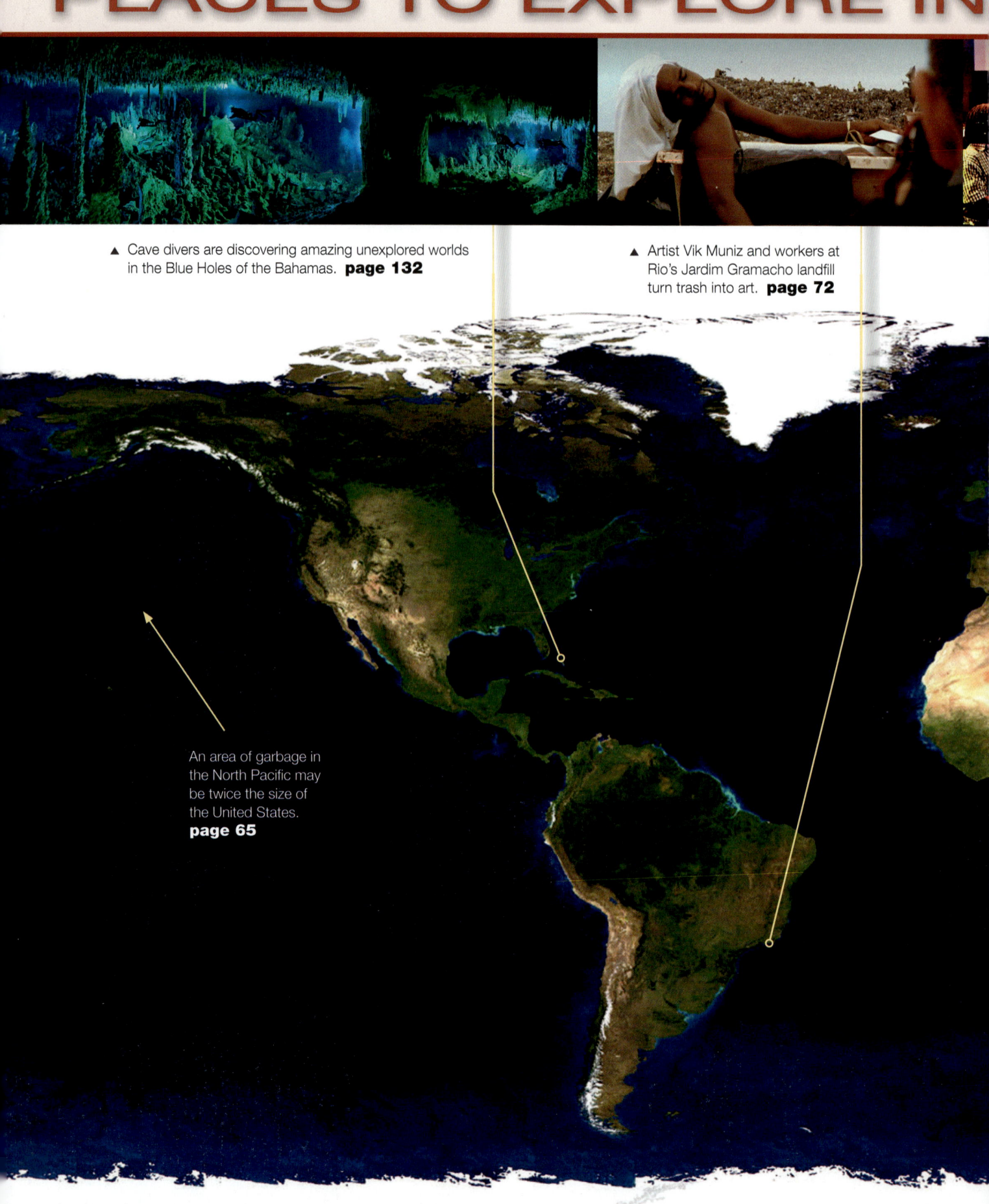

▲ Cave divers are discovering amazing unexplored worlds in the Blue Holes of the Bahamas. **page 132**

▲ Artist Vik Muniz and workers at Rio's Jardim Gramacho landfill turn trash into art. **page 72**

An area of garbage in the North Pacific may be twice the size of the United States. **page 65**

PATHWAYS

▲ An unusual group of musicians from the Congo are taking street music to the world. **page 145**

▲ In Mongolia, mobile "tent schools" make education available to everyone. **page 33**

▲ Will humans one day leave our planet to live on Mars? **page 112**

The world's smallest primate is found only in the jungles of Madagascar. **page 129**

Scope and Sequence

Unit	Academic Pathways	Vocabulary
 **1** **Life in a Day** Page 1 **Academic Track:** Interdisciplinary	**Lesson A:** Skimming for gist / Guessing meaning from context **Lesson B:** Reading interviews **Lesson C:** Understanding the writing process / Writing sentences about a single topic	Understanding meaning from context / Matching words with definitions / Applying vocabulary in a personalized context **Word Link:** word forms, *un-* **Word Partners:** *schedule*
 **2** **Learning Experiences** Page 21 **Academic Track:** Sociology/Education	**Lesson A:** Understanding the main ideas of paragraphs / Making inferences **Lesson B:** Understanding news reports **Lesson C:** Planning your writing / Writing sentences about goals	Understanding meaning from context / Using vocabulary to complete definitions / Applying vocabulary in a personalized context **Word Link:** *-in* **Word Usage:** *record* **Word Partners:** *trip*
 **3** **Family Ties** Page 41 **Academic Track:** History/Anthropology	**Lesson A:** Finding the right meaning / Identifying fact and speculation **Lesson B:** Synthesizing map and textual information **Lesson C:** Expressing speculation / Writing descriptive sentences about family	Understanding meaning from context / Using vocabulary to complete definitions / Applying vocabulary in a personalized context **Word Link:** *migr* **Word Partners:** *common*
 **4** **The Trouble with Trash** Page 61 **Academic Track:** Environmental Science/Sociology	**Lesson A:** Finding supporting ideas / Analyzing causes and effects **Lesson B:** Understanding a multimodal text **Lesson C:** Using details to clarify ideas / Writing sentences to make suggestions	Understanding meaning from context / Applying vocabulary in a personalized context **Word Partners:** *cause, despite*
 **5** **The World in Our Kitchen** Page 81 **Academic Track:** Interdisciplinary	**Lesson A:** Scanning for key details / Reflecting critically **Lesson B:** Identifying pros and cons in a passage **Lesson C:** Using synonyms to avoid repetition / Writing sentences to express an opinion	Understanding meaning from context / Applying vocabulary in a personalized context **Word Partners:** *basic, trend*

Reading	Writing	Viewing	Critical Thinking
Responding to statistics Predicting for main idea Understanding the gist Identifying key details Organizing information in a Venn Diagram **Skill Focus:** Skimming for gist	**Goal:** Writing sentences about daily activities **Grammar:** Simple present of *be* and other verbs **Skill:** Understanding the writing process	**Video:** *BioBlitz: Life in 24 Hours* Viewing for general understanding Viewing for specific information Relating video content to a reading text	Making inferences Analyzing and discussing information Synthesizing information to identify similarities Analyzing stages in a process **CT Focus:** Guessing meaning from context
Interpreting maps Predicting for main idea Scanning for specific information Identifying key details Differentiating main ides from supporting details **Skill Focus:** Understanding the main ideas of paragraphs	**Goal:** Writing sentences about personal goals **Grammar:** Using *want* and *need* **Skill:** Planning your writing	**Video:** *Alex the Parrot* Viewing to confirm predictions Viewing for specific information Relating video content to a reading text	Making inferences Analyzing reasons and motivations Synthesizing information to identify similarities **CT Focus:** Inferring character traits
Responding to texts and photos Scanning to make predictions Understanding the gist Identifying main ideas of paragraphs Identifying key details Identifying facts and speculations **Skill Focus:** Finding the right meaning	**Goal:** Writing descriptive sentences about family **Grammar:** Simple past of *be* and other verbs **Skill:** Speculating	**Video:** *The World in a Station* Viewing for general understanding Viewing for specific information Personalizing video content	Synthesizing information to make a decision Speculating about reasons **CT Focus:** Analyzing fact and speculation
Responding to texts and photos Using titles and visuals to make predictions Understanding the gist Identifying main ideas Scanning for key details Identifying supporting ideas Understanding information in graphs **Skill Focus:** Finding supporting ideas	**Goal:** Writing sentences to make suggestions **Grammar:** Giving advice and making suggestions **Skill:** Using details to clarify ideas	**Video:** *Trash People* Viewing to confirm predictions Viewing for general understanding Viewing for specific information Relating video content to reading texts	Analyzing solutions to problems Analyzing a graph to classify information Synthesizing information from multiple sources Evaluating possible solutions **CT Focus:** Analyzing causes and effects
Interpreting maps and charts Predicting the content of a reading Understanding the gist Identifying main ideas of paragraphs Sequencing steps in a process Identifying advantages and disadvantages **Skill Focus:** Scanning for key details	**Goal:** Writing sentences to express an opinion **Grammar:** Comparative forms of adjectives and nouns **Skill:** Using synonyms to avoid repetition	**Video:** *Earth University* Viewing to confirm predictions Viewing for general understanding Viewing for specific information Personalizing video content	Personalizing content of a reading Evaluating arguments for and against an issue Synthesizing map and textual information **CT Focus:** Reflecting on own preconceptions

Scope and Sequence

	Unit	Academic Pathways	Vocabulary
	**6** **Future Living** Page 101 Academic Track: Science/Sociology	**Lesson A:** Understanding pronoun reference Evaluating a writer's attitude **Lesson B:** Understanding a multimodal text **Lesson C:** Using pronouns to avoid repetition Writing sentences about the future	Understanding meaning from context Applying vocabulary in a personalized context **Word Partners:** *intelligence, plant* **Word Usage:** *average*
	**7** **Exploration and Discovery** Page 121 Academic Track: Interdisciplinary	**Lesson A:** Understanding prefixes Evaluating reasons **Lesson B:** Understanding an explanatory text and infographic **Lesson C:** Linking examples and reasons Writing sentences to give reasons	Understanding meaning from context Using new vocabulary in an everyday context **Word Link:** *re-* **Word Partners:** *follow,* phrasal verbs with *run*
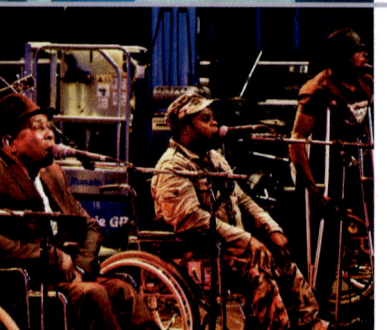	**8** **Musicians with a Message** Page 141 Academic Track: Art/Music	**Lesson A:** Taking notes Understanding idiomatic language **Lesson B:** Reading interviews and profiles **Lesson C:** Presenting one main idea in a paragraph Writing sentences to explain a preference	Understanding meaning from context Applying vocabulary in a personalized context Brainstorming ideas in a word web **Word Link:** *dis-* **Word Partners:** *issue*
	**9** **Behavior** Page 161 Academic Track: Life Science/ Anthropology	**Lesson A:** Recognizing noun clauses Making inferences from an interview **Lesson B:** Reading news articles about science **Lesson C:** Writing a topic sentence Writing a paragraph to compare animals	Understanding meaning from context Using new vocabulary in an everyday context **Word Usage:** *approach* **Word Partners:** *research, field*
	**10** **The Power of Image** Page 181 Academic Track: Interdisciplinary	**Lesson A:** Recognizing subordinating conjunctions Understanding mood **Lesson B:** Reading a personal narrative **Lesson C:** Using supporting ideas in a descriptive paragraph Writing a paragraph to describe a photograph	Understanding meaning from context Using new vocabulary in an everyday context Brainstorming words to describe emotions **Word Link:** *vis* **Word Usage:** *belong* **Word Partners:** *protect*

Reading	Writing	Viewing	Critical Thinking
Using texts and visuals to make predictions Scanning to make predictions Understanding the gist Identifying main ideas of paragraphs Identifying key details Sequencing events in a timeline **Skill Focus:** Understanding pronoun reference	**Goal:** Writing sentences to make predictions **Grammar:** Using *and*, *but*, and *so* **Skill:** Using pronouns to avoid repetition	**Video:** *Colonizing Mars* Viewing to confirm predictions Viewing for general understanding Viewing for specific information Relating video content to a reading text	Inferring and identifying reasons Personalizing information in a reading **CT Focus:** Evaluating a writer's attitude
Interpreting a timeline Using titles and visuals to make predictions Identifying main ideas Identifying key details Sequencing events in a timeline Labeling a diagram **Skill Focus:** Understanding prefixes	**Goal:** Writing sentences to give reasons **Grammar:** Giving reasons with *would like to* + *because* **Skill:** Linking examples and reasons	**Video:** *Madagascar Discovery* Viewing to confirm predictions Viewing for general understanding Viewing for specific information Relating video content to a reading text	Inferring and identifying reasons Personalizing information in a reading **CT Focus:** Evaluating reasons and motivations
Understanding a chronology Scanning to make predictions Understanding the gist Identifying main ideas of sections Identifying key details Using notes to understand key ideas **Skill Focus:** Taking notes	**Goal:** Writing sentences to explain a preference **Grammar:** Giving reasons using *therefore* and *since* **Skill:** Presenting one main idea in a paragraph	**Video:** *World Music* Brainstorming ideas related to the video Viewing for general understanding Viewing for specific information Relating video content to a reading text	Evaluating relative importance of issues Reflecting on language differences and similarities Using notes for a group discussion **CT Focus:** Interpreting idiomatic language
Responding to text and photos Understanding the gist Scanning to identify key details Identifying main ideas Understanding pronoun reference **Skill Focus:** Recognizing noun clauses	**Goal:** Writing a paragraph to make a comparison **Grammar:** Making comparisons **Skill:** Writing a topic sentence	**Video:** *Gorilla Toolmakers* Using prior knowledge Viewing for general understanding Viewing for specific information Relating video content to a reading text	Synthesizing information to make an evaluation Inferring implicit information Inferring a writer's assumptions **CT Focus:** Making inferences
Responding to photos Skimming/Scanning to make predictions Understanding the gist Identifying main ideas of paragraphs Relating key details to visuals Identifying events in a narrative **Skill Focus:** Recognizing subordinating conjunctions	**Goal:** Writing a descriptive paragraph about a photograph **Grammar:** Describing spatial relationships and emotions **Skill:** Using supporting ideas in a descriptive paragraph	**Video:** *Photo Camp* Viewing to confirm predictions Viewing for general understanding Viewing for specific information Analyzing information in a video Relating video content to a reading text	Applying information to a new context Analyzing and discussing reasons Evaluating photographs based on criteria **CT Focus:** Understanding mood

EXPLORE A UNIT

Each unit has three lessons.
Lessons A and B develop academic reading skills and vocabulary by focusing on two aspects of the unit theme. A video section acts as a content bridge between Lessons A and B. The language and content in these sections provide the stimulus for a final writing task (Lesson C).

The **unit theme** focuses on an academic content area relevant to students' lives, such as Sociology and Anthropology, Health Science, Business and Technology, and Environmental Science.

Academic Pathways highlight the main academic skills of each lesson.

Exploring the Theme provides a visual introduction to the unit. Learners are encouraged to think critically and share ideas about the unit topic.

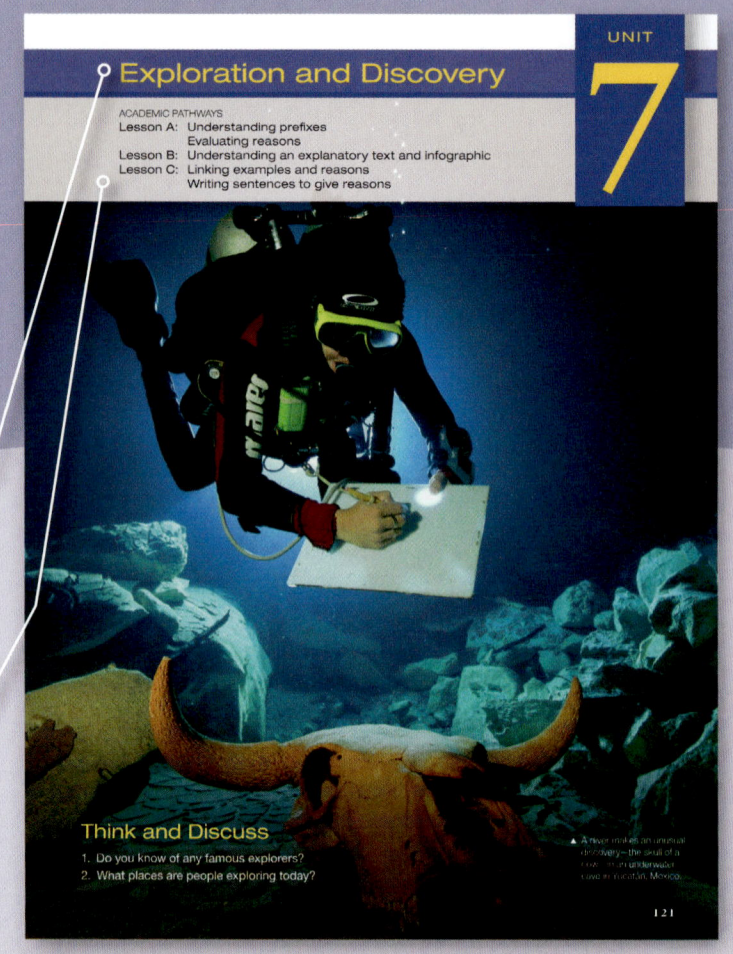

LESSON A

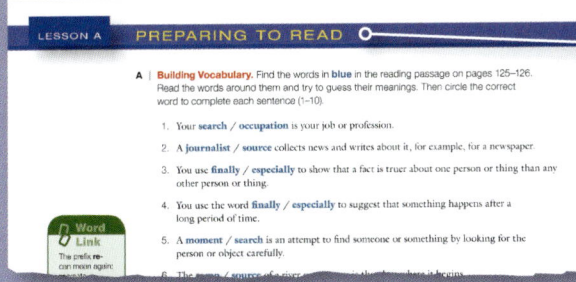

In **Preparing to Read**, learners are introduced to key vocabulary items from the reading passage. Lessons A and B each present and practice 10 target vocabulary items.

Reading A is a single, linear text related to the unit theme. Each reading passage is recorded on the audio program.

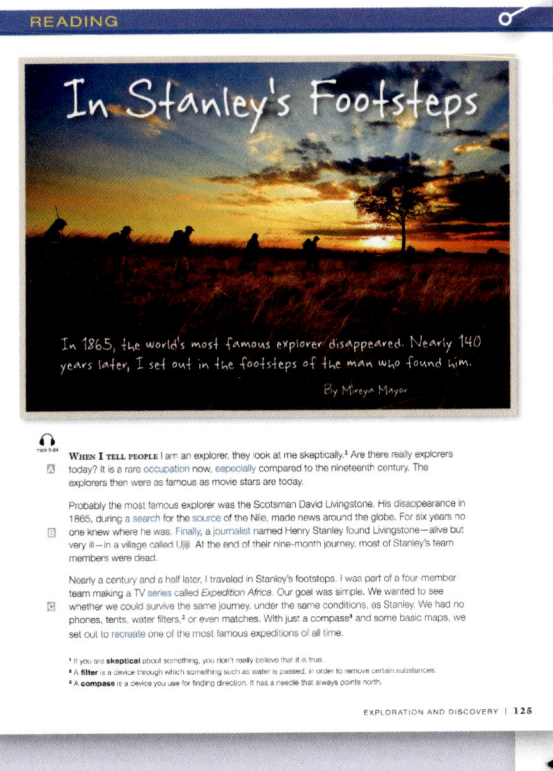

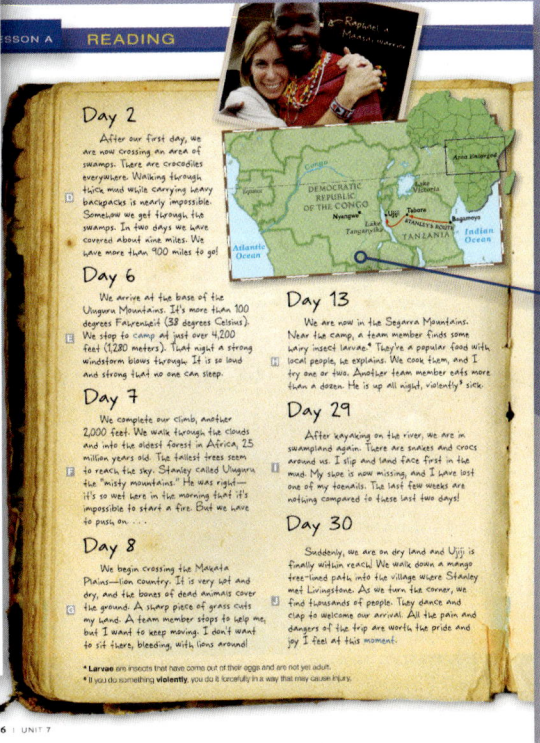

Maps and other graphic formats help to develop learners' visual literacy.

Guided comprehension tasks and reading strategy instruction enable learners to improve their academic literacy and critical thinking skills.

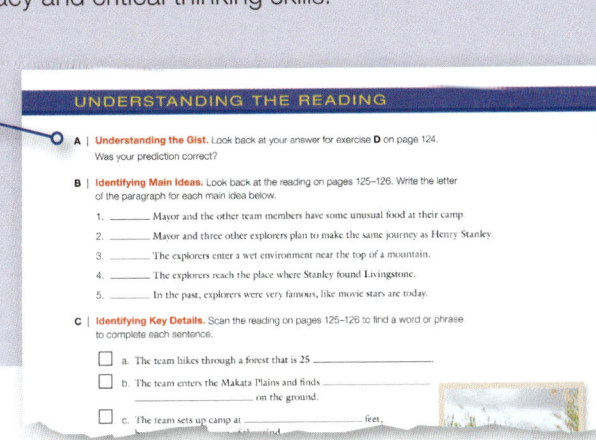

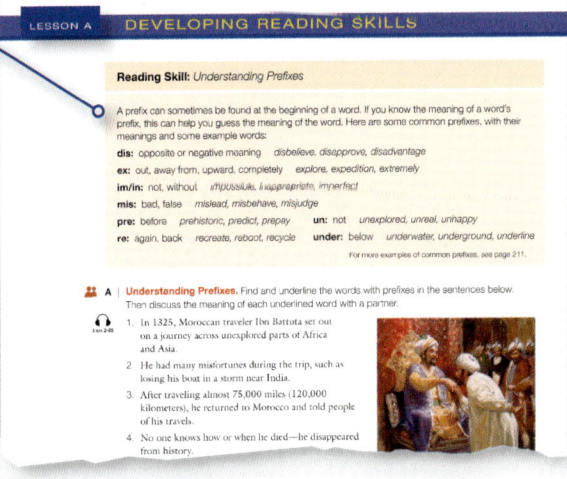

EXPLORE A UNIT

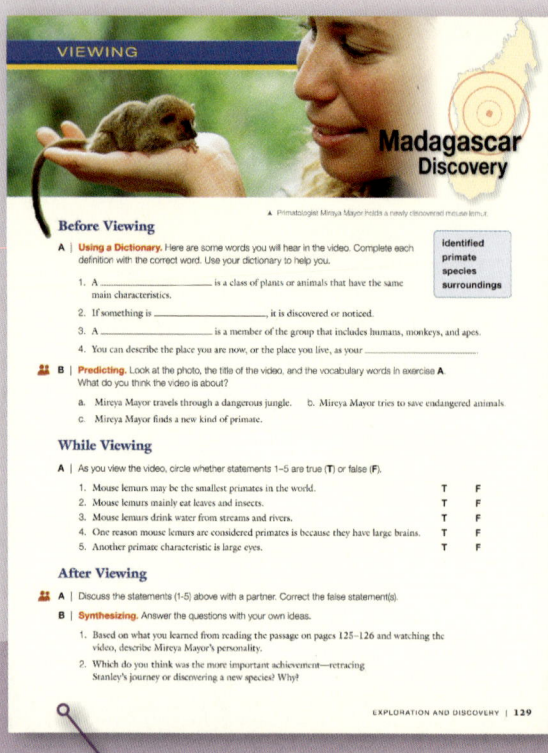

Viewing tasks related to an authentic National Geographic video serve as a content bridge between Lessons A and B. (Video scripts are on pages 203–208.)

Learners need to use their **critical thinking skills** to relate video content to information in the previous reading.

Word Link and **Word Partners** boxes develop learners' awareness of word structure, collocations, and usage.

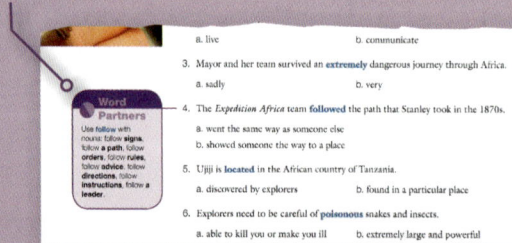

Guided pre-reading tasks and strategy tips encourage learners to think critically about what they are going to read.

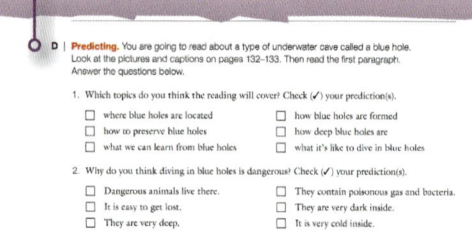

LESSON B

Lesson B's reading passage presents a further aspect of the unit theme, using a variety of text types and graphic formats.

Critical thinking tasks require learners to analyze, synthesize, and critically evaluate ideas and information in each reading.

Authentic charts and graphics from National Geographic support the main text, helping learners comprehend key ideas.

EXPLORE A UNIT | xiii

EXPLORE A UNIT

The **Goal of Lesson C** is for learners to relate their own views and experience to the theme of the unit by completing a guided writing assignment.

Integrated **grammar practice and writing skill development** provides scaffolding for the writing assignment.

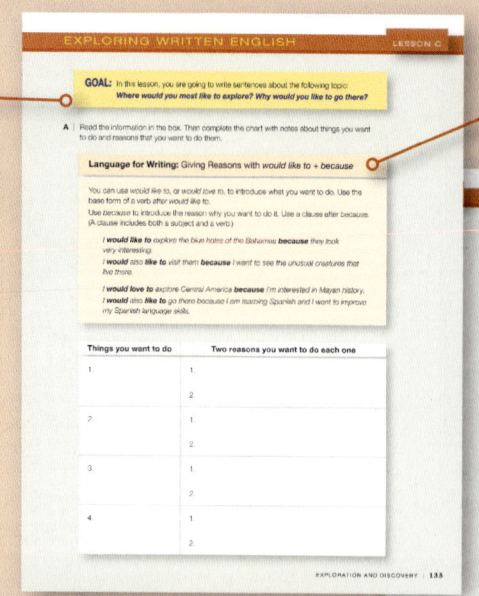

The **Independent Student Handbook** provides further language support and self-study strategies for independent learning. See pages 209–218.

Resources for *Pathways* Level 1

Video DVD with authentic National Geographic clips relating to each of the 10 units.

Teacher's Guide including teacher's notes, expansion activities, rubrics for evaluating written assignments, and answer keys for activities in the Student Book.

Audio CDs with audio recordings of the Student Book reading passages.

LESSON C

A **guided process approach** develops learners' confidence in planning, drafting, revising, and editing their written work.

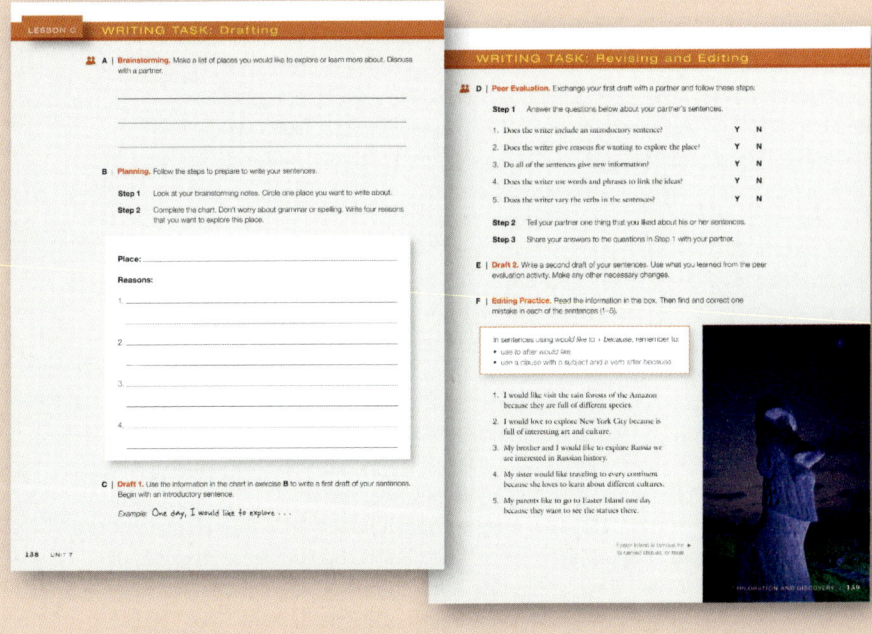

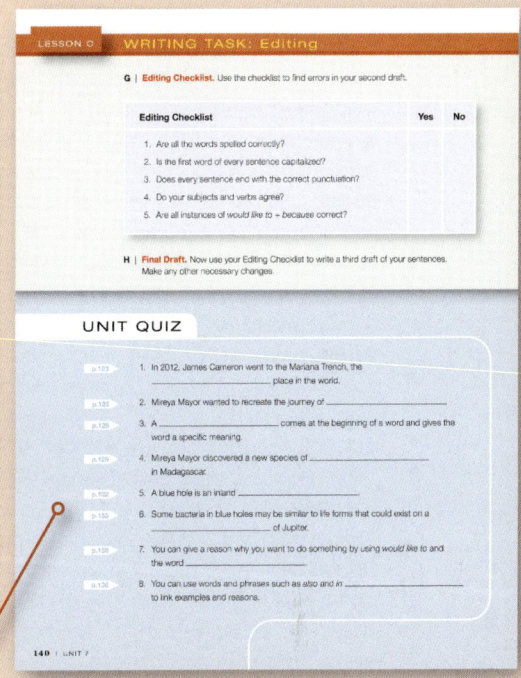

Unit Quiz provides an opportunity for learners to review some of the key ideas and language from the unit.

Assessment CD-ROM with Exam*View*® containing a bank of ready-made questions for quick and effective assessment.

Classroom Presentation Tool CD-ROM featuring audio and video clips, and interactive activities from the Student Book. These can be used with an interactive whiteboard or computer projector.

Online Workbook, powered by MyELT, with both teacher-led and self-study options. This contains the 10 National Geographic video clips, supported by interactive, automatically graded activities that practice the skills learned in the Student Books.

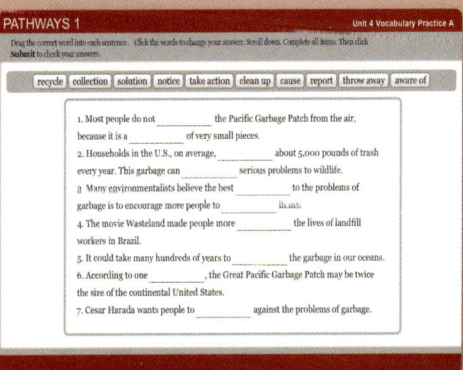

EXPLORE A UNIT | xv

Credits

TEXT CREDITS/SOURCES

5-6, Adapted from "Life in a Day: About the Production": http://movies.nationalgeographic.com/movies/life-in-a-day/about-the-production/; **12-13** Based on original interviews with Kakani Katija, Christine Lee, and Katsufumi Sato; **25-26:** Based on information from "The First Grader": http://movies.nationalgeographic.com/movies/the-first-grader/; **32-33:** Adapted from "Juan Martinez": http://www.nationalgeographic.com/explorers/bios/juan-martinez/; additional sources of information: http://www.ethiopiareads.org/programs/mobile (Ethiopia); http://www.koreatimes.co.kr/www/news/nation/2009/08/117_49729.html (Indonesian Tribe); http://www.unicef.org/education/mongolia_40960.html (Mongolia); **45-46:** Adapted from "From Africa to Astoria by Way of Everywhere" by James Shreeve: NGM October 2010; **52-53:** Adapted from "The Greatest Journey," by James Shreeve: NGM March 2006; additional information from "Atlas of the Human Journey": https://genographic.nationalgeographic.com/genographic/atlas.html; **65-66:** Adapted from "Great Pacific Garbage Patch": http://education.nationalgeographic.com/encyclopedia/great-pacific-garbage-patch/?ar_a=1&ar_r=3, and "Huge Garbage Patch Found in Atlantic, Too," by Richard A. Lovett: http://news.nationalgeographic.com/news/2010/03/100302-new-ocean-trash-garbage-patch/; **72-73:** Adapted from "Recycling: The Big Picture," by Tom Zeller, Jr.: NGM Jan 2008; other information adapted from: http://www.wastelandmovie.com/; **85-86:** Based on the TED talk by Thomas Thwaites, "How I Built a Toaster—From Scratch": http://www.ted.com/talks/thomas_thwaites_how_i_built_a_toaster_from_scratch.html; **92-93:** Adapted from "Eating Local Has Little Effect on Warming, Study Says," by Mason Inman: http://news.nationalgeographic.com/news/2008/04/080422-green-food.html; **105-106:** Adapted from "Robots: Us. And Them," by Chris Carroll: NGM Aug 2011. Additional information from NG Investigates: Future Tech, by Charles Piddock: Published by National Geographic Books, 2009; **112-113:** Adapted from "The Big Idea: Making Mars the New Earth," by Robert Kunzig: NGM Feb 2010; **125-126:** Adapted from "Pink Boots and a Machete: Chapter 13 (A Near Disaster, I Presume?), by Mireya Mayor. Published by National Geographic Books 2011; **132-133:** Adapted from "Deep Dark Secrets," by Andrew Todhunter: NGM Aug 2010; **145-146:** Based on information from "Benda Bilili": http://movies.nationalgeographic.com/movies/benda-bilili/; **152-153:** Adapted from "One on One: Jason Mraz," by Keith Bellows: National Geographic Traveler Mar 2011; additional sources of information: http://www.nationalgeographic.com/explorers/bios/thabethe-zinhle/ (Thabethe), and http://arnchornpond.com/ (Chorn-Pond); **165-166:** Adapted from "Cesar Milan – the Dog Whisperer," by Cathy Newman: NGM Dec 2006; **172-173:** Adapted from "Monkeys Show Sense of Fairness, Study Says," by Sean Markey: http://news.nationalgeographic.com/news/2003/09/0917_030917_monkeyfairness.html, and "Exposure to "Love Hormone" Increases Prosocial Behavior in Monkeys," by Alyson Foster: NG NewsWatch http://newswatch.nationalgeographic.com/2012/01/09/exposure-to-love-hormone-increases-prosocial-behavior-in-monkeys/; **185-188:** Based on the TED talk "David Griffin on How Photography Connects Us": http://www.ted.com/talks/david_griffin_on_how_photography_connects.html; **194-195:** Adapted from "Deadly Beauty," by Paul Nicklen and Kim Heacox: NGM Nov 2006.

NGM = National Geographic Magazine

PHOTO and ILLUSTRATION CREDITS

Cover: Julien Gille/iStockphoto, **IFC:** Mark Thiessen/National Geographic, **IFC:** Courtesy of Kevin Hand, **IFC:** Courtesy of Christine Lee, **IFC:** Rebecca Hale/National Geographic Image Collection, **IFC:** Charles Eshelman/Getty Images, **IFC:** Photograph courtesy Katsufumi Sato, **IFC:** Courtesy of Juan Martinez, **IFC:** www.markreadphotography.co.uk, **IFC:** National Geographic, **IFC:** AP Photo/Angela Rowlings, **i:** Jim Richardson / National Geographic Image Collection, **iv-v:** NASA Goddard Space Flight Center Image by Reto Stöckli (land surface, shallow water, clouds), **1:** Justin Guriglia/National Geographic, **2-3:** NASA, **3:** 2011 Randy Olson/National Geographic Image Collection, **5:** Vania da Rui, **6:** Courtesy of Mongrel Media, **6:** MM Film, s.r.o., **8:** Ludek Pesek/National Geographic, **9:** Stephen St. John/National Geographic, **12:** National Geographic, **12:** Robert Clark/National Geographic, **12:** Robert Clark/National Geographic, **13:** Courtesy of Christine Lee, **13:** Photograph courtesy Katsufumi Sato, **13:** O. Louis Mazzatenta/National Geographic Image Collection, **19:** Courtesy of Mongrel Media, **21:** Treadway, Alex/National Geographic, **23:** Justin Guriglia/National Geographic, **25:** Thomas Mukoya/REUTERS/Newscom, **26:** Courtesy of Kerry Brown, **28:** Meredith Davenport/National Geographic, **29:** Vincent J. Musi/National Geographic, **32:** REUTERS/Choi Bu-Seok, **33:** Courtesy of Juan Martinez, **33:** Oldrich Karasek/ TTL/PhotoShot, Inc., **34:** ethiopiareads.org, **37:** Treadway, Alex/National Geographic, **40:** ethiopiareads.org, **41:** Michelle Jones/National Geographic, **42:** Bruce Dale/National Geographic, **42:** Mike Theiss/National Geographic, **43:** Gordon Wiltsie/National Geographic, **43:** Randy Olson/National Geographic, **45:** Chris John/National Geographic, **46-47:** Steve Winter/National Geographic, **46-47:** Steve Winter/National Geographic, **46-47:** Steve Winter/National Geographic, **46-47:** Steve Winter/National Geographic, **49:** Alison Wright/National Geographic, **50:** Peter V. Bianchi/National Geographic Image Collection, **50:** Historical Art Collection (HAC) / Alamy, **52:** Kenneth Garretts/National Geographic, **53:** France Ministere de la Culture et de la Communication D.R.A.C./National Geographic, **57:** Hans Hildenbrand/National Geographic,

continued on p. 224

UNIT 1

Life in a Day

ACADEMIC PATHWAYS

Lesson A: Skimming for gist
Guessing meaning from context
Lesson B: Reading interviews
Lesson C: Understanding the writing process
Writing sentences about a single topic

Think and Discuss

1. Which part of your day do you like best? Which part do you like least? Why?
2. Think of someone you know who has an interesting life. Describe a day in the life of that person.

▲ A woman exercises as a new day begins in the Forbidden City, Beijing, China.

Exploring the Theme

A. Look at the information on these pages and answer the questions.

1. About how many more people are there in the world each day?
   How many children go to school? How many people visit social networking sites?
2. Does any of the information surprise you?

B. Answer the questions about yourself.

1. How often do you use a cell phone? What do you use it for?
2. Do you use the Internet every day? What kinds of things do you use it for?

More than **1,000,000,000** children go to school.

More than **4,000,000,000** people use a cell phone.

About **300,000,000** people visit social networking sites.

1,000 = one thousand
1,000,000 = one million
1,000,000,000 = one billion

Sources: www.umac.com, www.techrepublic.com, www.un.org, www.cbsnews.com

In one day on planet Earth...

The world's population grows by about

200,000 people.

◄ People and taxis crowd the streets of Kolkata, India, at the end of a busy day.

About **180,000**

people move into cities.

▲ This photograph, taken in 1968 from the *Apollo 8* spacecraft, showed for the first time the Earth as it looks from space.

LESSON A | PREPARING TO READ

A | Building Vocabulary. Find the words and phrases in **blue** in the reading passage on pages 5–6. Read the words around them and try to guess their meanings. Then circle the correct word or phrase to complete each sentence (1–10).

1. The **globe** / **team** is another way to describe the whole world or the Earth.
2. If something is **connected** / **normal**, it is usual and not very special.
3. A **result** / **project** is something that happens because of something else.
4. When two people or things are **connected** / **normal**, they are linked or joined together in some way.
5. When you **communicate** / **produce** with someone, you talk or write to that person.
6. When you **produce** / **arrive** somewhere, you get there from somewhere else.
7. A **globe** / **team** is a group of people who work together.
8. When you **connect** / **take care of** people, you look after them and make sure they are OK.
9. A **project** / **result** is a task or job that takes a lot of time and work.
10. When you **take care of** / **produce** something, you make it.

> **Word Link**
> When you learn a new word, use a dictionary to find other forms of the word, e.g.,
> (v.) arrive, (n.) arrival;
> (v.) produce, (n.) production;
> (v.) communicate, (n.) communication;
> (adj.) connected, (v.) connect, (n.) connection.

B | Using Vocabulary. Answer the questions. Share your ideas with a partner.

1. How do you usually **communicate** with your friends and family?
2. Who **took care of** you when you were young? Do you take care of anyone?
3. When do you work as part of a **team**?

C | Brainstorming. List things that you think most people around the globe do every day. Share your ideas with your partner.

> **Strategy**
> **Scanning for repeated words** can help you predict what a passage is about.

D | Scanning/Predicting. Scan the paragraphs on page 5 quickly. List nouns or verbs that appear two or more times.

_____

Now look at the words you wrote. What do you think the passage is about?

a. a day in the life of a movie director
b. a very unusual day on our planet
c. a movie about one day on Earth

READING

A DAY ON PLANET EARTH

▲ Skydiver Vania da Rui was one of thousands of contributors to the *Life in a Day* project.

A What happens in a single day on planet Earth? In 2010, a team led by film director Kevin Macdonald tried to find out. The team asked people around the world to film their life on a single day—July 24—and to send in their videos. As a result, people uploaded[1] 80,000 videos to YouTube—a total of more than 4,500 hours. The videos came from big cities and small villages, from people in 192 countries from Australia to Zambia. Macdonald's team used the videos to produce a 90-minute movie called *Life in a Day*.

B The movie begins as most days begin. People wake up, get dressed, wash their face, and brush their teeth. Parents take care of their children. People laugh and cry. As the day goes on, we see changes in people's lives. A man thanks the hospital workers who helped save his life. A woman learns that she is pregnant.[2] A man calls his mother and asks, "What should I say to the woman I love?"

[1] If you **upload** something, such as a photo or a movie, you put it on a website.
[2] If a woman or a female animal is **pregnant**, she has a baby or babies growing inside her.

LESSON A   READING

C   To make the movie, Macdonald understood that what may be normal to one person may be extraordinary to another. For example, the movie shows cultural differences such as the different ways that people travel to work. Macdonald explains, "What we might see as banal, living in our own culture, is not banal to somebody growing up in Dakar."

D   Macdonald's team also asked people the following questions: "What do you love most in the world, and what do you fear?" People speak of their love for family and friends, of football and fast cars, a pet cat, even a refrigerator. Children speak of being scared of imaginary monsters³ and of real-life lions. Some Ukrainian farmers worry that wolves are going to eat their goats. People around the globe talk about their fear of guns, of war, and of the loss of natural beauty.

▲ A man enjoys a watermelon in Piatichatki, Ukraine, on July 24, 2010

E   Macdonald says that *Life in a Day* was possible because of the way we are all connected. "The film is doing something that [was not] possible pre-Internet . . . The idea that you can ask thousands, tens of thousands, maybe hundreds of thousands of people all to contribute to a project and all to communicate about it and learn about it at the same time."

F   One of the people in the movie is a Korean cyclist named Okhwan Yoon. After traveling alone for nine years through 190 countries, he arrived on July 24 in Kathmandu, Nepal. "When I close my eyes," he says, "I can see all the different people in the world, from town to town, from country to country. I can feel it. I can touch it. I can see it." The *Life in a Day** team hopes that, after watching the movie, others may feel the same way.

" When I close my eyes, I can see all the different people in the world, from town to town, from country to country. "

— *Round-the-world cyclist Okhwan Yoon*

³ **Monsters** are creatures in stories that are ugly and scary.
* To view the full-length *Life in a Day* movie, visit: http://www.youtube.com/movie/life-in-a-day

UNDERSTANDING THE READING

A | Understanding the Gist. Look back at your answer for exercise **D** on page 4. Was your prediction correct?

B | Identifying Key Details. Read each statement below. Circle **T** for *true* and **F** for *false*.

1. The events in *Life in a Day* all happened on July 24, 2010.   T   F
2. The film shows people in many different countries.   T   F
3. People uploaded 80,000 hours of videos.   T   F
4. The filmmakers asked people to talk about things they love and fear.   T   F

C | Critical Thinking: Guessing Meaning from Context. Look at this example from the passage:

The team asked people around the world to film their life on a single day—July 24—and to send in their videos.

We can guess from the context ("July 24") that a single day probably means "one day." Now find and underline the following words in the reading. Use context to identify their meanings. Then match each word with its definition (1–6).

> **goes on** (paragraph B)   **extraordinary** (paragraph C)   **cultural** (paragraph C)
> **banal** (paragraph C)   **imaginary** (paragraph D)   **contribute** (paragraph E)

> **CT Focus**
>
> Use the context—the words around a word—to guess the meaning of a new word. The context can also help you decide the word's part of speech, e.g., noun, verb, adjective, etc.

1. _____ continues; doesn't stop
2. _____ not real; made-up; fictional
3. _____ very unusual or special
4. _____ boring; not interesting or unusual
5. _____ relating to how a group of people live
6. _____ (to) give something for a particular purpose

D | Critical Thinking: Analyzing. Read the last paragraph of the reading again. How do you think the filmmakers want people to feel after watching the film? Write three words or phrases. Share your ideas with a partner.

_____   _____   _____

E | Personalizing. Write answers to the questions. Then share your ideas with your partner.

1. Imagine you are making a video to send to a life-in-a-day project. What part of your daily life would you film? Explain.

   I would send a video of _____

   because _____.

2. Macdonald says, "The film is doing something that [was not] possible pre-Internet." What are two other things that were not possible before the Internet?

   _____

   _____

LIFE IN A DAY

LESSON A: DEVELOPING READING SKILLS

Reading Skill: *Skimming for Gist*

When we read a short passage such as an article or a story, we usually skim it first to find out what it is basically about. In other words, we look quickly at a passage without reading every word. We pay attention to key words and phrases such as repeated nouns. We also look for clues found in titles, photos, and subtitles that help us understand the overall topic. Knowing the gist of a passage can help you predict the kind of information you will learn before you read a passage in detail.

A | **Skimming.** Skim the paragraphs quickly. Pay attention to the words in **bold**. Then match each paragraph with one of the topics below.

track 1-02

CT Focus

Use context to guess the meaning of new words. What do you think *rotation* means?

A. We all know that a **single day** is **24 hours** long. However, that is only true about a day on the **planet Earth**. That's because it takes the Earth **24 hours** to make **one rotation**. Different **planets** take different amounts of time to **rotate**, or turn. So how long is one day on some of the **other planets** in our solar system? **One day** on the **planet Mercury** takes over **58 days** in Earth time. That's a long day, but **Venus** has the **longest day**. A day on the planet Venus is **243 Earth days** long. **Jupiter**, the largest planet, has the **shortest day**, just **9.9 Earth hours** long.

▲ A day lasts less than 10 hours on the planet Jupiter.

B. Are you about to have your **first baby**? Are you wondering what your **typical day** will be like? Well, it will definitely be very different from your **typical day** now. First, you won't **sleep** for eight hours at night and **stay awake** for the other 16 hours of the day. You will probably **sleep** when your **baby sleeps** and be **awake** when your **baby is awake**. **Babies** have different **sleep** patterns, but your baby will probably **sleep** for one to three hours at a time. When you are **awake**, you will probably spend a lot of your time **feeding your baby** and **changing diapers**. Expect to be **tired** most of the time. But you can also expect to feel incredible **happiness** when you look at your **beautiful new baby**.

A.
____ 1. how long a day is on other planets
____ 2. why a day on Earth is 24 hours long
____ 3. a normal day on the planet Jupiter

B.
____ 1. the normal day of a new parent
____ 2. how to take care of a baby
____ 3. why people need a lot of sleep

B | Now read the paragraphs in exercise **A** in detail. Were you correct about the gist of each one?

VIEWING

BioBlitz: Life in 24 Hours

▲ A wild deer appears in the early morning light in Rock Creek Park, District of Columbia, USA.

Before Viewing

A | Using a Dictionary. Here are some words you will hear in the video. Complete each definition with the correct word. Use your dictionary to help you.

> behavior   biodiversity   identify   stuff   volunteers

1. _____ is a collection of things or ideas.
2. If you study an animal's _____, you study the things it does and the way it acts.
3. _____ are people who do work without being paid for it; they do the work because they want to help other people.
4. _____ is the existence of many different kinds, or species, of plants and animals.
5. When you _____ something, you are able to say who or what it is.

B | Brainstorming. Think about a park in your town. List some plants, animals, and insects that you think live in the park. Share your ideas with a partner.

While Viewing

A | Read questions 1–4. Think about the answers as you view the video.

1. What did the people do in the park?
2. How long were the people in the park?
3. Why was Rock Creek a good park for a Bioblitz?
4. What is the main purpose of the Bioblitz?

After Viewing

A | Discuss your answers to questions 1–4 above with a partner.

B | Synthesizing. What do the BioBlitz and the movie *Life in a Day* have in common? Write the number of each idea in the correct place in the Venn diagram.

1. goes on for 24 hours
2. happens in a park
3. includes children
4. is about life in different countries
5. uses volunteers
6. shows behavior of living things
7. shows diversity
8. is about 90 minutes long

Life in a Day movie | Both | BioBlitz

LIFE IN A DAY | 9

LESSON B   PREPARING TO READ

A | Building Vocabulary. Read the definitions below of some of the words and phrases in the reading on pages 12–13. Complete each sentence (1–5) with the correct word or phrase.

> When you **balance** two things, they both have the same weight or importance.
>
> When one thing **depends on** a second thing, the first thing is affected by the second thing.
>
> If something happens **during** a period of time, it happens between the beginning and end of that period.
>
> An animal's **environment** is the place where it lives.
>
> If something is **unexpected**, you did not know that it would happen.

Word Link
The prefix *un-* can make an adjective negative, e.g., **un**expected, **un**happy, **un**identified, **un**explored.

1. An employee's paycheck _____ his or her work hours. When the employee works more hours, he or she gets a bigger paycheck.
2. Scientists usually like to study an animal in its natural _____. That way, they can see what it eats, where it sleeps, and how it lives.
3. It's important to _____ your work and your personal life. Don't work so much that you don't have time to be with your family and friends.
4. Some people sleep _____ the day and work at night.
5. Do you like _____ visits from your friends? Or do you like it when people call you before they come over?

B | Building Vocabulary. Read the sentences below. The words and phrases in **bold** are from the reading on pages 12–13. Write each word or phrase next to the correct definition.

> Builders have to **measure** each piece of wood before they cut it. Each piece of wood has to be the right size.
>
> When drivers **realize** they are going the wrong way, they usually look at a map or ask for directions.
>
> Do you have a busy **schedule** on the weekend? Or do you have a lot of free time then?
>
> Do you usually **spend time** with your friends during the weekend?
>
> A rainy day in the middle of the summer is often a **surprise**.

1. _____: to find how big or small something is
2. _____: to do something or be with certain people for a while
3. _____: an event, a fact, or a piece of news that you did not think will happen
4. _____: to become aware that something is true, or to understand it is true
5. _____: a plan or an outline of times when things will happen

C | Using Vocabulary. Answer the questions in complete sentences. Then share your sentences with a partner.

1. Describe something **unexpected** that happened to you in the past.

   _____

   _____

2. What things does an ability to learn a new language **depend on**?

   _____

   _____

3. Think of two animals and describe their natural **environments**.

   _____

   _____

4. How do you remember your **schedule**? For example, do you use a wall calendar? Do you use a calendar on your phone?

   _____

   _____

5. What kinds of things do you do for fun **during** your vacation?

   _____

   _____

> **Word Partners**
> Use **schedule** with: (adj.) **busy** schedule, **regular** schedule; (n.) **change of** schedule, schedule **of events**, **train** schedule; (prep.) **ahead of** schedule, **behind** schedule, **on** schedule.

D | Predicting. Look at the title, subheads, and photos in the reading on pages 12–13. What kind of reading is it?

a. three scientific news reports

b. an opinion article about a scientific topic

c. a set of interviews with scientists

> **Strategy**
> Use clues in **titles, subheads, and photos** to get an idea of the overall gist of a reading. These clues will help you know what to expect when you read in more detail.

LESSON B READING

A Day in a Life

WHAT IS IT LIKE to be a National Geographic Explorer? Three scientific explorers around the world describe their daily life.

Name: Kakani Katija
Job: Bioengineer

Kakani Katija studies the movements of jellyfish and other ocean animals.

Where do you work?

Sometimes I work in my office or with animals in a laboratory. I spend a lot of time in the ocean, too. I dive with animals to learn how they swim and eat.

What time do you normally start and end your workday?

I often keep a 9-to-5 schedule. When I am studying animals in the ocean, my start and end times depend on the behavior of the animals.

What's the best thing about your job?

The best thing is finding answers to a question that truly interests me. I also get to see things in nature that nobody else gets to see.

What's the most difficult thing about your job?

It's tough to balance my work schedule, travel, and time with my family.

What's one of the strangest things that happened to you at work?

One night I was diving in Woods Hole, Massachusetts. I was measuring a jellyfish. Suddenly, a crab swam up. It grabbed the jellyfish in its claws and ate him! It was a big surprise!

Scientists like Kakani ▶ Katija look for designs in nature that engineers can use. An example is this animal, called a boxfish. Mercedes-Benz used the boxfish's design to make a new type of car (right).

12 | UNIT 1

Name: Christine Lee
Job: Bioarchaeologist

Christine Lee studies the skeletons of early humans to understand how they lived.

Where do you work?

I work on archaeological excavations[1] in China and Mongolia. I also work in a professor's office and in a laboratory.

What time do you normally start and end your workday?

If I am on an archaeological excavation, I usually work from sunrise to sundown. In the laboratory, I work as long as the laboratory is open.

What's the best thing about your job?

Finding a story that has been buried for hundreds or thousands of years.

What's the toughest thing about your job?

Cold weather, no bathrooms!

What's one of the strangest things that happened to you at work?

When I was working on two children's skeletons, the skulls started moving back and forth. Luckily, I realized there was a rainstorm coming. The wind was moving the skulls!

Name: Katsufumi Sato
Job: Behavioral ecologist

Katsufumi Sato studies the behavior of animals in their natural environment.

▲ Katsufumi Sato with one of the tools he uses to record animal behavior.

Where do you work?

That depends on the animals that I am studying. For example, when I studied penguins, I went to Antarctica. When I studied tiger sharks, I went to a tropical island.

What time do you normally start and end your workday?

When I am in Tokyo, I go to my office at the university at 9:00 A.M. and come home at 9:00 P.M. However, when I am at a study site, animals decide my schedule. When I study nocturnal animals, I work during the night and sleep in the daytime.

What's the best thing about your job?

I really enjoy visiting different places in the world and experiencing unexpected things.

What's the most difficult thing about your job?

I get seasick on the ocean!

> It's amazing to look at a skull and realize I'm the first person to see that face in 2,000 years.

[1] In an **archaeological excavation**, scientists look for things buried in the ground, such as pots and bones, in order to learn about the past.

LESSON B: UNDERSTANDING THE READING

A | Understanding the Gist. Look back at your answer for exercise **D** on page 11. Was your prediction correct?

B | Identifying Key Details. Write the letter of each description in the correct place in the Venn diagram.

a. scientist
b. bioengineer
c. ecologist
d. archaeologist
e. works in China and Mongolia
f. studies humans
g. works in an office
h. studies animals' behavior
i. schedule depends on animals
j. gets seasick

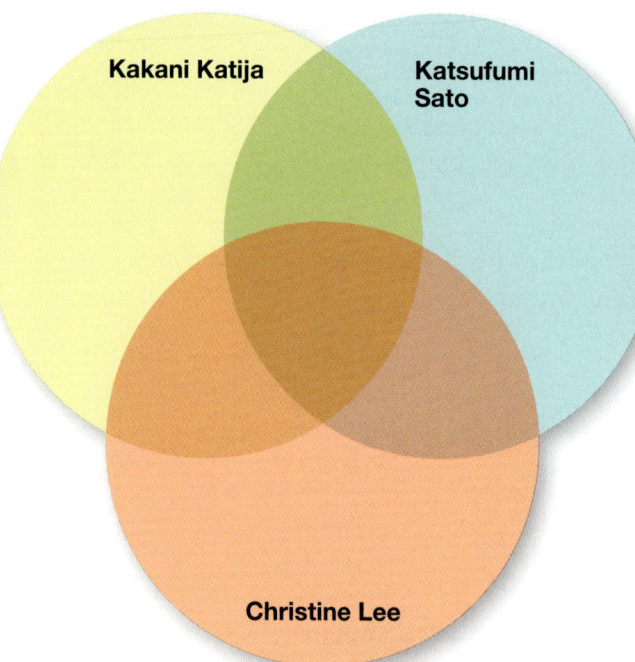

C | Critical Thinking: Guessing Meaning from Context. Find and underline these words on pages 12–13. Use context to identify their meanings. Then match each word to its definition.

| buried | dive | engineers | laboratory | nocturnal | skeleton |

1. _____: covered up; hidden
2. _____: staying awake during the night
3. _____: all the bones in a person's or an animal's body
4. _____: people who design or build machines or other things
5. _____: go down under the surface of a sea or a lake
6. _____: a room or building where scientific work is done

D | Synthesizing. Discuss these questions in small groups.

1. What is similar about the two reading passages and the video in this unit?
2. Which person in the unit do you think has the most interesting job? Who has the most difficult job? Why do you think so?

EXPLORING WRITTEN ENGLISH

LESSON C

GOAL: In this lesson, you are going to plan, write, revise, and edit sentences on the following topic:

Which three of your daily activities might be interesting to someone from another country? Why do you think they might be interesting?

A | Read the information below. Then complete each sentence (1–7) with the correct simple present form of a verb from the box. You will use two verbs twice.

Language for Writing: Simple Present of *Be* and Other Verbs

Use the simple present for habits and daily routines:

> Sometimes I **work** in my office.
> I **don't work** in a laboratory.
> I **go** to my university at 9:00 A.M. and **come** home at 9:00 P.M.
> Animals **decide** my schedule.

Also use the simple present for facts or things that are generally true:

> The average American **eats** about 90 grams of sugar per day.
> Planet Earth **takes** about 24 hours to make one rotation.
> Jupiter **doesn't have** a 24-hour day.
> This **is** really where the wild things are.

For more explanation and examples, see page 214.

---

be   communicate   find   go   have   ~~leave~~   not work   ride   work

---

Example: Every day, I ____leave____ my house at 7:00 A.M.

1. I _____ with my friends by email.
2. We _____ all connected through the Internet.
3. A day on Jupiter _____ less than 10 Earth hours long.
4. She _____ on weekends. She only _____ from Monday to Friday.
5. In a BioBlitz, teams of scientists, parents, kids, and volunteers all _____ to a park or a neighborhood and try to _____ everything that's alive there.
6. I _____ two jobs. My wife also _____ two jobs.
7. I _____ the train to work every morning.

B | Write four sentences using the simple present. Use the verbs in parentheses.

1. (go) _____
2. (have) _____
3. (be) _____
4. (eat) _____

LIFE IN A DAY

LESSON C EXPLORING WRITTEN ENGLISH

C | Write complete sentences to answer the questions below.

Example: What is your name?
    My name is John.

Where do you live?
    I live in Los Angeles.

1. What is your name?
    _____

2. Where do you live?
    _____

3. Where are you from?
    _____

4. What do you usually do on weekends?
    _____

5. How do you get to class every day?
    _____

6. Where do you study?
    _____

D | Ask and answer the questions in exercise **C** with a partner. Then write your partner's answers.

Example:
    My partner's name is John.
    John lives in Los Angeles.

1. _____
2. _____
3. _____
4. _____
5. _____
6. _____

Writing Skill: *Understanding the Writing Process*

In this lesson, you are going to learn about the stages in the writing process: brainstorming, planning, drafting, revising, and editing.

In the **brainstorming** stage, you list all the ideas you can think of about a topic. You might also do some journal writing or free writing about the topic. You don't have to write complete sentences, and you should not worry about spelling, grammar, or punctuation.

In the **planning** stage, you choose the ideas from your brainstorming list and/or your journal writing that you want to include in your writing. If you are writing a paragraph or a longer piece, you can organize your ideas in an outline or another type of graphic organizer before you begin writing.

In the **drafting** stage, you write your first draft. Don't worry too much about spelling, grammar, or punctuation. Focus on getting your ideas down on paper.

In the **revising** stage, you write your second draft. Focus on making your ideas clear and adding details. You may also write additional drafts if necessary.

In the **editing** stage, you check your writing for spelling, grammar, and punctuation errors and create your final draft.

E | Write the correct stage from the box above next to each description (1–5).

1. _____ writing your ideas in sentences for the first time
2. _____ choosing ideas to include in your writing
3. _____ making changes to your first draft
4. _____ correcting things such as spelling and grammar errors
5. _____ listing your ideas about a topic

F | **Critical Thinking: Evaluating.** Talk with a partner. Why do you think the stages below are important for the writing process? Complete the sentences with your ideas.

1. Brainstorming is important because _____
   _____.

2. Revising is important because _____
   _____.

3. Editing is important because _____
   _____.

LESSON C | WRITING TASK: Drafting

A | Brainstorming. Brainstorm a list of things that you do in a normal day.

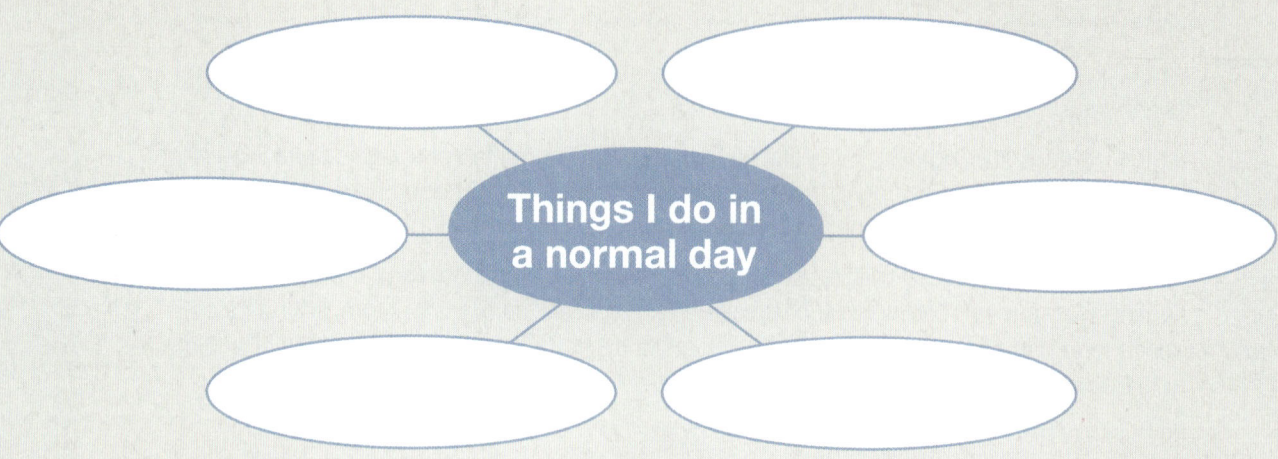

B | Planning. Follow the steps to make notes for your sentences.

Step 1   Look at your brainstorming notes from exercise **A**. Underline three daily activities that you think someone from another country might find interesting.

Step 2   Decide how you want to organize your ideas. For example, do you want to put the activities in the order that you do them every day? Or do you want to save the most interesting activity for last?

Step 3   Complete the chart.

Things I do in a normal day:	Why I think these might be interesting to someone from another country:
take a boat across the lake to get to work	not many people take boats to work
1.	
2.	
3.	

C | Draft 1. Use the information in your chart to write a first draft of your sentences.

WRITING TASK: Revising and Editing

D | Peer Evaluation. Exchange your first draft with a partner and follow these steps:

Step 1 Read your partner's sentences. Then answer the questions below about them.

1. Are the sentences about daily activities?   Y   N
2. Does your partner explain why someone from another country might find each activity interesting?   Y   N
3. Does your partner organize the sentences in an order that makes sense?   Y   N

Step 2 Tell your partner one thing that you liked about his or her sentences.

Step 3 Share your answers to the questions in Step 1 with your partner.

E | Draft 2. Write a second draft of your sentences. Use what you learned from the peer evaluation activity. Make any other necessary changes.

F | Editing Practice. Read the information in the box. Then find and correct one simple present mistake in each of the sentences (1–8).

> In sentences using the simple present, remember to:
> - use the correct form of *be*: *am*, *is*, or *are*.
> - use the correct form of other verbs, for example, *go/goes*, *eat/eats*, *talk/talks*.
> - use the correct form of *do* and the base form of a verb in negative statements, for example, *don't take/doesn't take*.

1. I cooks food for 500 people every day.
2. I think most people doesn't cook for that many people.
3. My husband drive me to work every morning.
4. He be a bus driver.
5. I don't works in an office.
6. I working in a laboratory.
7. My wife and I has three daughters.
8. My daughter doesn't has a job.

LIFE IN A DAY | 19

LESSON C — WRITING TASK: Editing

G | Editing Checklist. Use the checklist to find errors in your second draft.

Editing Checklist	Yes	No
1. Are all the words spelled correctly?		
2. Is the first word of every sentence capitalized?		
3. Does every sentence end with the correct punctuation?		
4. Do your subjects and verbs agree?		
5. Did you use the simple present correctly?		

H | Final Draft. Now use your Editing Checklist to write a third draft of your sentences. Make any other necessary changes.

UNIT QUIZ

p.3   1. Each day, there are about 200,000 more _____ in the world.

p.6   2. The filmmakers asked people to share their _____. Some people talked about guns and war. Some children talked about imaginary monsters.

p.6   3. According to director Kevin Macdonald, the movie *Life in a Day* was not possible before the _____.

p.8   4. _____ is looking at a passage quickly to find out what it is about.

p.9   5. Hundreds of _____ take part in the BioBlitz project; they receive no money for taking part.

p.10 6. A plan that lists when things will happen is called a _____.

p.13 7. Katsufumi Sato studies animals in their natural _____.

p.17 8. In the writing process, the step between drafting and editing is called _____.

Learning Experiences

UNIT 2

ACADEMIC PATHWAYS
Lesson A: Understanding the main ideas of paragraphs
            Making inferences
Lesson B: Understanding news reports
Lesson C: Planning your writing
            Writing sentences about goals

▲ Students get help from a teacher at a school in the West Khasi Hills of India.

Think and Discuss

1. What important things do people learn in school? What important things do they learn outside of school?
2. What were the three most useful things you learned in school?

Exploring the Theme

A. Look at the **Measuring Global Literacy** map and answer the questions.

1. In which parts of the world are there many literate people—people who can read and write?
2. In which places are there many illiterate people—people who cannot read and write?

B. Look at the **School Enrollment for Girls** map and answer the questions.

1. What does the dark green color show in this map?
2. What does the yellow color show?

Reading and Writing Around the World

About one billion adults around the world cannot read and write.[1] Two-thirds of these people are women, and 90 percent of them live in poor countries. Countries with many literate people—people who can read and write—are usually wealthier than countries with many illiterate people.

[1] Source: United Nations

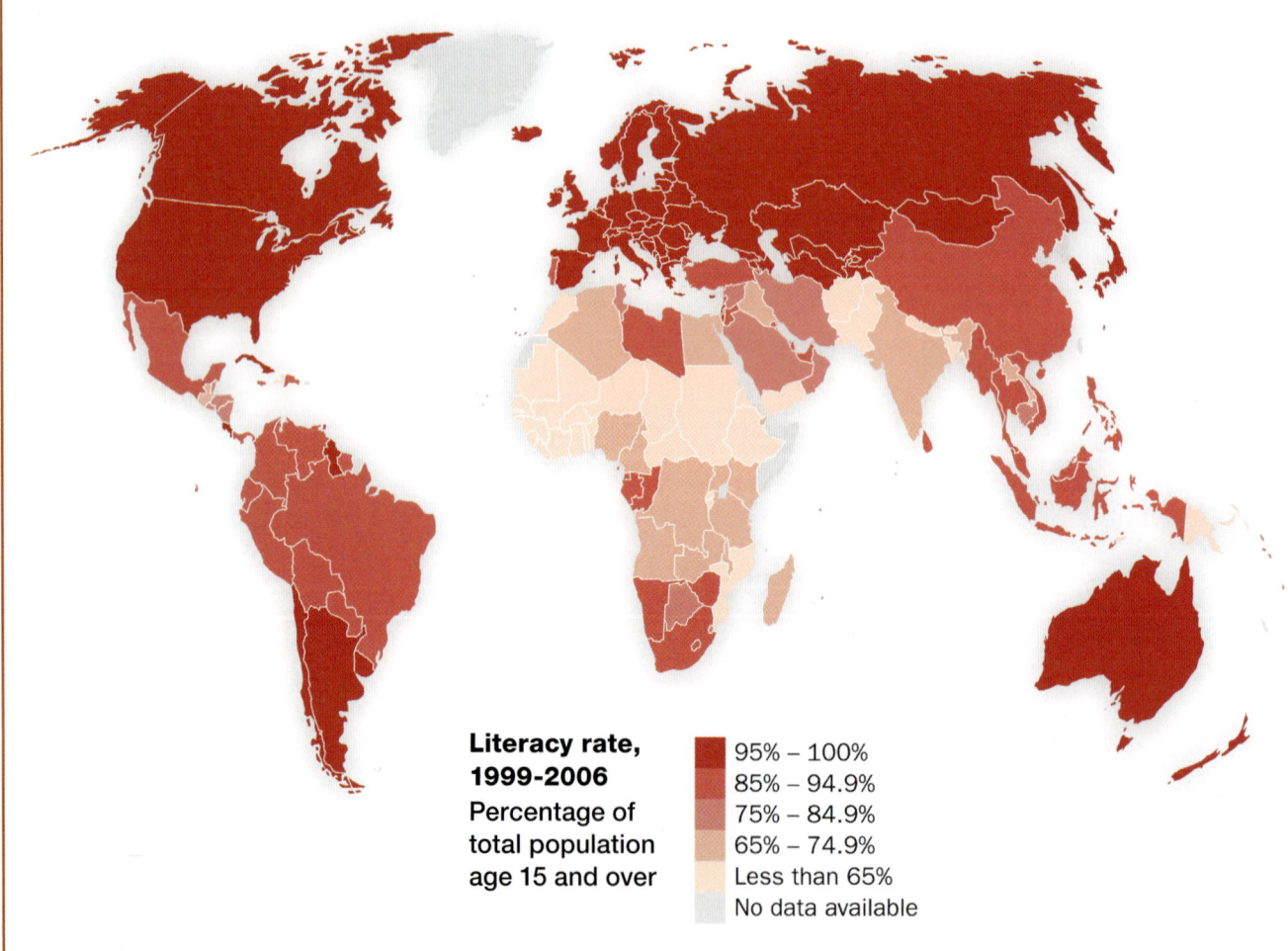

Measuring Global Literacy

Literacy rate, 1999-2006
Percentage of total population age 15 and over

- 95% – 100%
- 85% – 94.9%
- 75% – 84.9%
- 65% – 74.9%
- Less than 65%
- No data available

Girls in School

More boys than girls attend school in poor countries. In 2008, 96 girls for every 100 boys were enrolled at primary school—the early years of school. There were 95 girls for every 100 boys in secondary school—the later years of school.

School Enrollment for Girls

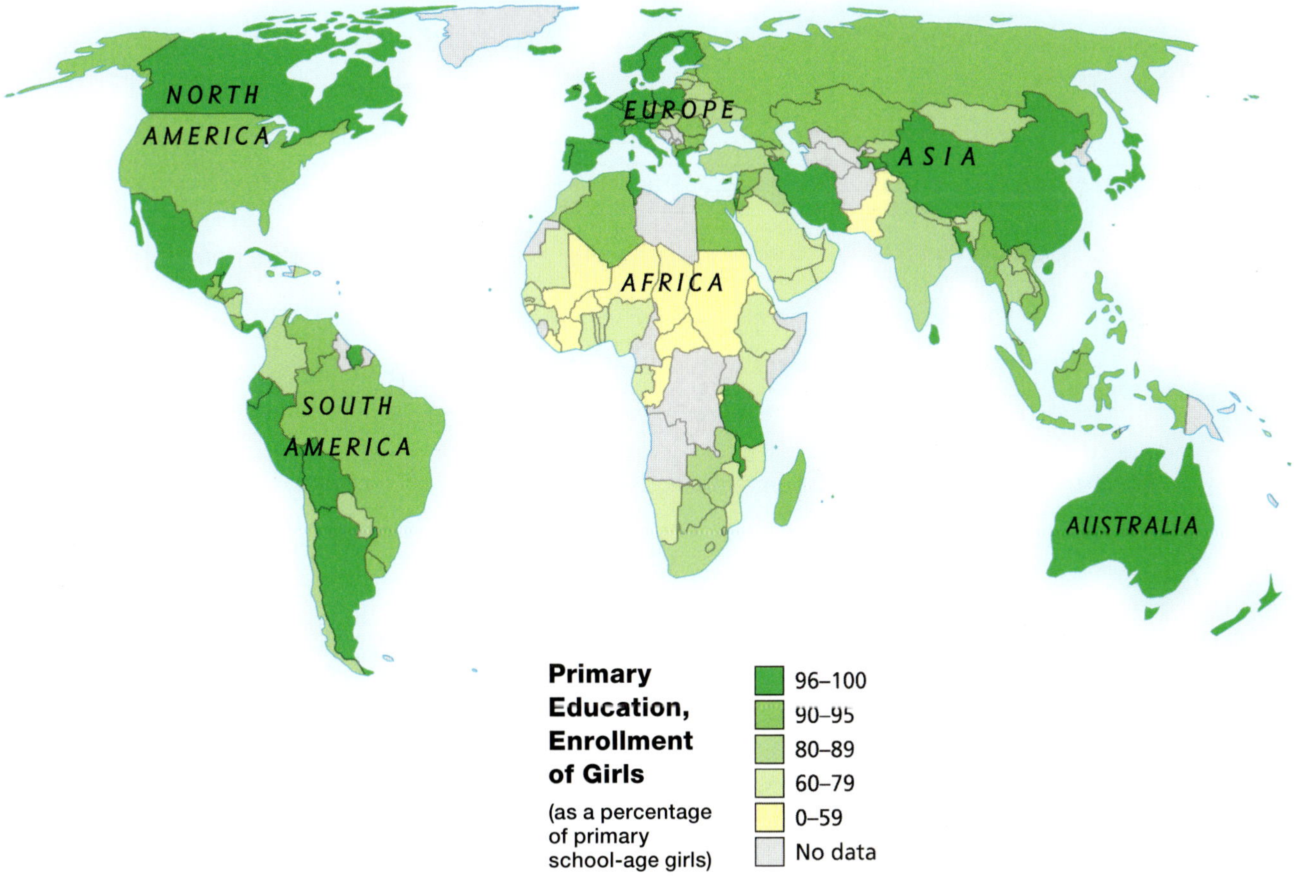

Primary Education, Enrollment of Girls

(as a percentage of primary school-age girls)

- 96–100
- 90–95
- 80–89
- 60–79
- 0–59
- No data

LEARNING EXPERIENCES | 23

LESSON A PREPARING TO READ

A | Building Vocabulary. Find the words in **blue** in the reading passage on pages 25–26. Read the words around them and try to guess their meanings. Then match the sentence parts below to make definitions.

_____ 1. The **principal** of a school   a. are normal, and not special in any way.
_____ 2. A **resident** of a house or an area b. is the group of people who control and organize it.
_____ 3. **Ordinary** people and things   c. you think it is true.
_____ 4. The **government** of a country   d. is the person who lives there.
_____ 5. If you **believe** something,   e. is the person in charge of it.

> **Word Link**
> The prefix *in-* can mean "not," e.g., **in**complete, **in**correct, **in**dependent, **in**direct.

B | Building Vocabulary. Find the words and phrases in **blue** in the reading passage on pages 25–26. Read the words around them and try to guess their meanings. Then complete the sentences.

| attend | decide to | independent | motivated | primary |

1. Countries become _____ when they are no longer governed by another country.
2. Some adults _____ go back to school to get better jobs.
3. In _____ school, young children normally learn to read and write.
4. Many young children _____ school near their homes.
5. _____ students study hard and want to learn.

C | Using Vocabulary. Answer the questions. Share your ideas with a partner.

1. Do you know any people who are very **motivated**? Describe them.
2. What kind of **primary** school did you attend? Describe it.
3. Do you remember the **principal** of your first school? What was he or she like?

D | Brainstorming. List some reasons to go to primary school. Share your ideas with your partner.

_____
_____

> **Strategy**
> **When you scan,** you read quickly to find specific information. For example, to scan for names, look for proper nouns starting with capital letters.

E | Scanning/Predicting. Read the title and subheads and scan the first page of the following reading passage. Look for a repeated name, and the country he is from.

Name: _____ Country: _____

What do you think the reading passage is mainly about?

a. an unusual parent   b. an unusual student   c. an unusual teacher

24 | UNIT 2

READING

The World's Oldest First Grader

track 1-04

"You're never too old to learn." One man in Kenya proved this famous saying.

A

ON JANUARY 12, 2004, Kimani Maruge knocked on the door of the primary school in his village in Kenya. It was the first day of school, and he was ready to start learning. The teacher let him in and gave him a desk. The new student sat down with the rest of the first graders—six- and seven-year-old boys and girls. However, Kimani Maruge was not an ordinary first grader. He was 84 years old—the world's oldest first grader.

Fighting to stay in school

B

Kimani Maruge was born in Kenya in 1920. At that time, primary education in Kenya was not free, and Maruge's family didn't have enough money to pay for school. When Maruge grew up, he worked hard as a farmer. In the 1950s, he fought with other Kenyans against the British colonists. After years of fighting, Kenya became independent in 1963.

C

In 2003, the Kenyan government began offering free primary education to everyone, and Maruge wanted an education, too. However, it wasn't always easy for Maruge to attend school. Many of the first graders' parents didn't want an old man in their children's class. School officials[1] said that a primary education was only for children. But the school principal, Jane Obinchu, believed Maruge was right. With her help, he was able to stay in school.

---

[1] An **official** is a person who has an important position in an organization, such as a government or a school.

▲ Kenyan actor Oliver Litondo played Kimani Maruge in the 2010 movie *The First Grader*.

D Maruge was a motivated and successful student. In fact, he was one of the top five students in his first grade class. In second grade, Maruge became the school's student leader. He went as far as seventh grade, the final year of primary school. Over the years, Maruge studied Swahili,[2] English, and math. He wanted to use his education to read the Bible and to study veterinary[3] medicine.

E In 2008, there were problems in Kenya after an election. People were fighting and burning houses in Maruge's village. Maruge moved to a refugee camp for safety and lived in a tent. However, even during those difficult times he continued to go to school. Later that year, he moved to a home for the elderly. He continued going to school, and even taught other residents of the home to read and write.

Inspired[4] to Learn

F In 2005, Maruge flew in a plane for the first time in his life. He traveled to New York City, where he gave a speech at the United Nations. He spoke about the importance of education and asked for help to educate the people of Kenya. Maruge also wanted to improve primary education for children in Africa.

G Maruge died in 2009, at age 89. However, his story lives on. The 2010 movie *The First Grader* showed Maruge's amazing fight to get an education. Many older Kenyans decided to start school after seeing *The First Grader*. One of those people was 19-year-old Thoma Litei. Litei said, "I knew it was not too late. I wanted to read, and to know more language, so I came [to school] to learn. That is why it is important for his story to be known."

[2] **Swahili** is a language spoken in much of East Africa.
[3] **Veterinary** refers to the medical treatment of animals.
[4] If someone or something **inspires** you, they give you new ideas or make you want to do something.

UNDERSTANDING THE READING

A | Understanding the Gist. Look back at your answers for exercise **E** on page 24. Were your answers correct?

B | Identifying Key Details. Complete each statement with information from the reading passage.

1. On January 12, 2004, Kimani Maruge was _____ years old.
2. Before 2003, primary education in Kenya was not _____.
3. The school _____ helped Maruge to stay in school.
4. Maruge continued to attend school, even when people were _____ _____ in his village.
5. Maruge spoke at the U.N. about the importance of _____.
6. Maruge inspired many older Kenyans. For example, after Thoma Litei saw *The First Grader*, he decided to _____.

C | Critical Thinking: Analyzing/Inferring. What kind of person is Maruge? Check (✓) the adjectives that describe him. (Look up words you don't know in a dictionary.) Find examples in the reading passage for the words you checked.

1. ✓ motivated — He was one of the top five students in his first grade class.
2. ☐ ordinary _____
3. ☐ persistent _____
4. ☐ hardworking _____
5. ☐ caring _____
6. ☐ brave _____
7. Your idea: _____

D | Critical Thinking: Making Inferences. With a partner, think about the reasons for Maruge's actions. With your partner, complete these sentences. Look at the words you checked in exercise **C** for ideas.

I think Maruge was a successful student because _____.

I think he continued studying because _____.

I think he spoke at the U.N. because _____.

E | Personalizing. What do you think each of these sayings means? Which one do you agree with the most? Are there any similar sayings in your own language?

"You're never too old to learn."   "You can't teach an old dog new tricks."

> **CT Focus**
>
> **Inferring the character traits** of a person in a story can help you understand the reasons for his or her actions. As you read, ask yourself: What kind of person is this? What are the motivations for his or her actions?

LEARNING EXPERIENCES

LESSON A DEVELOPING READING SKILLS

Reading Skill: *Understanding the Main Ideas of Paragraphs*

The main idea of a paragraph is the most important idea. It's the idea that the paragraph focuses on. A good paragraph usually has one main idea. Other ideas in the paragraph support the main idea; they describe or explain the main idea.

A | Understanding the Main Idea. Read the paragraph. Then check (✓) the paragraph's main idea.

track 1-05

In my opinion, older adults should attend school with children. There are two reasons for this. First, older students can teach many things to children. For example, older people have more experience in life than children do. As a result, they often know more than children do about subjects such as literature and history, and they can help children with these subjects. Children can teach things to older adults, too. Children often learn new technology faster than adults do, so they can teach older adults how to use new technologies. For example, children can help adults use educational software or e-books. For these reasons, it's a good idea for children and older adults to learn together in the same classroom.

▲ 69-year-old Candida Rumbo is one of more than 1.2 million adult students who have learned to read and write at new schools in Venezuela.

☐ Older adults sometimes do better than children in literature and history.
☐ Children learn new technology faster than adults do.
☐ It's a good idea for older adults and children to attend school together.

B | Identifying the Main Idea. Look again at paragraph **D** on page 26. Check the main idea of the paragraph.

☐ Maruge was one of the top students in his class.   ☐ Maruge was a successful student.
☐ Maruge was a student leader at his school.

C | Matching. Look back at the reading on pages 25–26. Match each main idea below to one of these paragraphs from the reading: **A**, **C**, **E**, and **G**.

_____ 1. Maruge was an inspiration to other adult Kenyans.
_____ 2. Maruge faced many challenges when he started school.
_____ 3. Maruge was not an ordinary first grader.
_____ 4. Maruge did not stop studying, even when it was difficult.

VIEWING

Alex the Parrot

▲ Many parrots, such as this African Gray Parrot, can say simple words. But do they understand what they are saying?

Before Viewing

A | Using a Dictionary. Here are some words you will hear in the video. Write each word next to the correct definition. Use your dictionary to help you.

cognitive
mimic
reasoning
specific

1. _____: concluding something after thinking about all the facts
2. _____: copy or repeat sounds or actions
3. _____: relating to the processes of knowing, and understanding
4. _____: particular; not general

B | Thinking Ahead. When a parrot talks, do you think it understands what it is saying? Discuss with a partner.

While Viewing

A | As you view the video, circle whether statements 1-4 are true (**T**) or false (**F**).

1. Alex amazed scientists because he could talk. T F
2. When Alex sees two objects, he can say which object is bigger. T F
3. When Alex identifies objects by color and size, he shows cognitive skills similar to those of young children. T F
4. Alex learned about 50 words during his life. T F

After Viewing

A | Discuss the statements (1–4) above with a partner. Correct the false statement(s).

B | Synthesizing. In what ways was Alex extraordinary? In what ways was Kimani Maruge extraordinary?

Alex was extraordinary because _____.

Maruge was extraordinary because _____.

LEARNING EXPERIENCES | 29

LESSON B   PREPARING TO READ

A | Building Vocabulary. Read the sentences below. Look at the words around the **bold** words and phrases to guess their meanings. Then circle the best definition.

1. Kimani Maruge spoke to the United Nations because he wanted **aid**, for example, more money and training, to help educate children in Africa.

   a. help   b. problems

2. Free primary education is now **available** to all children in Kenya. Before 2003, families paid for primary education.

   a. something you cannot have   b. something you can get

3. People in Korea gave books to schools in Indonesia, and Indonesians taught Koreans a traditional dance. This **exchange** helped them learn about each other's culture.

   a. giving and receiving things at the same time

   b. trying many different things at the same time

4. **Mobile** libraries bring books to children in many small communities. These libraries travel from town to town in cars, vans, or trucks.

   a. staying in one place   b. moving from place to place

5. A **program** in Los Angeles helps children learn about the environment by taking them to nearby mountains and beaches.

   a. set of books   b. set of activities

6. If you **record** people speaking a disappearing language, you can keep important information about both the language and its speakers.

   a. save for the future   b. talk to

7. Japanese grammar **is similar to** Korean grammar. For example, in both languages, verbs come at the ends of sentences.

   a. has features that are the same   b. has features that are different

8. One **skill** that teens can get from outdoor education is how to survive in difficult situations.

   a. an ability   b. a job

9. Parents can help to **solve** their children's learning problems by volunteering in the classroom.

   a. find an answer to a problem   b. make a problem worse

10. Taking a **trip** to a foreign country is a good way to practice a second language, but it is too expensive for many people.

    a. a book about a particular place   b. a visit to a particular place

> **Word Usage**
>
> **Record** can be a noun or a verb, but the stress is different. **Re**cord is a noun. (We have a **re**cord of this language.) Re**cord** is a verb. (They are going to re**cord** the Cia Cia language for future generations.)

30 | UNIT 2

B | Using Vocabulary. Answer the questions in complete sentences. Then share your sentences with a partner.

1. What was the last **trip** you took? Where did you go? What did you do?

   _____
   _____

2. What kinds of **skills** do you need to be a language teacher?

   _____
   _____

3. Is your native language **similar to** English or another language? Give examples.

   _____
   _____

4. What was the last problem you **solved**? How did you **solve** it?

   _____
   _____

5. What are the best ways to **record** new vocabulary that you want to use in the future?

   _____
   _____

> **Word Partners**
> Use **trip** with nouns, verbs, and adjectives: *(n.)* **business** trip, **camping** trip, **field** trip; *(v.)* **plan a** trip, **take a** trip, **make a** trip; *(adj.)* **long** trip, **safe** trip, **short** trip.

C | Scanning/Predicting. Read the main title of the reading passage on pages 32–33. Then scan the passage for names of countries. Check (✓) the countries you find. Then answer the question below.

☐ Indonesia   ☐ Korea   ☐ Japan   ☐ Mongolia

☐ the United States   ☐ Kenya   ☐ Ethiopia   ☐ Mexico

What do you think the stories in this passage are about?

1. new ways to teach languages
2. learning about the natural world
3. educational programs around the world

> **Strategy**
> When you are scanning for place names, remember to pay attention to nouns beginning with capital letters.

LEARNING EXPERIENCES | 31

LESSON B   READING

Global Education

News Stories from the World of Learning

▲ Seoul city Mayor Oh Se-hoon shows examples of Hangul to students from the Indonesian Cia Cia tribe, during a 2009 exchange visit to Korea.

Buton Island, Sulawesi, Indonesia
Indonesian Tribe Uses Korean to Save Its Native Language

A The Cia Cia tribe of Buton Island, Indonesia, speaks a language that has no written form. The language—also called Cia Cia—is in danger of disappearing. Fewer people speak it with each passing generation. When a language such as Cia Cia disappears, some of the history and culture of the speakers can disappear, too.

B In 2009, the Cia Cia tribe decided to record their language using Hangul, an alphabet from Korea. Hangul is a phonetic system—the written symbols have a direct match to language sounds. Many of the sounds of Hangul are similar to ones in Cia Cia.

C The Cia Cia sent members of their tribe to the Korean capital, Seoul, to learn Hangul. The tribe also received textbooks, teachers, and aid from Korea. A group of Cia Cia primary students began learning how to read, write, and pronounce Hangul.

D The Cia Cia people hope that the written system will strengthen their language so that it does not die out in the future. At the same time, the cultural exchange allows the Cia Cia and Korean people to learn more about each other's history and traditions.

South Central Los Angeles, USA
Nature Inspires Inner-City Kids

E Juan Martinez grew up poor in South Central Los Angeles. As a child, he was surrounded by gangs, drugs, and violence. But a school trip to the mountains of Wyoming helped him see the world differently.

F The experience also gave Martinez a career. He decided to start a program to help young people in cities get outdoors. Martinez's program takes them to the beach and to the mountains near Los Angeles. He shows them the positive value of nature, not just environmental problems. He also helps the teens develop their leadership and teamwork skills.

G By connecting kids to the environment, Martinez is helping to change lives. "Just one person showing an interest and giving [young people] an opportunity can change everything," says Martinez.

▲ Youth leader Juan Martinez

Awassa, Ethiopia; Western Mongolia
Traveling Schools Bring Education to Remote Villages

H In Ethiopia, many schools don't have libraries, which makes learning difficult. A program called Ethiopia Reads is helping to solve this problem using mobile libraries. Ethiopia Reads has an unusual way to get books to children in remote areas: Donkeys pull carts filled with children's books to rural schools and villages.

I In western Mongolia, nomadic[1] families move with their herd animals several times a year. This makes it difficult for young children to get to school. So a UNICEF program is bringing schools to the children. Teachers use *gers*—traditional Mongolian tents—as classrooms. The "tent schools" travel with the nomadic families. In this way, UNICEF aims to make education available to all Mongolian children, wherever they live.

[1] **Nomadic** people travel from place to place rather than living in one place all the time.

◄ A tent school in Mongolia

LESSON B | UNDERSTANDING THE READING

A | Understanding the Gist. Look back at your answers for exercise **C** on page 31. Was your prediction correct?

B | Identifying Main Ideas. Read the sentences about the paragraphs on pages 32–33. Check (✓) the sentence if it expresses the **main** idea of the paragraph (not a supporting detail).

☐ Paragraph A: The Cia Cia language is in danger of disappearing.
☐ Paragraph B: The Hangul alphabet is from Korea.
☐ Paragraph E: A school trip helped Juan Martinez see the world in a new way.
☐ Paragraph F: Juan Martinez started an environmental education program to help teens in cities.
☐ Paragraph H: Mobile libraries bring books to children in remote areas of Ethiopia.
☐ Paragraph I: *Gers* are traditional Mongolian tents.

Write the main idea(s) of the paragraph(s) above that you didn't check.

_____
_____

C | Identifying Key Details. Read each statement below. Then circle **T** for *true* and **F** for *false*.

1. Hangul is the name of a Korean alphabet.   T   F
2. The written symbols of Hangul are similar to the written symbols of Cia Cia.   T   F
3. Juan Martinez grew up in the mountains of Wyoming.   T   F
4. Teens in Martinez's program learn how to work as a team.   T   F
5. A donkey cart is one way that Ethiopia Reads brings books to Ethiopian children. T   F

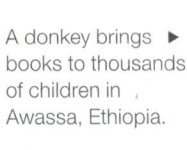 **D | Critical Thinking: Inferring/Synthesizing.** Discuss the questions below in small groups.

1. How do you think Juan Martinez and Kimani Maruge are similar? How are they different?
2. Did someone inspire you when you were in primary school or high school? In what way(s)?

◀ A donkey brings books to thousands of children in Awassa, Ethiopia.

EXPLORING WRITTEN ENGLISH

LESSON C

GOAL: In this lesson, you are going to plan, write, revise, and edit sentences on the following topic: *Describe an educational goal and explain what you need to do to achieve it.*

A | Read the information in the box. Then unscramble the sentences (1–5).

> **Language for Writing:** Using *want* and *need*
>
> Use *want* and *need* with an infinitive (*to* + base verb form) to describe things you *would like to* do (i.e., you have a choice) and things you *have to* do (i.e., you don't have a choice):
>
> *Older Kenyans saw* The First Grader, *and now they* want to go *back to school.*
> want + infinitive
>
> *I* need to study *English so I can improve my grade.*
> need + infinitive
>
> You can also use *want* and *need* with noun phrases:
>
> *The students want* new laptops.   *The school needs* more money *to pay its teachers.*
>
> Note that *need* is stronger or more important than *want*. For example, maybe you don't *want to* study for a test, but you *need to* study in order to get a good grade.

Example: leadership skills / teach / wants / the teacher / to

   The teacher wants to teach leadership skills.

1. to school / to / some older Kenyans / want / go

   _____.

2. this month / an exam / take / to / need / we

   _____.

3. to / in Ethiopia / build / Ethiopia Reads / wants / libraries / more

   _____.

4. a writing system / find / needs / the Cia Cia tribe / to

   _____.

5. learn / the students / to / about the environment / want

   _____.

LEARNING EXPERIENCES | 35

LESSON C — EXPLORING WRITTEN ENGLISH

B | Choose *want* or *need* to complete each sentence.

Example: The tribe **wants** / **(needs)** a writing system for their language or it will disappear.

1. You can't attend a good university with a low TOEFL score; you **want** / **need** to have a high score.

2. I **want** / **need** to learn Spanish because it's a beautiful language.

3. You don't **want** / **need** to have a college degree to work in a hotel.

4. My brother doesn't **want** / **need** money for college because our family is wealthy.

C | Think about things that you *want* to do in the next five years and things that you *need* to do. Complete the chart.

Things I *want* to do in the next 5 years	Things I *need* to do in the next 5 years
visit Mexico	get a college degree

Now compare your chart with a partner's. Ask and answer questions about the information.

A: *What do you want to do in the next five years?*
B: *I want to visit Mexico.*

A: *What do you need to do in the next five years?*
B: *I need to get a college degree.*

Now write two sentences using *want* + infinitive and two sentences using *need* + infinitive about the information in your chart.

_____
_____
_____
_____

Writing Skill: *Planning Your Writing*

To plan your writing, first brainstorm a list of ideas about your topic. Then put your ideas in an order that makes sense. The ideas should connect in a logical way. For example, you can organize reasons in order of importance. You may choose to put the most important idea first and the least important idea last. You can also order the steps in a process; in other words, the first step in a process is the first step you write about.

D | Look at these lists of ideas on two different topics. Which one is a list of reasons? Which one is a list of steps?

_____ reasons   _____ steps

a. How do you choose a college?
- ☐ complete and submit your applications
- ☐ decide what you want to study
- ☐ after you visit, choose the five best colleges
- ☐ do online research; choose 10 colleges that have the courses you want
- ☐ visit as many of your choices as possible

b. Why is it important to learn a second language?
- ☐ you can study in another country
- ☐ you can make friends with people from another country
- ☐ it helps you understand more information online
- ☐ you sometimes have better job opportunities
- ☐ it makes travel more fun

E | Now put the lists in order:
- Number the steps in order of time—the first step is number 1, and so on.
- Number the reasons in order of importance—the most important item is number 1. Use your own opinions for ordering the reasons. Share your ideas with a partner.

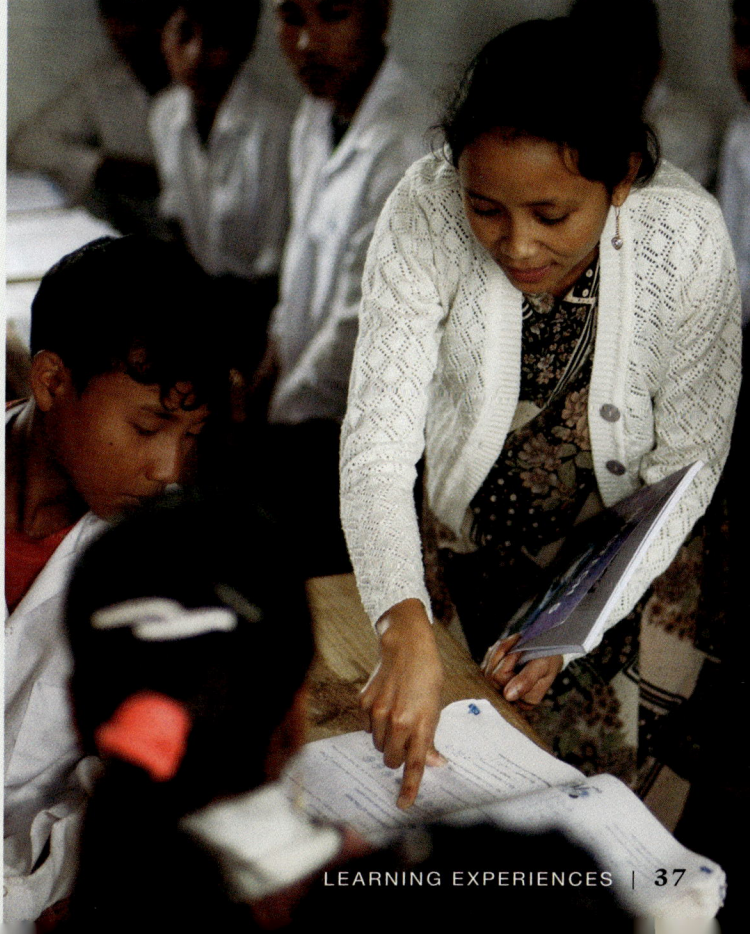

LESSON C | **WRITING TASK: Drafting**

A | Brainstorming. Think about your educational goals. Write your ideas in the chart and then share them with a partner.

Things I want to learn (examples: a subject, a language, a skill)	**Places I want to go to learn** (examples: a country, a school, a training program)	**Things I need to do or get** (examples: a degree, a certificate, a diploma)
Web design	a university in Canada	a new computer a technology certificate

B | Planning. Follow the steps to make notes for your sentences. Use the chart.

Step 1 Look at your brainstorming notes in exercise **A**. Underline your most important educational goal. What do you want to learn? Write it in the planning chart below.

Step 2 Make a list of actions—things you need to do in order to achieve your goal.

Step 3 Now look at your list and answer this question: Are all of your ideas related to your goal? Draw a line through any ideas that do not belong.

Step 4 Organize your ideas. Number them to show the correct order.

Topic: Describe an educational goal and explain what you need to do to achieve the goal.

1. What is your educational goal?

   I want to _____.

2. List at least four things that you need do in order to achieve your goal:

   I need to _____.

   _____.

   _____.

   _____.

C | Draft 1. Use the information in the chart in exercise **B** to write a first draft of your sentences.

WRITING TASK: Revising and Editing

D | Peer Evaluation. Exchange your first draft with a partner and follow these steps:

Step 1 Read your partner's sentences. Tell him or her one thing that you liked about them.

Step 2 List your partner's goal and steps in the space below.

1. My partner wants to
   _____

2. He/She needs to
   _____
   _____
   _____
   _____

Step 3 Compare your notes with the notes your partner completed on page 38. The two sets of notes should be similar. If they aren't, discuss how they differ.

Step 4 Now answer these questions about your partner's sentences:

1. Is the goal clear?   Y   N
2. Does your partner clearly describe the actions?   Y   N
3. Are all the actions related to the main goal?   Y   N
4. Are the actions organized in a logical way?   Y   N

Step 5 Share your answers in Step 4 with your partner.

E | Draft 2. Write a second draft of your sentences. Use what you learned from the peer evaluation activity.

F | Editing Practice. Read the information in the box below. Then find and correct one mistake with *need* or *want* in each of the sentences (1–5).

> In sentences using *want* or *need*, remember to:
> - use an infinitive after *want* and *need*.
> - use *need* if it is something you must do because you don't have a choice.

1. You need getting a passport before you can study in Canada.
2. The student wants to take an entrance exam when he applies to college.
3. The organization wants builds more libraries in Ethiopia.
4. Maruge went to primary school because he wanted learning to read.
5. The Cia Cia want saving their language for future generations.

LESSON C WRITING TASK: Editing

G | Editing Checklist. Use the checklist to find errors in your second draft.

Editing Checklist	Yes	No
1. Are all the words spelled correctly?		
2. Do your subjects and verbs agree?		
3. Is the first word of every sentence capitalized?		
4. Does every sentence end with the correct punctuation?		
5. Did you use *want* and *need* correctly?		

H | Final Draft. Now use your Editing Checklist to write a third draft of your sentences. Make any other necessary changes.

UNIT QUIZ

p.22 1. _____ is the ability to read and write.

p.25 2. In 1963, Kenya became _____.

p.26 3. Kimani Maruge went to New York and spoke at the United Nations about _____.

p.28 4. The _____ is the most important idea in a paragraph.

p.29 5. Alex the parrot could identify objects by their _____ and size.

p.32 6. Many of the sounds of Hangul are _____ the sounds in Cia Cia.

p.33 7. Traveling libraries and schools are bringing education to children in places such as _____ and _____.

p.35 8. If you have to do something, you

   want / **need** to do it.

Family Ties

UNIT 3

ACADEMIC PATHWAYS
Lesson A: Finding the right meaning
Identifying fact and speculation
Lesson B: Synthesizing map and textual information
Lesson C: Expressing speculation
Writing descriptive sentences about family

▲ Emerson Jones stays warm in his father's jacket during a family trip to the Southern California coast, U.S.A.

Think and Discuss

1. What do you know about your family history?
2. How do you get information about your family history?

Exploring the Theme

Read the information on these pages and discuss the questions.

1. What is genealogy?
2. How do you think the people in each photo are related?
3. Do you know the names of your relatives from two generations ago? Three generations? More?

A Trip in Time

Look in the mirror. What do you see? Maybe you have your grandmother's eyes or your father's smile. We share some of our looks and much more with our family members. From one generation[1] to the next, families pass down physical traits, favorite foods, traditions, and stories.

Your family's past is made up of many stories. For example, who were your mother's grandmothers? Where did they live, and what were they like? Your family's history may be a mystery to you. However, there are ways to learn about it. The study of family history is called *genealogy*. It starts with your parents and grandparents, and it can take you back in time.

[1] A **generation** includes all the people in a group or a country who are of a similar age.

3 ▷ generations of an Inuit family in Nunapitchuk, Alaska, U.S.A.

2 generations of Peruvians—a mother and her child—at a market in Cusco. ▽

4 generations of women in the Darhad Valley, Mongolia.

5 generations of the Walker family in Gold Beach, Oregon, USA.

LESSON A PREPARING TO READ

A | Building Vocabulary. Find the words in **blue** in the reading passage on pages 45–46. Read the words around them and try to guess their meanings. Then match the sentence parts below to make definitions.

1. Something **ancient** is ___
2. Your **ancestor** is ___
3. An **immigrant** is ___
4. If something is **major**, ___
5. If you **discover** something, ___

a. very old or from a long time ago.
b. you find it or learn about it for the first time.
c. a person in your family who lived before you.
d. a person who left one country to come to live in a different country.
e. it is very important.

> **Word Link**
> The word root *migr* means "moving or changing," e.g., im**migr**ant, im**migr**ate, im**migr**ation, **migr**ant, **migr**ate, **migr**ation.

B | Building Vocabulary. Find the words in **blue** in the reading passage on pages 45–46. Read the words around them and try to guess their meanings. Then complete the sentences.

| information | migrate | recent | section | trace |

1. _____ about something is a set of facts about it.
2. A _____ is one part of something.
3. If something is _____, it happened a short time ago.
4. If people _____, they move from one place to another.
5. If you _____ the origin or development of something, you find out how it started or developed.

C | Using Vocabulary. Answer the questions. Share your ideas with a partner.

1. Where did your **recent ancestors** live?
2. How do you think people can get **information** about their **recent ancestors**?
3. How do you think people can find out about their **ancient ancestors**?

D | Brainstorming. List things that you think people would like to know about their ancestors. Share your ideas with your partner.

_____   _____   _____

_____   _____   _____

E | Scanning/Predicting. Scan the reading passage on pages 45–46 and answer the questions.

1. Who is Spencer Wells? _____
2. Where is he? _____
3. What is he doing? _____

READING

▲ The DNA patterns of these Namibian tribesmen date back to a time before modern humans left Africa.

track 1-07

A IN JULY 2008, a crowd of people gathered in the Astoria section of Queens, New York, for the 30th Avenue Street Festival. Through the multicultural crowd walked a tall, blond man. As he walked through the market, he stopped to talk to people. Then, if they were willing,[1] he asked them for a few cells from the inside of their cheeks.

B The tall man in the crowd was Spencer Wells, the director of National Geographic's Genographic Project. Wells and his team are collecting DNA in cheek swabs[2] and blood samples from hundreds of groups around the globe. Wells and other scientists believe that human DNA patterns today can help us trace the history of human migration.

C As ancient human populations migrated out of Africa, they split off from each other and discovered new lands (see pages 52–53). Over the years, each branch developed different DNA patterns. In recent centuries, these migration paths have come together in places with large immigrant populations, such as New York City. "From the beginning of the project," Wells says, "I've wondered if it would be possible to sample all the major lineages[3] on Earth on a single street." On 30th Avenue he almost did just that. With information from their DNA, Wells was able to connect people in Astoria with nearly all the world's major migrations.

D Astoria, in fact, is one of the most ethnically varied[4] places on Earth. Marriages between ethnic groups have been common there for generations. This exchanging of DNA makes retracing the past very challenging. However, that doesn't stop Wells. Will the Genographic team be able to create the first ever complete human history? Wells is hopeful that it will. As he says, [this study of DNA] "is really the story of all of us."

---

[1] If someone is **willing** to do something, they agree to do it.
[2] A **cheek swab** is a small piece of cotton used to take a sample from the inside of someone's cheek.
[3] Someone's **lineage** is the series of families from which they are directly descended.
[4] If a place is **ethnically varied**, there are many different racial or cultural groups living there.

LESSON A READING

From Africa to Astoria

E In total, 193 people gave DNA samples in Astoria. The chart below shows the migration paths of four people. All four, like the rest of us, can trace their earliest **ancestors** to East Africa. The path of Michelle's ancestors leads from Africa directly to the Americas. The ancestors of Pedro, Atsushi, and Alma first moved out of Africa into the Middle East. Their family trees then split in different directions. For example, Pedro's ancestors probably crossed central Asia and Siberia and arrived in the Americas about 15,000 years ago.

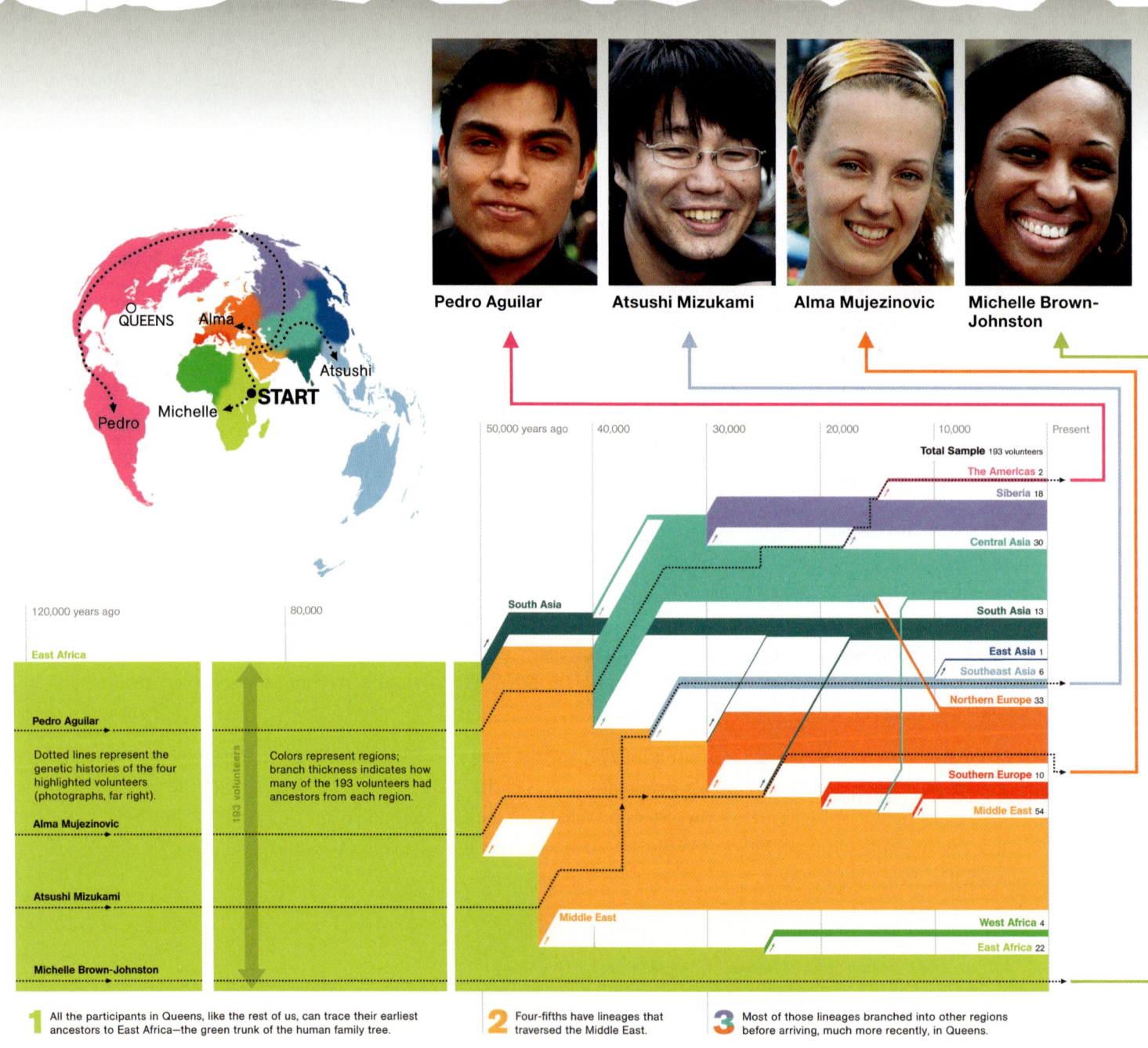

1 All the participants in Queens, like the rest of us, can trace their earliest ancestors to East Africa—the green trunk of the human family tree.

2 Four-fifths have lineages that traversed the Middle East.

3 Most of those lineages branched into other regions before arriving, much more recently, in Queens.

46 | UNIT 3

UNDERSTANDING THE READING

A | Understanding the Gist. Look back at your answers for exercise **E** on page 44. Were your answers correct?

B | Identifying Main Ideas. Choose the correct main idea for each paragraph.

1. **Paragraph B**

    Spencer Wells wants to _____.

    a. ask people about their family
    b. learn about human history
    c. learn about his own family history

2. **Paragraph C**

    One neighborhood in New York has _____.

    a. samples from many migration paths
    b. a population with very simple DNA patterns
    c. people from most countries in Africa

C | Identifying Key Details. Read the statements (1-4) about the information on page 46. Match each person (a-d) to the correct statement.

a. Pedro   **b.** Atsushi   **c.** Alma   **d.** Michelle

___ 1. This person's ancestors came to North America from Northern Europe.
___ 2. This person's ancestors came to North America directly from East Africa.
___ 3. This person's ancestors left the Middle East about 35,000 years ago.
___ 4. This person's ancestors crossed central Asia and Siberia.

D | Critical Thinking: Fact vs. Speculation. Work with a partner. Read each statement about the reading. Write **F** for *fact* and **S** for *speculation*.

___ 1. Wells and his team are collecting DNA from people around the globe.
___ 2. Human DNA patterns today could help us create the first ever complete human history.
___ 3. Astoria is one of the most ethnically varied places on Earth.
___ 4. Pedro's ancestors probably left Siberia about 15,000 years ago.

E | Personalizing. What would you like to know about your ancient ancestors? Write your question. Share your ideas with a partner.

Did/Were my ancient ancestors _____

_____?

> **CT Focus**
>
> As you read, it's important to identify which statements are **facts** (things that are certainly true) and which are opinions, ideas, questions, or other types of **speculations**. Speculations often include words such as *think*, *believe*, *maybe*, *perhaps*, and *might*.

FAMILY TIES | 47

LESSON A: DEVELOPING READING SKILLS

Reading Skill: *Finding the Right Meaning*

Remember that many words have more than one meaning. So, when you look up a word with more than one definition, pay attention to the context of the word. The context can give you an idea of what the word might mean. Then read all of the definitions in the dictionary so you can be sure you understand the word correctly.

single

1 ADJECTIVE   You use **single** to show that you are talking about only one person or thing.
I haven't seen a single person all day.

2 ADJECTIVE   If you are **single**, you are not married. *I'm married, but my sister is single.*

3 ADJECTIVE   A **single** room or bed is for one person only.
This single bed is too small for two people.

A | Matching Definitions. Look at the definitions for the words *cell* and *branch*. Then write the number of the correct definition as the word is used in each sentence.

cell

1 NOUN   A **cell** is the smallest part of an animal or a plant.
The scientists studied the sick animal's blood cells.

2 NOUN   A cell is a small locked room in a prison or a police station.
There are two prisoners in the cell right now.

_____ a. The thief escaped from his **cell** last night.
_____ b. Too much sun can damage your skin **cells**.

branch

1 NOUN   A **branch** of a tree is the part that has leaves, flowers, or fruit.
In the winter, the branches of the apple trees don't have any leaves on them.

2 NOUN   A **branch** of a family is a section of the family who are all related to the same ancestor.
One branch of my grandfather's family moved to Germany in the 1800s.

3 NOUN   A **branch** of a business is one section of the business.
I work in the New York branch of our firm.

_____ a. Three **branches** of my family stayed in Korea, but my parents left in 1972.
_____ b. I'd love to work in the London **branch** of our company.
_____ c. Birds like to sit in the upper **branches**.

B | Finding Definitions. Look up the words below in a dictionary. Write two definitions and sample sentences for each word.

cross VERB   **trace** VERB   **direction** NOUN

VIEWING

The World in a Station

▲ About 125,000 people pass through New York City's Grand Central Terminal every day.

Before Viewing

A | Using a Dictionary. Here are some words you will hear in the video. Complete each definition with the correct word. Use your dictionary to help you.

> anonymously
> heritage
> separate

1. A person's _____ is their ethnic or cultural background.
2. If people or things _____, they move apart, away from each other.
3. If you do something _____, you do it without giving your name or personal information.

B | Brainstorming. Why do you think a train station in New York City is a good place to find volunteers for the Genographic Project? Write three reasons and share your ideas with a partner.

_____   _____   _____

While Viewing

A | As you view the video, circle whether statements 1–4 are true (**T**) or false (**F**).

1. A group of Dee Dee's ancestors left Africa about 5,000 years ago.   T   F
2. Frank's ancestors were some of the first people to migrate to the Americas.   T   F
3. Cecile's family is mainly from Nepal.   T   F
4. Some of J.W.'s ancestors were probably the first humans to plant seeds.   T   F

After Viewing

A | Discuss the statements (1–4) above with a partner. Correct the false statement(s).

B | Synthesizing. Think about what you learned in the reading on pages 45–46 and the video. Imagine you are doing research for the Genographic Project in your area. Complete the sentences below.

1. I would go to _____ to find volunteers because _____.
2. I **think** / **don't think** a lot of people in my area would volunteer because _____
_____.

FAMILY TIES | 49

LESSON B — PREPARING TO READ

CT Focus

Is "So some of my ancestors were probably hunters" a fact or a speculation? How about "Archaeologists found a lot of mammoth remains there"?

A | Building Vocabulary. The words in **blue** below are from the reading passage on pages 52-53. Match each word with its definition.

I found out that some of my ancestors lived in an **area** that is now part of Siberia. Archaeologists found a lot of mammoth **remains** there. They also found a lot of **objects** such as spears and knives. So some of my ancestors were **probably hunters**.

_____ 1. **area**　　a. a thing that has a shape and size

_____ 2. **remains**　　b. a person who chases and kills wild animals for food

_____ 3. **object**　　c. likely or possibly, but not certainly or surely

_____ 4. **probably**　　d. a particular part of a town, a country, a region, or the world

_____ 5. **hunter**　　e. the parts of a human or an animal that are left after the human or animal dies

▲ Early humans hunted mammoths for food.

Word Partners

Use **common** with *(n.)* common **ancestor**, common **language**, common **enemy**, common **goal**, common **interests**, common **understanding**; *(prep.)* (to have something) **in** common.

B | Building Vocabulary. Read the definitions below for some of the words in the reading passage on pages 52-53. Then use the words to complete the paragraph.

If something is **alive**, it is living, not dead.
If something is **common**, it is shared by two or more people or groups.
Someone's **descendants** are that person's children, grandchildren, and all the family that live after them.
A **journey** is a trip from one place to another place.
If you **reach** a place, you arrive at or get to the place.

I recently did some research about my family history, and I found out that a famous actor and I have a _____ ancestor. We have the same great-great-grandfather! He came on a ship from England two hundred years ago. When he was _____, the _____ from England to the United States was very long and difficult. His ship took two months to _____ New York! I was very excited to learn this information. I wonder if, two hundred years from now, my _____ will be doing research about me!

C | Using Vocabulary. Answer the questions below in complete sentences. Then share your sentences with a partner.

1. How many of your grandparents' **descendants** can you list?

   _____

   _____

2. Describe the **area** you live in. For example, is it busy? Quiet? Crowded?

   _____

   _____

3. Name five **objects** that you usually carry with you every day.

   _____

   _____

4. What are some **common** interests that you share with your friends?

   _____

   _____

5. Describe your usual **journey** to school or work.

   _____

   _____

D | Thinking Ahead. The reading on pages 52–53 gives information about things that happened a long time ago. How much do you know about ancient history? Circle your answers to the questions below.

1. The oldest known human ancestor lived in **East Africa** / **Europe** .
2. The common male ancestor of all humans alive today lived about **5,000** / **60,000** years ago.
3. Humans probably migrated from Asia to North America **by boat** / **by land** .

E | Predicting. Look at the pictures and subheads on pages 52–53 quickly. What do you think the topic of the reading is?

a. the history of one person's ancestors

b. the history of human migration

c. the history of one major human lineage

FAMILY TIES | 51

LESSON B READING

Our Family Journey

A STUDIES OF MODERN DNA and ancient human remains tell us that all humans today come from a small group of African ancestors. Over 50,000 years ago, these ancestors began an amazing journey. After leaving Africa, they split into groups and entered new lands. By crossing from continent to continent, our ancestors migrated to all parts of the globe.

① Oldest Humans

B Omo I and Omo II are the oldest known fossil remains of modern humans like ourselves. Scientists believe Omo I and Omo II lived about 195,000 years ago.

② Distant Relative

C The common male ancestor of every living man lived in Africa about 60,000 years ago. This man was not the first human—he had human ancestors. Also, he was not the only man alive at that time. However, his descendants are the only ones still alive in the present day.

③ Leaving Africa

D The first large group of migrants left Africa about 50,000 years ago. They probably traveled through southern Arabia, across India, and into Southeast Asia.

④ First Australians

E Some of the early migrants reached Australia. Scientists have discovered stone objects and other remains in the area of Lake Mungo. The findings show that people cooked fish and other animals there about 45,000 years ago.

⑤ Across Asia

F About the same time, other groups of migrants moved across central Asia. Scientists call this area a "migration superhighway." Some humans went west, but mountains and forests made reaching Europe difficult. Most migrants went east, across flat lands called the Eurasian steppes. As they moved north, they made clothing to keep warm in the colder weather.

6 Mammoth Hunters

Discovery of hunting tools shows that humans reached Siberia about 40,000 years ago. The hunters probably followed migrating mammoths. Scientists found similar hunting tools in North America. These findings tell us the hunters' descendants were probably the first people to reach North America.

7 Early Art

In 1994, scientists found the world's oldest artwork in a French cave called Chauvet-Pont-d'Arc. Early humans painted hundreds of animals on the cave walls, including lions, rhinos, and mammoths. Scientists also found the oldest human footprints here. They are probably the footprints of a child who lived about 26,000 years ago.

9 Journey's End

In 1976, 13,000-year-old human remains were found by a river in the Monte Verde area in southern Chile. South America was the last continent reached by humans in their migration around the globe.

◂ These tools of early Americans, discovered in Cactus Hill, Virginia, may be some of the oldest yet found in the Americas.

8 Into America

About 25,000 to 30,000 years ago, the sea level was about 300 feet (90 meters) lower than it is now. At that time, a 620-mile (1,000-kilometer) "land bridge" connected Asia and North America. Humans probably migrated from Asia to North America by this bridge.

FAMILY TIES | 53

LESSON B | UNDERSTANDING THE READING

A | Understanding the Gist. Look back at your answer for exercise **E** on page 51. Was your prediction correct?

B | Identifying Sequence. Number the events below in the correct order (1-8).

_____ 1. Humans traveled from Asia to North America.
_____ 2. Humans lived in the area that is now France.
_____ 3. The male ancestor that we are all related to was alive in Africa.
_____ 4. Humans arrived in Australia.
_____ 5. Humans reached South America.
__1__ 6. Omo I and Omo II were alive.
_____ 7. Humans reached Siberia.
_____ 8. A group of humans began the first journey out of Africa.

C | Identifying Fact and Speculation. Work with a partner. Look back at the reading on pages 52–53. Write three more facts and three more speculations in the chart.

Facts	Speculations
In 1994, scientists found the world's oldest artwork in a French cave called Chauvet-Pont-d'Arc.	Scientists believe Omo I and II lived about 195,000 years ago.

D | Critical Thinking: Speculating. Discuss your answers to these questions with a partner.

1. Think about the art that was found in the cave in France. Why do you think people drew those pictures?
2. Why do you think some humans left Africa 50,000 years ago? Why do you think different migrant groups went in different directions?

E | Synthesizing. Discuss these questions in small groups.

1. Of the different people mentioned in this unit, whose ancestors do you think had the most difficult journey?
2. Based on the information in the readings and video, what do you think are some reasons to study ancient human history?

EXPLORING WRITTEN ENGLISH

LESSON C

GOAL: In this lesson, you are going to write sentences about the following topic:
Choose three members of your family and write facts or speculations about each one.

A | Read the information in the box. Then use the simple past of the verbs in parentheses to complete the sentences (1–8).

Language for Writing: Simple Past of *Be* and Other Verbs

Use the simple past to talk about completed actions in the past:

*When she **was** young, her family **moved** to a city in the north.*

The past forms of *be* are *was / wasn't* and *were / weren't*.

Add *-ed* to the base form of a regular verb to form the simple past. Add *-d* if the verb already ends in *-e*:

travel—travel**ed**   discover—discover**ed**   migrate—migrate**d**   move—move**d**

Make spelling changes with verbs that:
- end in consonant + *-y*:   try—tr**ied**   carry—carr**ied**   study—stud**ied**
- end in consonant + vowel + consonant: ro**b**—ro**bbed**   stop—sto**pped**

Some verbs have irregular past forms:

come—came	eat—ate	feel—felt	find—found
go—went	have—had	know—knew	make—made
meet—met	read—read	see—saw	take—took
think—thought			

For negative statements, use *did not (didn't)* + the base form of a verb:

*She **didn't have** any brothers or sisters.*

For more explanation, examples, and a list of irregular past tense verbs, see page 215.

1. I _____ _____ (*move*) to this country in 2012.

2. Last year, I _____ (*decide*) to learn about my family history.

3. I _____ (*study*) the information that I _____ (*find*) online.

4. I _____ (*learn*) that my grandparents _____ (*come*) from Poland.

5. They _____ (*be*) farmers when they _____ (*live*) there.

6. My mother's grandparents _____ (*make*) the journey to this country 75 years ago.

7. On the way here, they _____ (*stop*) in Japan for three months.

8. My great-grandparents _____ (*have*) five children.

LESSON C   EXPLORING WRITTEN ENGLISH

B | Write sentences using the simple past. Use the verbs in parentheses.

1. (go) _____
2. (see) _____
3. (find out) _____
4. (not be) _____
5. (be) _____
6. (not meet) _____
7. (not know) _____

Writing Skill: *Speculating*

In this lesson, you are going to learn different ways to express speculation. To show that you believe something is true, but you are not sure, use these words and phrases:

My great-grandparents **probably** *came here in 1920.* **I believe** *they arrived from Brazil.*
I think *they were farmers.* **It might be true that** *they lived in Mexico for a few years.*
It's possible that *they came here on a ship.*

Probably shows a little more certainty than the other phrases.

When you are speculating about someone or something, use a different word or phrase for speculating in each sentence.

I think *they lived in Russia.* **It's possible that** *they were farmers.*

C | Work with a partner. Rewrite each sentence below to express speculation.

1. My friend's mother lived in England when she was a child.
   _____

2. My great-grandparents came from Korea.
   _____

3. My ancestors were hunters.
   _____

4. My grandfather has a lot of old photographs of his recent ancestors.
   _____

D | **Critical Thinking: Analyzing.** Read the information below. Then complete each sentence to write a fact or a speculation statement.

1. I found my great-grandmother's passport. It lists her birth year as 1902.

   _____My great-grandmother_____ was born in 1902.

2. My father knows how to grow fruits and vegetables. His father taught him. I'm not sure what my grandfather's job was.

   _____ was a farmer.

3. My mother went to elementary school and junior high school in Tokyo. She went to high school in New York. She still lives in New York.

   _____ came to New York when she was a teenager.

4. My great-grandmother died in 1950. My mother was born in 1962.

   _____ never met her grandmother.

5. My great-grandfather was very interested in Egyptian history. My father says his grandfather traveled a lot when he was a young man.

   _____ visited Egypt when he was young.

Studying old photographs can help us trace our family history. This early color photo from the 1920s shows two men riding camels past the Sphinx and Great Pyramid at Giza, Egypt. ▼

FAMILY TIES | 57

LESSON C — WRITING TASK: Drafting

A | Brainstorming. Brainstorm a list of your family members. Include parents, grandparents, aunts, uncles, sisters, brothers, and cousins.

_____

_____

_____

_____

B | Planning. Follow the steps to make notes for your sentences.

Step 1   Look at your brainstorming notes. Circle the three people you want to write about.

Step 2   Complete the chart below with information about the three family members. These can be facts or speculations. Write notes, not full sentences. Don't worry about grammar, spelling, or punctuation.

Step 3   Choose and underline two pieces of information for each person in your chart.

Family member	
Information	
Family member	
Information	
Family member	
Information	

C | Draft 1. Use the information in the chart in exercise **B** to write a first draft of your sentences.

WRITING TASK: Revising and Editing

D | **Peer Evaluation.** Exchange your first draft with a partner and follow these steps:

Step 1 Read your partner's sentences. Then answer the questions below about them.

1. Does the writer describe three family members?   Y   N
2. Do the sentences give facts and speculations about the family members?   Y   N
3. Are words and phrases for expressing speculation used correctly?   Y   N
4. Does the writer use more than one way to express speculation?   Y   N

Step 2 Tell your partner one thing that you liked about his or her sentences.
Step 3 Share your answers to the questions in Step 1 with your partner.

E | **Draft 2.** Write a second draft of your sentences. Use what you learned from the peer evaluation activity. Make any other necessary changes.

F | **Editing Practice.** Read the information in the box. Then find and correct one simple past mistake in each of the sentences (1–5).

> In sentences using the simple past, remember to:
> - use the correct form of *be*: *was* or *were*.
> - make spelling changes when necessary, for example, *carry/carried*.
> - use the correct form of irregular verbs, for example, *go/went*, *come/came*, *have/had*.

1. My grandparents was born in Seoul, Korea.
2. My mother study science when she was in college.
3. My grandmother taked her children south after the war.
4. My aunt and uncle come to America last year.
5. I discoverd a lot of interesting information about my family history.
6. I think my great-grandmother studed medicine and worked in a hospital.

LESSON C   **WRITING TASK: Editing**

G | **Editing Checklist.** Use the checklist to find errors in your second draft.

Editing Checklist	Yes	No
1. Are all the words spelled correctly?		
2. Is the first word of every sentence capitalized?		
3. Does every sentence end with the correct punctuation?		
4. Do your subjects and verbs agree?		
5. Are the simple past verb forms correct?		

H | **Final Draft.** Now use your Editing Checklist to write a third draft of your sentences. Make any other necessary changes.

UNIT QUIZ

p.42 1. The study of family history is called _____.

p.44 2. Your great-grandparents and their parents are your _____.

p.45 3. Scientists are using samples of people's _____ to learn about human history.

p.47 4. A statement that expresses something that is not certain is called a _____.

p.49 5. If two things move apart, they _____.

p.50 6. If you think something is _____ true, you think it is true but are not totally sure.

p.52 7. All humans alive today have one _____ male relative who lived in Africa about 60,000 years ago.

p.53 8. Scientists found ancient _____ on the walls of a cave in France in 1994.

The Trouble with Trash

UNIT 4

ACADEMIC PATHWAYS
Lesson A: Finding supporting ideas
Analyzing causes and effects
Lesson B: Understanding a multimodal text
Lesson C: Using details to clarify ideas
Writing sentences to make suggestions

Think and Discuss

1. What kinds of garbage can you use again? How can you use them?
2. What kinds of problems result from throwing away garbage?

▲ A sherpa sorts plastics, metals, and other trash left by climbers on Mount Everest.

Exploring the Theme

A. Read the photo caption below and answer the questions.

1. What do you throw away? What do you recycle?
2. Do you throw away more items than you recycle?

B. Look at the information on page 63 and answer the questions.

1. What recyclable material made Cheung Yan rich?
2. How did a 14-year-old girl earn enough money to help buy a house?

Throw Away or Recycle?

The photo shows the amount of items an average family in a wealthy country, such as the United States, typically throws away and recycles in one year. On the right is 5,300 pounds (2,400 kilograms) of trash. On the left is 1,100 pounds (500 kilograms) of glass, paper, metal, and plastic that will be recycled.

From Trash to Cash

You might think trash is just something you throw away. But some people have found creative ways to turn trash into cash.

Trash made **Cheung Yan** one of the richest women in the world. Cheung Yan buys paper garbage in the United States and sends it to her factories in China. In her factories, the paper becomes cardboard boxes. Companies in China use her cardboard boxes to send products made in China, such as TVs and microwaves, to Europe and the United States. When people in the United States throw the boxes away, Cheung Yan buys them, and her trash-to-riches process starts all over again. Cheung Yan's company made $3.8 billion in 2011.

Collecting trash helped 14-year-old **Willow Tufano** buy a house. Willow collected things on the sidewalk in her neighborhood that people didn't want anymore, items such as furniture and electronics. "It's amazing the things they throw away," Willow said. If the items were broken, Willow fixed them. Then she sold the items on the Internet. She earned $6,000 from her sales. Her mother added another $6,000, and together they bought an inexpensive house in Port Charlotte, Florida. Willow continues to make money by renting the house to tenants.

LESSON A: PREPARING TO READ

A | Building Vocabulary. Find the words and phrases in **blue** in the reading passage on pages 65–66. Read the words around them and try to guess their meanings. Then circle the correct word or phrase to complete each sentence (1–10).

1. If you **take action / clean up**, you remove dirt or other unwanted items.
2. If you **collect / notice** something, you see it.
3. When you **clean up / collect** things, you bring them together.
4. To **cause / be aware of** something is to make it happen.
5. If you have a **solution / report** for a problem, you have a way to remove it.
6. When you **recycle / throw away** things such as paper or plastic, you use them again.
7. When you **notice / take action**, you do something for a particular purpose.
8. When people **throw away / notice** things, they get rid of them because they no longer need them.
9. A **solution / report** is information about something that has already happened, or is happening now.
10. To **be aware of / cause** a problem is to know about it.

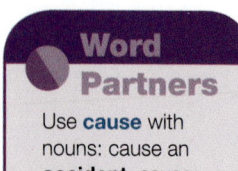

Word Partners
Use **cause** with nouns: cause an **accident**, cause **problems**, cause a **reaction**.

B | Using Vocabulary. Answer the questions. Share your ideas with a partner.

1. What problems **are** you **aware of** in your community?
2. What kinds of things do you **throw away**?
3. Think about a recent problem that you fixed. What was the **solution**?

C | Brainstorming. What kinds of everyday items are made of plastic? Share your ideas with a partner.

_____
_____
_____
_____

D | Predicting. Read the title of the passage on page 65. Then look at the pictures and the captions. What do you think the reading is mainly about?

a. causes of pollution around the world
b. a large pile of garbage on land
c. a large area of garbage in an ocean

READING

track 1-09

Garbage Island

A YOU CAN'T SEE IT from the air. It's almost impossible to see from a ship. But somewhere in the North Pacific is a giant island of garbage, floating just below the ocean's surface.

What is the island made of—and how did it get there?

B The garbage island is not really an island, but a collection of millions of bits of plastic and other objects. Pacific Ocean currents bring the objects together and cause them to spin around in a giant circle. The spinning movement stops the garbage from escaping. New objects enter the spinning water, and the island grows larger.

Who discovered the island?

C A racing-boat captain named Charles Moore found the island in 1997. He was sailing from Hawaii to California after competing in a boat race. As Moore crossed the North Pacific, he noticed many pieces of plastic around his boat. Scientists began to study the area and named it the "Great Pacific Garbage Patch."

Where does all the plastic come from?

D Much of the garbage comes from everyday objects that people throw away, such as shopping bags and water bottles. Some of these objects eventually reach the ocean. Garbage from the western coast of North America takes about six years to reach the Great Pacific Garbage Patch. Objects from East Asia take about a year. Other garbage comes from ships passing through the area.

How big is the Great Pacific Garbage Patch?

E No one really knows. Some scientists say it is about 270,000 square miles (700,000 square kilometers). Other reports say it may be up to 20 times larger—twice the size of the continental United States.

▶ There are millions of plastic bottles floating in the Pacific Ocean.

THE TROUBLE WITH TRASH | 65

LESSON A   READING

◀ In 2008, filmmaker Joel Paschal traveled across the North Pacific Garbage Patch on this boat, called "Junk." Like David de Rothschild, he hopes to make people aware of environmental problems in the Pacific. Paschal's boat is made of 20,000 plastic bottles and other garbage.

The Great Pacific Garbage Patch is not the only big garbage island. Scientists believe there are also garbage islands in the Atlantic and Indian Oceans.

Why is the Garbage Patch difficult to see?

F   It is possible to see some of the larger objects floating on the surface. However, mostly the garbage is made of tiny pieces of plastic called microplastics. These pieces are too small to see. Also, much of the garbage is floating below the ocean surface, so the Garbage Patch is difficult to see from the air or by satellite.[1]

Is the Garbage Patch dangerous?

G   The larger pieces of garbage are a problem for wildlife. For example, sea turtles often think plastic bags are jellyfish, their favorite food. They eat the plastic and die. Seabirds may die if they try to eat the plastic rings that hold six-packs of soda together.

H   In addition, the microplastics near the ocean surface block sunlight from reaching deeper water. The lack of sunlight kills very small sea creatures called plankton and algae. As these animals die, there is less food for larger fish such as tuna.

Are there any solutions?

I   Cleaning up a giant island of plastic garbage in the ocean isn't easy. But making people aware of the problem will help. One environmentalist, David de Rothschild, is sailing around the world in a boat made of plastic bottles. He hopes to use the boat, which he calls "Plastiki," to teach people about the problem of ocean garbage.

J   Another idea is to recycle the plastic garbage. Environmental engineer Cesar Harada is building a robot that collects pieces of plastic. Harada hopes to use his robot in the Pacific. Harada also has a website for reporting environmental problems. He says, "Everybody can become an environmental activist. You don't have to be part of an NGO[2] [or] a government . . . you can just actively report and take action against environmental problems."

[1] A **satellite** is an object sent into space to collect information.
[2] **NGO** is an abbreviation for Non-Governmental Organization.

UNDERSTANDING THE READING

A | Understanding the Gist. Look back at your answer for exercise **D** on page 64. Was your prediction correct?

B | Getting the Main Idea. What is the main idea of the reading? Circle the best answer.

a. There is an island of plastic garbage in the Pacific Ocean, and nobody knows where it came from.

b. Plastic garbage formed an island in the Pacific Ocean, and it is now causing environmental problems.

c. Charles Moore discovered an island of plastic garbage in the Pacific Ocean in 1997.

C | Identifying Key Details. Read each statement below. Then circle **T** for *true* and **F** for *false*.

1. The garbage island is a collection of objects spinning in the water.   T   F
2. A scientist discovered the Great Pacific Garbage Patch.   T   F
3. It takes a year for garbage from the western United States to reach the island.   T   F
4. No one really knows how big the island is.   T   F
5. Most of the garbage in the island is large pieces of plastic.   T   F
6. Sea animals sometimes eat the garbage and die.   T   F
7. Rothschild is making plastic bottles to send around the world.   T   F
8. Harada's robot collects plastic for recycling.   T   F

D | Critical Thinking: Analyzing Causes and Effects. Work with a partner. Find and underline information in the reading passage that describes the causes of garbage islands. Then complete the graphic organizer.

> **CT Focus**
>
> When you **analyze the cause or effect** of an event, you identify the reasons why it happened and the results. Ask yourself: Why did this event happen? What were some of the results?

Causes of Garbage Islands	Effects of Garbage Islands
• People throw away _____. • Ocean currents bring the objects together and cause them to _____.	• Some sea animals _____ the plastic and die. • Small pieces of plastic float on the ocean _____ and block _____. This also kills sea animals.

E | Critical Thinking: Analyzing Problems and Solutions. Work with a partner. In the reading passage, underline some possible solutions to the problem of garbage islands. Then write an answer to this question: What can people do to help clean up the oceans?

LESSON A: DEVELOPING READING SKILLS

Reading Skill: *Finding Supporting Ideas*

Supporting ideas tell the reader more about the main idea of a paragraph. Supporting ideas usually answer questions such as "What?", "How?", and "Why?" about the main ideas in a reading passage.

Supporting ideas can do the following:

- give reasons for ideas—in other words, answer the question "Why?"
- give examples of ideas—descriptions of specific things that show you what the main idea means. Examples can answer questions such as "What?" and "How?"

Read the following paragraph:

track 1-10

There are certain things our community can do to become more environmentally responsible. It's important that we become more environmentally responsible to make our city a better place to live now and in the future. First, we should start recycling more and throwing away less. We can collect cans, bottles, paper, and metal from homes and businesses and send them to the city's recycling center. We can also clean up the air and save resources by finding better ways of getting around town. For example, we can drive our cars less and walk or ride bicycles more. Finally, we can help to teach the community about the importance of caring about our environment. We can start environmental education programs for children, including trips to nearby mountains and beaches. If we educate children, they will feel a closer connection to the natural world.

The **green** sentences in the paragraph give reasons for ideas—**why** the community should be more environmentally responsible and why we should take children on trips outside the city. The **blue** sentences give examples—**what** items the writer suggests people recycle, **how** to get around without cars, and **how** to teach people about the environment.

A | Matching. Match the supporting ideas with the main ideas.

_____ 1. Plastic is bad for the environment.
_____ 2. Recycling creates jobs.
_____ 3. Recycling improves the quality of the air.

a. Recycling employs over 1.1 million people in the United States, according to the U.S. Recycling Economic Information Project.

b. According to the EPA, in 2009, recycling helped to reduce 178 million metric tons of carbon emissions.

c. Plastic does not break down quickly.

B | Finding Supporting Ideas. Find supporting ideas in the reading passage on pages 65–66 to answer these questions.

1. Paragraph B: How do garbage islands keep growing?

   _____

2. Paragraph G: Why is the garbage island dangerous for animals?

   _____

3. Paragraph I: Why did David de Rothschild build a boat made of plastic?

VIEWING

Trash People

▲ H. A. Schult's "Trash People" have travelled to cities all over the world, including Rome, Italy, in 2007.

Before Viewing

A | Using a Dictionary. You will hear these words and phrases in the video. Complete each sentence with the correct word or phrase. Use your dictionary to help you.

| garbage collectors | landfill |
| sculpt | transform |

1. If you _____ something, you make a solid piece of art.
2. _____ take trash away from people's homes.
3. If you _____ something, you change it.
4. When people place large amounts of trash in deep holes in the ground, they create a _____.

B | Brainstorming. Work with a partner. What are some different things that an artist might do with trash? Write your ideas on the lines.

take photos of it, _____

While Viewing

A | Read questions 1–3. Circle the best answer(s) as you watch the video.

1. What is H. A. Schult doing with trash?
   a. making sculptures of famous people   b. making sculptures of ordinary people
2. Where does Schult get his trash?
   a. from a landfill   b. from garbage collectors
3. According to the video, which countries have Schult's sculptures been to?
   a. Egypt   b. China   c. Russia   d. the United States
   e. South Africa f. Switzerland g. Germany   h. France

After Viewing

A | Discuss your answers to questions 1–3 above with a partner.

B | Synthesizing/Evaluating. Think about Rothschild's, Harada's, and Schult's ideas for taking action against the problems of garbage. Which idea do you think is best? Why?

THE TROUBLE WITH TRASH | 69

LESSON B — PREPARING TO READ

A | Building Vocabulary. Read the definitions below of some of the words and phrases in the reading passage on pages 72–73. Complete each sentence (1–5) with the correct word or phrase.

> A **company** is a business that sells things.
> When you **deal with** something, you work with or use it.
> When you **create** something, you make it.
> When you **combine** things, you join them.
> **Material** is something you use to make things.

1. Some artists _____ different types of garbage to make art objects. For example, H. A. Schult puts metal and plastic together to make sculptures of people.

2. A recycling _____ makes money by processing garbage, for example, by cleaning pieces of glass and then selling them.

3. Artists _____ new and interesting things from everyday objects. For example, H. A. Schult makes sculptures from garbage.

4. Recyclers often _____ dangerous objects. For example, they work with glass and sharp pieces of metal.

5. To make his sculptures, H. A. Schult uses many types of _____, such as paper, glass, plastic, and metal from landfills.

B | Building Vocabulary. Find the words in **blue** in the reading passage on pages 72–73. Read the words around them and try to guess their meanings. Then match the sentence parts below to make definitions.

Word Partners
Use **despite** with a noun or a noun phrase followed by a comma: despite **the danger**, despite **the late hour**, despite **all the problems**, despite **the fact that the work is very dangerous**.

1. You use the word *despite* _____
2. If you **receive** something, _____
3. If you feel **proud**, _____
4. An **organization** _____
5. An **image** _____

a. you feel pleased about something that you did.
b. to introduce a contrasting idea.
c. is a picture.
d. you get it after someone sends it to you.
e. is an official group of people.

70 | UNIT 4

C | Using Vocabulary. Answer the questions in complete sentences. Then share your sentences with a partner.

1. What kinds of objects do you **deal with** every day?
2. What colors do you **combine** to get orange? What colors do you **combine** to get purple?
3. Do you **create** any kind of art? What do you **create**?
4. Do you have a favorite **image**? Describe it.
5. Do you feel **proud** of the work you do in your English classes? Explain.

D | Predicting. Answer the questions about the photo below. Then share your answers with a partner. Are your predictions similar?

1. Where do you think the people are? What kind of place is it?
2. The man standing in front is Vik Muniz. What do you think his job is?
3. Who are the people behind him? What do you think they are doing?

LESSON B READING

The Art of Recycling

Brazilian artist Vik Muniz combines everyday objects and situations in unusual ways. Through his art, Muniz makes people think differently about their everyday lives—even their own garbage.

72 | UNIT 4

◀ Artist Vik Muniz photographed a landfill worker in the style of a famous French painting, *The Death of Marat* (left). He then made a huge image of the worker on the floor of his studio using garbage from the landfill (far left). A photograph of this artwork sold for $50,000.

🎧 track 1-11

A BEGINNING IN 2007, artist Vik Muniz worked on a two-year project at one of the largest landfills in the world. The landfill, called Jardim Gramacho, receives about 70 percent of the garbage from Rio de Janeiro. About 3,000 garbage pickers, known as *catadores*, work at the landfill. Their job is to hunt through the garbage for recyclable cans, bottles, and other materials. They then make money by selling the objects to recycling companies.

B The catadores' work is dirty and dangerous, and most of them only receive between $20 and $25 a day. However, many catadores are proud of their work, despite the hard conditions. Valter dos Santos, a worker at Jardim Gramacho for more than 25 years, told Muniz: "I am proud to be a picker. I try to explain to people [that recycling prevents] great harm to nature and the environment. People sometimes say, 'But one single [soda] can?' One single can is of great importance! [T]hat single can will make the difference."

C Muniz became friends with dos Santos and other catadores. They allowed him to take their photographs at the landfill. The workers then helped Muniz create huge images of these photos on the floor of Muniz's studio. They used material from the landfill to add color and depth to the images. As Muniz explained, "I want[ed] to be able to . . . change the lives of people with the same materials they deal with every day."

D His images did change the catadores' lives in many ways. One of the pictures sold for £28,000 ($50,000) at a London art auction. Muniz gave the money to the catadores' workers organization. Because other people saw the pictures as works of art, the catadores began to see themselves differently. "Sometimes we see ourselves as so small," says Irma, a cook at Gramacho, "but people out there see us as so big, so beautiful."

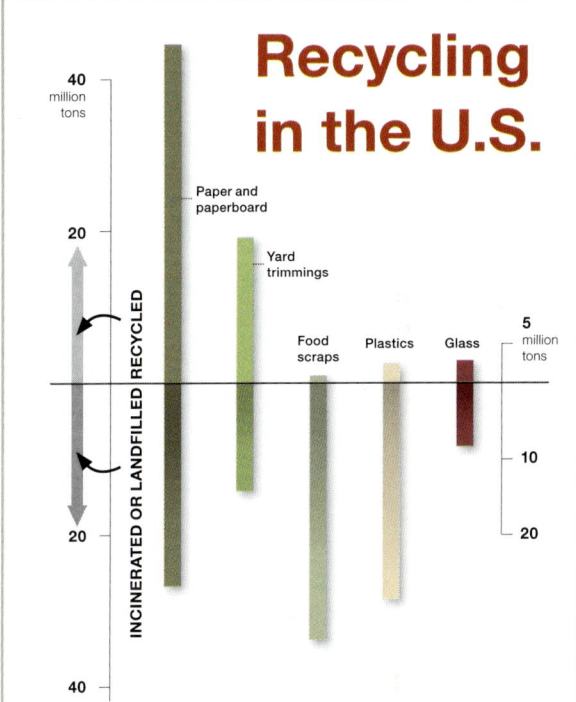

What Gets Recycled?

U.S. households produce large amounts of waste every day. In 2000 alone, the EPA (Environmental Protection Agency) reports American households and businesses produced 243 million tons (220 metric tons) of garbage, or about 4.3 pounds (1.9 kilograms) per person. Much of this waste comes from paper and yard trimmings (the material left after people clean up their gardens—for example, dead plants and cut grass). Other waste is from plastics, glass, and food scraps. Some of this waste, particularly paper and yard waste, gets recycled. The rest is usually incinerated (burned) or put into landfills—deep holes in the ground.

LESSON B — UNDERSTANDING THE READING

A | Understanding the Gist. Look back at your answers for exercise **D** on page 71. Were your predictions correct?

B | Scanning for Key Details. Complete the following sentences about "The Art of Recycling." Note the paragraph where you find the information.

1. The catadores of Jardim Gramacho work at one of the largest _____ in the world.   Paragraph: _____

2. Vik Muniz and the catadores used garbage to add _____ and _____ to the large images on Muniz's studio floor.
   Paragraph: _____

3. Most catadores only receive between _____ and _____ a day.   Paragraph: _____

4. Muniz made money from one of his images, and he gave the money to the catadores' _____.   Paragraph: _____

C | Identifying Supporting Ideas. Find supporting ideas in the reading passage on pages 72–73 to answer these questions.

1. What do catadores do? Find two supporting ideas that explain what they do.

   _____.

2. Why is Valter dos Santos proud to be a picker? Find a supporting idea that gives a reason.

   _____.

3. How did Muniz's images help the catadores? Find a supporting idea that gives an example.

   _____.

D | Critical Thinking: Analyzing Graphs. What usually gets recycled in the United States? What usually is incinerated (burned) or goes into landfills? Put each item in the chart.

| paper   glass   food scraps   plastic   yard waste |

Mostly recycled	Mostly incinerated or landfilled

E | Critical Thinking: Synthesizing. How are Rothschild's, Schult's, and Muniz's ideas for solving the problem of garbage similar? Write **R**, **S**, and/or **M** for each sentence, and discuss in a group.

_____ They are using art to solve the problem.

_____ They are making people aware of the problem.

_____ They are using trash to solve the problem.

EXPLORING WRITTEN ENGLISH

LESSON C

GOAL: In this lesson, you are going to plan, write, revise, and edit sentences on the following topic: **What should we do to be more environmentally responsible?**

A | Read the information in the box. Then unscramble the sentences (1–5).

> **Language for Writing:** *Giving Advice and Making Suggestions*
>
> *Should*, *ought to*, and *could* are useful for talking about people's actions.
> We use *should* and *ought to* to give advice:
>
> > People **should** stop wasting resources.
> >
> > We **shouldn't** waste fuel.
> >
> > We **ought to** drive less.
>
> We use *could* to make suggestions. Making suggestions is not as strong as giving advice.
>
> > We **could** take public transportation instead of driving.
>
> The base form of the verb always follows *should*, *ought to*, and *could*.
>
> Note: *Shouldn't/Should not* is more common than *ought not to*. We do not use the negative form of *could* to make suggestions.
>
> For more explanation and examples, see page 216.

Example: bring / our own bags / should / to the store / we

We should bring our own bags to the store.

1. start / the school / could / a recycling program

   _____

2. solar energy / use / the school / should

   _____

3. ought to / we / broken things / repair

   _____

4. shouldn't / plastic bags / stores / use

   _____

5. people / turn down / ought to / the heat

   _____

LESSON C — EXPLORING WRITTEN ENGLISH

B | Use *should* and *could* and the cues below to write sentences.

Example: We / buy / used furniture. (*advice*)

We should buy used furniture.

1. We / make people aware of / the problem of garbage islands. (*suggestion*)
   _____

2. We / not waste food. (*advice*)
   _____

3. People / buy fewer things. (*suggestion*)
   _____

4. People / not buy / water in plastic bottles. (*advice*)
   _____

5. Students / use / recycled paper in school. (*advice*)
   _____

6. Art students / make / art objects from trash at school. (*suggestion*)
   _____

C | Think about environmental problems at your school, or in your city or town. What *should*, *ought*, and *could* you do to make it a better place? Think about making it a cleaner, more attractive, safer, or healthier place. Make notes about possible solutions in the chart.

Problems at My School	Possible Solutions
not enough trees	plant more trees

Compare your ideas in small groups. Which ideas are the best?

Now write three sentences about the ideas in your chart using *should* or *ought to*, and three sentences using *could*.

Example: _We should plant more trees at my school._

76 | UNIT 4

Writing Skill: *Using Details to Clarify Ideas*

Details help the reader clearly understand your ideas. Details can be adjectives that describe your key ideas. They can also be facts about your key ideas, or examples of your key ideas. You can use the phrases *such as* and *for example* to introduce examples.

Compare these sentences:

Harada invented a robot. → Harada invented a <u>garbage-collecting</u> robot. (adjective)

My family buys a lot of plastic water bottles. → My family buys <u>30</u> plastic water bottles <u>a week</u>. (fact)

My community recycles things. → My community recycles things, <u>such as paper, glass, and plastic</u>. (examples)

D | Identifying Details. Check (✓) the sentences that have details. Then underline the detail words.

☐ 1. We can reuse plastic containers and fill them with leftover food.
☐ 2. We should recycle more things.
☐ 3. We can fix broken items, such as clothes and toys, and reuse them or sell them.
☐ 4. We should recycle items, for example, newspapers, glass, and plastic.
☐ 5. People should drive one day less each week.
☐ 6. People should be aware of environmental problems, such as garbage islands.
☐ 7. We shouldn't waste resources.
☐ 8. People shouldn't throw things away.

E | Matching. Match the sentences and the details. Then rewrite the sentences using the details.

Sentences	Details
_____ We should recycle bottles.	a. such as sea turtles and birds
_____ Garbage islands are a problem for wildlife.	b. such as paper, plastic, and glass
_____ We should try to recycle more of our waste.	c. plastic water bottles

1. _____
2. _____
3. _____

LESSON C WRITING TASK: Drafting

A | Brainstorming. Being environmentally responsible means paying attention to and taking care of the environment. Brainstorm a list of all the things people should do to become more environmentally responsible. Use the ideas in this unit and your own ideas.

clean up trash,

_____

_____

B | Planning. Follow the steps to make notes for your sentences.

Step 1 Look at your brainstorming notes in exercise **A**. Put a check mark next to five or more of the most important things that people should do to become more environmentally responsible. Complete the sentence in item 1 in the chart below with the number of ideas you have.

Step 2 List the things that you *should*, *ought to*, and *could* do to be more environmentally responsible.

Step 3 Check your list of ideas. Do they all relate to your first sentence? Are there any sentences that aren't related?

Step 4 Look at your brainstorming notes again. What details can you add to each item in your list? Use details to make your ideas clearer.

1. There are _____ things that we should do to become more environmentally responsible.

2. What should we do to be more environmentally responsible?

_____

_____

_____

_____

_____

_____

C | Draft 1. Use the information in the chart in exercise **B** to write a first draft of your sentences.

WRITING TASK: Revising and Editing

D | Peer Evaluation. Exchange your first draft with a partner and follow these steps:

Step 1 Answer the questions below about your partner's sentences.

1. Are the sentences about things that people should do to become more environmentally responsible? Y N
2. Does the first sentence explain what the rest of the sentences are about? Y N
3. Do the sentences have details that give you a clear pictureof the writer's main idea? Y N

Step 2 Tell your partner one thing that you liked about his or her sentences.

Step 3 Share your answers to the questions in Step 1 with your partner.

E | Draft 2. Write a second draft of your sentences. Use what you learned from the peer evaluation activity. Make any other necessary changes.

F | Editing Practice. Read the information in the box. Then find and correct one mistake with *should*, *ought to*, and *could* in each of the sentences (1–8).

> In sentences with *should*, *ought to*, and *could*, remember to:
> - use the base form of the verb after *should*, *ought to*, and *could*.
> - use *to* with *ought*.

1. People could to recycle computer paper by printing on both sides.
2. The school ought turn off the lights at night.
3. We shouldn't takes long showers.
4. We should to use public transportation and not drive to work.
5. We ought buy less and recycle more.
6. Students could to plant more trees at their school.
7. We could saving energy if we unplug our computers at night.
8. People should being more aware of the environment.

LESSON C WRITING TASK: Editing

G | Editing Checklist. Use the checklist to find errors in your second draft.

Editing Checklist	Yes	No
1. Are all the words spelled correctly?		
2. Is the first word of every sentence capitalized?		
3. Does every sentence end with the correct punctuation?		
4. Do your subjects and verbs agree?		
5. Did you use *should*, *ought to*, and *could* correctly?		

H | Final Draft. Now use your Editing Checklist to write a third draft of your sentences. Make any other necessary changes.

UNIT QUIZ

p.63 1. Cheung Yan made money by _____ paper garbage in the U.S. and recycling it as cardboard _____.

p.64 2. When you _____ things, you use them again.

p.64 3. When you _____ things _____, you don't use them again.

p.65 4. There is a giant area of garbage in the North _____.

p.68 5. A _____ explains or gives reasons or examples for the main idea in a paragraph.

p.69 6. German artist H. A. Schult uses garbage to make _____ of people.

p.70 7. The word *despite* introduces a _____ idea.

p.73 8. Jardim Gramacho is a large _____ that receives garbage from Rio de Janeiro.

UNIT 5

The World in Our Kitchen

ACADEMIC PATHWAYS
Lesson A: Scanning for key details
Reflecting critically
Lesson B: Identifying pros and cons in a passage
Lesson C: Using synonyms to avoid repetition
Writing sentences to express an opinion

Think and Discuss

1. Where do you buy your fruits and vegetables?
2. Are any of your fruits and vegetables grown locally (from places near where you live)? Which come from other countries?

▲ Fresh tomatoes are loaded onto an old cart, ready to be taken to a market in Yogyakarta, Indonesia.

Exploring the Theme

A. Look at the information on these pages and answer the questions.

1. Which countries buy a lot of grains from other countries? Why?
2. What does the map show? Where does most of your country's food come from?
3. Which countries produce a lot of iron and copper? Can you think of any items that use those materials?

Basic Foods

Grains are the edible parts (the parts we can eat) of cereal plants such as rice, corn, and wheat. We get most of our food energy from grains. Countries such as Japan and Korea do not have much land for farming, so they import grains from other countries. The largest exporter of grains is the United States.

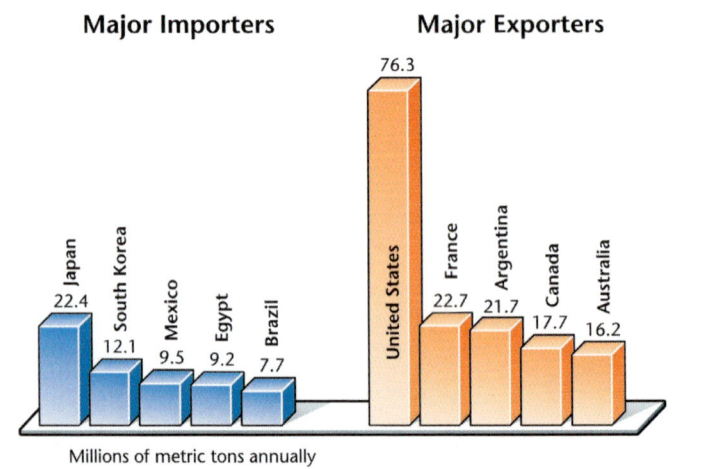

Major Importers
- Japan: 22.4
- South Korea: 12.1
- Mexico: 9.5
- Egypt: 9.2
- Brazil: 7.7

Major Exporters
- United States: 76.3
- France: 22.7
- Argentina: 21.7
- Canada: 17.7
- Australia: 16.2

Millions of metric tons annually

A strong wind helps these Chinese farmers collect grains of millet, a cereal crop grown for food.

Global Trade

Millions of tons of **grain**, **meat**, and **fish** move around the globe every year. North America, for example, buys about $14 billion worth of agricultural products from Asia every year. It sells more than twice that amount to Asia, about $33 billion worth of food.

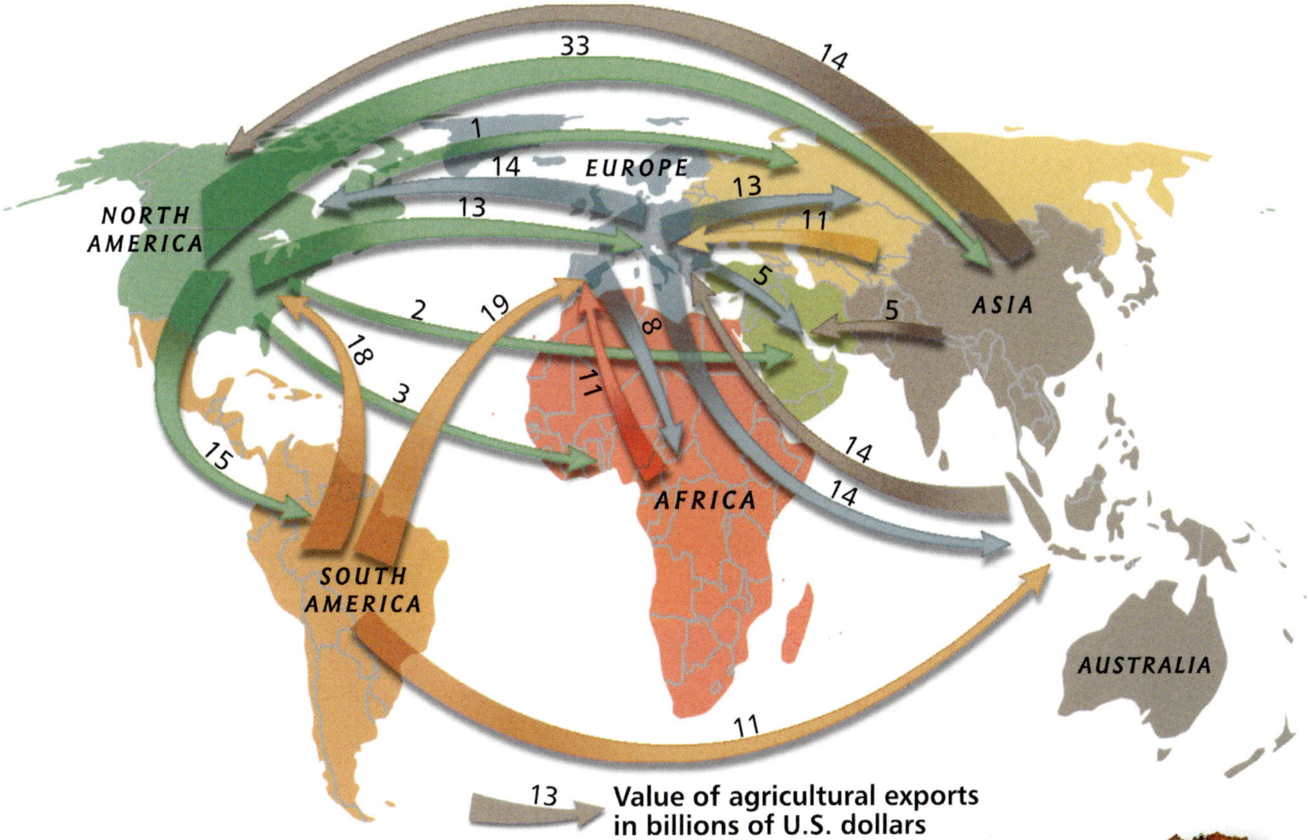

Value of agricultural exports in billions of U.S. dollars

Raw Materials

Iron and **copper** are used to make many items that we use every day. But where do these two metals come from?

People have mined and used copper for over 10,000 years. Major producers of copper are Chile, Peru, and the United States.

Much of the world's iron comes from China. Other major producers are Japan, Russia, and India. Iron is useful for making steel, which is used to make many kitchen items such as knives, forks, and spoons.

◀ A gecko licks food from a plate and fork left at an outdoor cafe in Hawaii.

THE WORLD IN OUR KITCHEN | **83**

LESSON A PREPARING TO READ

A | Building Vocabulary. Find the words in **blue** in the reading passage on pages 85–86. Read the words around them and try to guess their meanings. Then match the sentence parts below to make definitions.

> **Word Partners**
>
> Use **basic** with: (n.) basic **foods**, basic **knowledge**, basic **materials**, basic **needs**, basic **services**, basic **skills**.

_____ 1. An **item** is
_____ 2. A **century** is
_____ 3. If something is **electric**,
_____ 4. If you **melt** something,
_____ 5. If something is **basic**,

a. you change it from a solid to a liquid.
b. one thing in a list or a group of things.
c. it is very simple and important.
d. you usually have to plug it in to use it.
e. a period of 100 years, for example, from 1901 to 2000.

B | Building Vocabulary. Find the words in **blue** in the reading passage on pages 85–86. Read the words around them and try to guess their meanings. Then complete the sentences.

| appreciate | consider | honest | instructions | task |

1. A set of _____ is information about how to do something.
2. A _____ is a kind of activity or work.
3. If you _____ something, you think about it.
4. If you are _____, you tell the truth and do not steal or cheat.
5. If you _____ something, you are grateful for it and know it is valuable.

C | Using Vocabulary. Answer the questions. Share your ideas with a partner.

1. What are three **basic items** that you need every day?
2. What kinds of things do you read **instructions** for?
3. What are three things that you **appreciate**?

D | Brainstorming. Discuss the questions below with a partner.

1. List three electric items in your home.

   _____ _____ _____

2. What do you think each item is made of?

E | Predicting. The reading on pages 85–86 is about a man who tried to build a toaster. What materials do you think he needed to build it? Make a list with a partner.

84 | UNIT 5

READING

▲ The tools Thomas Thwaites used to build his toaster

track 1-12

A IN THE BOOK *Mostly Harmless*, by Douglas Adams, a man from 20th-century Earth travels to a strange planet. The people on the planet don't have technology. At first, the man thinks he can become the people's leader because he knows about technology. However, he soon realizes he can't create technology by himself. As Adams writes in the book, "[By himself], he couldn't build a toaster. He could just about make a sandwich, and that was it."

B In 2010, a British designer named Thomas Thwaites was inspired by this story. After reading it, he decided to build an electric toaster by himself, using raw materials.[1] To begin his "Toaster Project," Thwaites looked at all the toasters in a store. He bought the cheapest toaster because he thought that it would be the easiest one to build. He took it apart to see what it was made of. Although the toaster seemed simple, it had 400 different pieces! These pieces were made from about a hundred different materials from all over the world.

C Thwaites decided to start by making a few basic materials. As he later said, "I didn't have the rest of my life to work on this project. I had maybe nine months." Three of the materials were steel, for the heating grill; plastic, for the toaster's casing and cord; and copper, to make the internal wires and the pins of the electric plug.

[1] **Raw materials** are in their natural state before being processed or used in manufacturing.

THE WORLD IN OUR KITCHEN | 85

LESSON A   READING

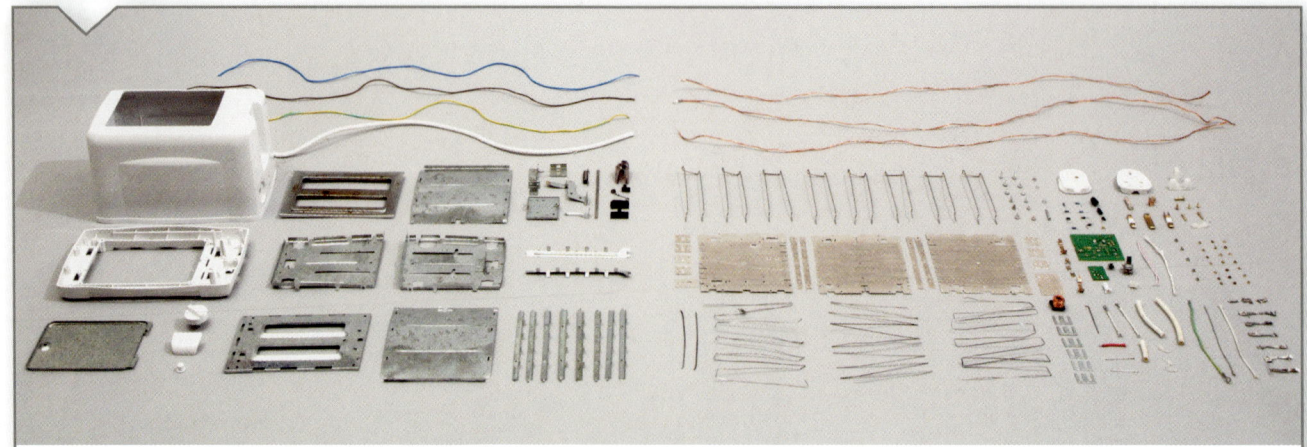

How to Make a **Toaster**

▲ A typical toaster has about 400 parts.

D   First, Thwaites needed some steel. In an old book, he found instructions for making steel from iron using fire and a leaf blower.² So he went to a mine in England to get some iron. Then he worked for a day and a half in his mother's backyard trying to make steel from iron. It was slow work, and he needed to use a microwave to finish the task. Finally, he made his first piece of steel. It was the size of a small coin.

E   After steel, Thwaites needed some copper. He went to a mine in Wales that was once the largest copper mine in the world. He collected mine water with dissolved³ copper in it. Thwaites used the copper from the water to make wires and the pins for the toaster's electric plug.

F   Thwaites then needed some plastic. He considered that, in the future, we will find a lot of plastic in the ground. It will be there because of all the plastic garbage that we put into landfills today. In that way, plastic will be a kind of raw material. So he went to a waste-processing plant⁴ and found some used plastic. He melted the plastic and shaped it to form the toaster's casing.

G   At last, Thwaites had some basic materials. He began to put together the parts to create a toaster. The end result wasn't pretty, but would it work? Thwaites plugged it in, and it started toasting! Unfortunately, after about five seconds, the wires melted. As Thwaites says, "I considered it a partial success, to be honest."

H   A toaster is one of the simplest kitchen items. However, Thwaites worked for several months to make a toaster that worked for a few seconds. The next time you use a toaster—or any everyday item—consider what it is made of and where the materials come from. You might appreciate your piece of toast just a little more!

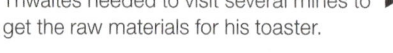

▶ Thwaites needed to visit several mines to get the raw materials for his toaster.

² A **leaf blower** is a gardening tool that blows air to push leaves into a pile.
³ If a substance **dissolves** in liquid, it becomes mixed with the liquid and can no longer be seen.
⁴ A **plant** is a factory or a place where power or material is produced.

UNDERSTANDING THE READING

A | Understanding the Gist. Look back at your answer for exercise **E** on page 84. Were your predictions correct?

B | Identifying Main Ideas. Look back at the reading on pages 85–86. Match each main idea below to one of these paragraphs from the reading: **B**, **C**, **F**, **G**, and **H**.

_____ 1. Thwaites decided to make some basic materials.

_____ 2. Even simple items take a lot of effort to make, and they require a lot of raw materials.

_____ 3. Thwaites found plastic at a waste-processing plant.

_____ 4. Thomas Thwaites decided to try to make a toaster.

_____ 5. With his basic materials, Thwaites put together a toaster.

C | Identifying Key Details. Scan the reading on pages 85–86 to find information to complete each sentence.

☐ a. Thwaites discovered that the toaster had more than ___400___ pieces.

☐ b. It took Thwaites _____ days to make a piece of steel.

[1] c. Thwaites was inspired by a _____ called *Mostly Harmless*.

☐ d. Thwaites's toaster worked for _____ seconds.

☐ e. Thwaites started the Toaster Project in _____.

☐ f. Thwaites used plastic to make the _____ of the toaster.

☐ g. Thwaites used copper to make _____ and _____.

☐ h. Thwaites went to a _____ to look at the toasters.

☐ i. Thwaites took a toaster apart to see what it was _____.

D | Sequencing. Now number the sentences in exercise **C** to order the steps in Thwaites's process. The first step is numbered for you.

E | Critical Thinking: Reflecting. Work with a partner. Discuss your answers to the questions below.

1. Think of the household items that you use the most often. Which three items do you appreciate the most? Why?

2. Where are the items made? Do you know what the items are made of? Where do you think the different parts come from?

> **Strategy**
>
> To understand a **process**, look for certain words that writers often use to introduce the steps, such as *to begin*, *first*, *next*, *then*, *after*, and *finally*.

> **CT Focus**
>
> As you read, **reflect** on whether the information changes how you feel about the topic or issue. Did you learn something new? Does it change your opinion?

LESSON A
DEVELOPING READING SKILLS

Reading Skill: *Scanning for Key Details*

Scanning helps you find important, or *key*, details quickly. When you scan, you move your eyes quickly over the reading and look for specific things. For example, you can look for **numbers** to find times, dates, and distances, or **capitalized words** to find names of people and places. You can also look for **nouns** and **verbs** that appear several times.

A | Scanning for Key Details. Look at the chart below. Scan this paragraph for the information you need to complete the chart.

track 1-13

People in different countries spend very different amounts of money on household items such as food and fuel. For example, in the West African country of Mali, each person spends about US $1.69 a day on household items. That amounts to US $616 a year for each person in Mali. In contrast, the average person in Japan spends about US $42.03 a day on household goods. That's an average of US $15,342 a year for every individual in Japan. Individuals in the United States spend more on household items than the residents of any other country. The average person living in the United States spends about US $29,000 a year on items such as food and fuel. That's about US $79.45 a day.

Source: *National Geographic State of the Earth 2010*

Country: _____ Yearly spending: _____ Daily spending: _____

Country: _____ Yearly spending: _____ Daily spending: _____

Country: _____ Yearly spending: _____ Daily spending: _____

B | Scanning for Key Details. Look at the concept map below. Scan the reading on pages 85–86 to complete the missing information.

Material: _____
- found some in water from a _____ in _____
- used for the pins for the electric _____
- also needed for the internal _____

Material: _____
- found some at a plant for processing _____
- Thwaites _____ it and used it to make the toaster's _____.

Material: steel
- found some iron in a _____ in _____
- used it to make steel using _____ and a _____

Thwaites' final product wasn't pretty—but it did work, for a few seconds! ▶

VIEWING

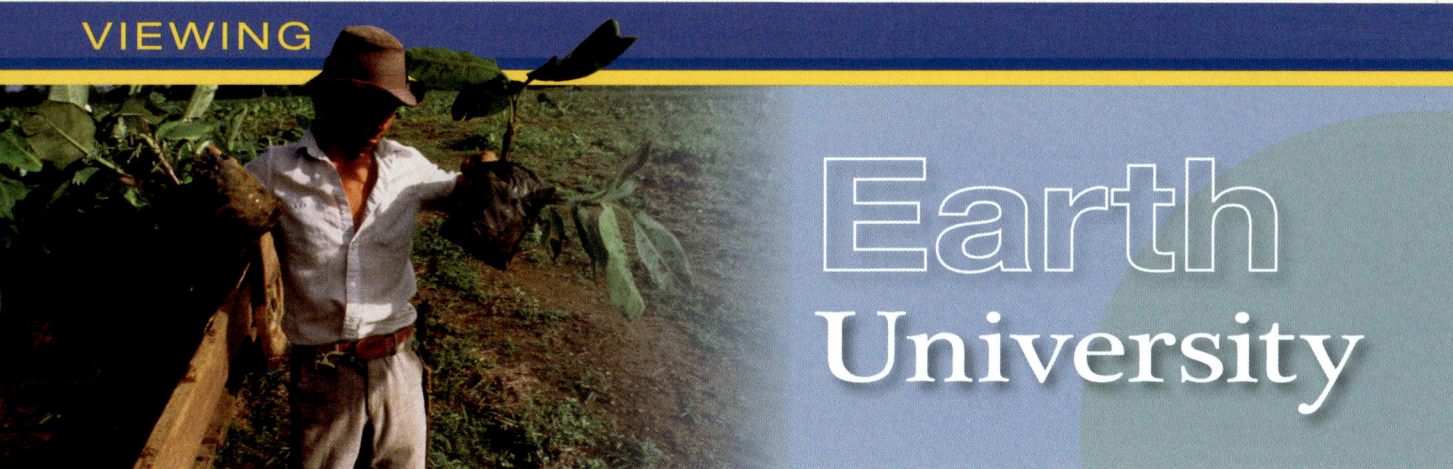

Earth University

▲ A banana farmer in Costa Rica examines one of his fresh products.

Before Viewing

A | Using a Dictionary. Here are some words you will hear in the video. Complete each definition with the correct word. Use your dictionary to help you.

> community   ecology   methods   profit   sustainable

1. _____ is the study of the relationships between living things and their environment.
2. If something is _____, it uses natural products for a long time without hurting the environment.
3. _____ is the money you make from a business.
4. A _____ is a group of people who live in a particular area or are alike in some way.
5. _____ are ways of doing things.

B | Predicting. Work with a partner. Look at the photo, the title of the video, and the words in exercise **A**. What do you think the video is going to be about? Share your ideas with a partner.

a. an ecology class in a large community
b. a place where students teach people in a community how to farm
c. a university where people learn sustainable farming methods

While Viewing

A | Read items 1–6. Think about the answers as you view the video.

_____ 1. Earth University is in   a. Costa Rica.
_____ 2. Students learn to farm without harming   b. a banana farm.
_____ 3. Most of the students are from   c. the environment.
_____ 4. Students spend six days a week in   d. Latin America.
_____ 5. Students try out sustainable methods on   e. scholarships for poor students.
_____ 6. Profits from the banana farm support   f. the classroom and on a farm.

After Viewing

A | Discuss your answers to the questions (1–6) above with a partner.

B | Personalizing. Answer the questions with your own ideas.

1. Do you grow any of your own food? Why, or why not?
2. Do you think you would like to attend Earth University? Why, or why not?

THE WORLD IN OUR KITCHEN | **89**

LESSON B

PREPARING TO READ

A | Building Vocabulary. Read the sentences below. Look at the words around the **bold** words to guess their meanings. Then circle the best definition.

1. Fast food often has a lot of **chemicals** added to it, for example, chemicals to make it sweeter.

    a. substances used in food processing

    b. substances found only in vegetables

2. Vegetarians have different reasons for not eating meat. Some are **concerned** about the treatment of animals on farms. Others become vegetarians for health reasons.

    a. confused   b. worried

3. Food companies often add a lot of sugar and salt to make their food taste better to their **consumers**.

    a. people who buy something or use a service

    b. people who sell or provide goods or services

4. Large food producers have a **corporate** responsibility to make healthy and safe food for their customers.

    a. relating to the environment   b. relating to large companies

5. Shopping at small family-owned grocery stores can help your city's **economy** because the money goes directly to local businesses.

    a. the system for making and using goods and money

    b. a system for paying businesspeople for their work

6. Countries that grow more food than their people need usually **export** food.

    a. sell goods to another country   b. buy goods from another country

7. Food with too much sugar, salt, or fat can be **harmful** to your health. It can cause problems such as high blood pressure and heart disease.

    a. dangerous   b. helpful

8. Many countries cannot grow their own crops, so they **import** wheat, corn, and other grains and vegetables.

    a. sell goods to another country   b. buy goods from another country

9. People who want to lose weight sometimes look for the latest **trends** in dieting and exercise.

   a. traditional or usual ways of doing something

   b. new and popular ways of doing something

10. It's important to **trust** the store where you buy your food. Does the store sell healthy, fresh food? Are the store's prices fair?

    a. believe that someone is honest and will not try to harm you

    b. buy goods and services from someone in your own town or city

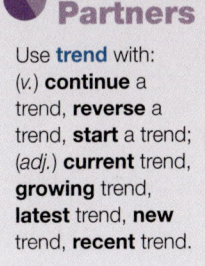

Word Partners

Use **trend** with:
(v.) **continue** a trend, **reverse** a trend, **start** a trend; (adj.) **current** trend, **growing** trend, **latest** trend, **new** trend, **recent** trend.

B | Using Vocabulary. Answer the questions in complete sentences. Then share your sentences with a partner.

1. What are three popular current **trends**?

   _____

   _____

2. What are some foods that can be **harmful** to your health?

   _____

   _____

3. What are some global issues that you are **concerned** about?

   _____

   _____

4. Which sources of information do you **trust** the most?

   _____

   _____

C | Scanning/Predicting. Read the main title and the subheads of the reading passage on pages 92–93. Then scan the passage for words that appear two or more times. What do you think the passage is mainly about?

   a. reasons why more people are eating locally grown food

   b. some ways that corporate farms harm the environment

   c. examples of the kinds of food that are very healthy to eat

THE WORLD IN OUR KITCHEN | 91

LESSON B READING

From Farm to Fork

A **WALK INTO ANY LARGE FOOD STORE** and you will probably find items imported from different countries. In today's global economy, a single store might sell beef from Australia, oranges from Brazil, and vegetables from France.

B However, an increasing number of people are concerned about the globalization of food. In particular, they are concerned about food produced by large, corporate farms. Their concerns have started a trend—the locavore movement. Locavores are people who choose to eat food products from small, local farms. Why would someone become a locavore?

1. The Environmental Argument

C Food products often travel large distances to reach a store. An orange, for example, might travel by truck from a farm to a packaging plant.[1] It might then be exported by plane to another country, where it reaches a store and then, finally, a consumer. Some food items travel long distances even within a country. Food items sold in the United States often travel more than 1,000 miles (1,600 kilometers) from farm to kitchen.

D Locavores argue that transporting goods over large distances is harmful to the environment. Burning airplane fuel,[2] for example, produces greenhouse gas emissions.[3] Locally produced products, on the other hand, consume much less fuel for transport. Because the distance from farm to consumer is shorter, local products also use less paper and plastic for packaging. In addition, small, local farms normally use fewer oil-based fertilizers and pesticides[4] than corporate farms.

[1] A **packaging plant** is a large factory where food is wrapped and made ready for transportation or sale.
[2] **Fuel** is a substance such as coal, oil, or gasoline that is burned to provide heat or power. Cars and airplanes use fuel to run.
[3] **Greenhouse gas emissions** are gases that are released into the air and cause a slow rise in Earth's temperature. The main greenhouse gas is carbon dioxide.
[4] **Pesticides** are chemicals that farmers and gardeners use to kill insects.

▲ A pumpkin farmer in Minnesota, USA, prepares to take his produce to a local outdoor market.

However, not everyone agrees that eating locally has a major effect on the environment. A recent study by Carnegie Mellon University shows that what you eat may be more important than where the food comes from. Beef production, for example, requires a lot of food, water, and land. Cows also produce methane, a greenhouse gas. Removing red meat from your diet, the study concludes, is probably better for the global climate than deciding to eat only locally produced foods.

2. The Health Argument

Locavores argue that eating locally is also good for your health. "The local food movement did not develop because of concerns about climate and greenhouse gas emissions," says economist David Morris. "It developed because people don't trust multinational[5] companies. They [want] to know the supplier [of their food]. People feel that [local food] is safer, and it's fresher."

Local products are fresher, locavores argue, because they don't have to travel so far. The products spend less time in storage[6] and transport, so they need fewer preservatives[7] and other chemicals. Locavores also argue that locally produced food items taste better. Fruit and vegetables, for example, can lose flavor and nutrients[8] during transportation and storage.

However, not all places have the right climate or agricultural land to produce a variety of food all year. So locavores may not have many in-season products to choose from. In addition, food produced on big, corporate farms is often cheaper. Corporate farms can produce large amounts of food at a time, which results in lower costs for the farms and lower prices for consumers. Despite these factors, the locavore movement continues to grow worldwide.

---

[5] A **multinational** company is one that has offices in many different countries.
[6] If you put something in **storage**, you keep it in a special place until it is needed.
[7] **Preservatives** are chemicals that keep things in good condition. Food producers use preservatives to keep food fresh.
[8] **Nutrients** are substances in food, such as vitamins and minerals, that help plants and animals grow and stay healthy.

LESSON B | UNDERSTANDING THE READING

A | Understanding the Gist. Look back at your answer for exercise **C** on page 91. Was your prediction correct?

B | Identifying Main Ideas. Read the sentences about paragraphs in the reading passage on pages 92–93. Write **M** if it expresses the *main idea* of the paragraph. Write **D** if it expresses a *detail*.

1. _____ A: Most people can buy food from around the world.
2. _____ D: Small farms use less airplane fuel than corporate farms.
3. _____ E: Cow farmers use a lot of resources to raise their cows.
4. _____ F: Locally grown food may be healthier than food from corporate farms.
5. _____ G: Locally grown food is often fresher and tastes better.

C | Classifying. Scan the reading on pages 92-93 to find advantages and disadvantages of being a locavore. Use the information to complete the chart.

Advantages of Being a Locavore	Disadvantages of Being a Locavore

D | Critical Thinking: Evaluating. Work with a partner. Discuss your answers to the questions below.

1. Do you think the writer provides a stronger argument *for* the locavore movement or *against* the locavore movement? Or does the writer provide a balanced viewpoint?
2. Think about the two main arguments for the locavore movement: health and environment. Which one do you think is the stronger reason?
3. Can you think of any advantages or disadvantages of the locavore movement that the writer doesn't mention?

E | Critical Thinking: Reflecting. Write answers to the questions.

1. How do you choose the food you eat?
2. Has this reading made you think differently about food? Explain your answer.

F | Synthesizing. Look back at the map on page 83. Discuss this question in small groups: How does the information in the map support the details in the reading passage?

EXPLORING WRITTEN ENGLISH

LESSON C

GOAL: In this lesson, you are going to write sentences about your opinion on the following topic:
Which is better—buying mostly local food or buying mostly non-local food?

A | Read the information in the box. Then write the comparative forms of the adjectives in the chart below. Use a dictionary to help you.

> **Language for Writing:** *The Comparative Forms of Adjectives and Nouns*
>
> We use the comparative form to talk about differences between two people or things.
>   Asia is **bigger than** Europe.   Europe is a **smaller** continent **than** Asia.
>   Corporate farms produce **more** food **than** smaller farms.
>
> - For most one-syllable adjectives and some two-syllable adjectives, add -*er*. If the adjective ends in an -*e*, just add -*r*:
>   small—small**er**   quiet—quiet**er**   nice—nic**er**   simple—simple**r**
>
> - Make spelling changes with adjectives that
>   - end in consonant + -*y*:   happy—happ**ier**   busy—bus**ier**
>   - end in consonant + vowel + consonant: big—big**ger**   sad—sad**der**
>
> - Some adjectives have irregular comparative forms:
>   good—**better**   bad—**worse**   far—**farther**
>
> - For adjectives with three or more syllables and most two-syllable adjectives that don't end in a -*y*, use *more* (or *less*):
>   **more** basic   **more** honest   **more** important   **more** responsible   **more** sustainable
>
> - For nouns, use *more* (or *less*):
>   Corporate farms use **more fuel than** local farms.
>
> For more explanation and examples, see pages 216–217.

Adjective	Comparative Form	Adjective	Comparative Form
1. hungry	_____	9. expensive	_____
2. bad	_____	10. easy	_____
3. large	_____	11. basic	_____
4. cheap	_____	12. thin	_____
5. sustainable	_____	13. close	_____
6. fresh	_____	14. harmful	_____
7. safe	_____	15. flat	_____
8. concerned	_____	16. far	_____

LESSON C EXPLORING WRITTEN ENGLISH

B | Use the comparative form of the adjectives and nouns in parentheses to complete the sentences.

Example: Eating fresh fruit is _____better_____ (*good*) than eating fast food.

1. Organic food may be _____ (*safe*) than food containing chemicals.
2. Vegetables are a _____ (*healthy*) choice than candy.
3. Refrigerators use _____ (*electricity*) than toasters.
4. Locally grown food may have _____ (*nutrients*) than food from corporate farms.
5. Locavores have _____ (*variety*) to choose from than people who also eat food from large farms.
6. Food from corporate farms normally contains _____ (*chemicals*) than locally grown food.

C | Write a sentence containing a comparative adjective or noun to express each idea below.

1. Johnson's Farm is five miles away. Mega Corporate Farm is 300 miles away.
   _____
2. Local farms are very sustainable. Some corporate farms are not very sustainable.
   _____
3. Food from corporate farms is cheap. Food from local farms is usually not cheap.
   _____
4. Organic produce can be expensive. Non-organic produce is not usually very expensive.
   _____
5. Large corporate farms use a lot of fertilizer. Small, local farms usually do not use much fertilizer.
   _____
   _____

D | Write three sentences using comparative adjectives. Write three sentences using comparative nouns. Write about the food you buy and eat.

1. _____
2. _____
3. _____
4. _____
5. _____
6. _____

Writing Skill: *Using Synonyms to Avoid Repetition*

Synonyms are two or more words that have the same or similar meanings. You can use synonyms to avoid repetition and improve your writing. Look at the difference between these sets of sentences.

Some people prefer to buy organic food.
These people prefer to eat food that is grown without pesticides.
They want their families to eat food that is safe and free of pesticides.

Some people prefer to buy organic food.
These people choose to eat food that is grown without pesticides.
They want to feed their families food that is safe and free of chemicals.

Note that when you use a synonym, you may need to change the word order as well. For example, in the sentences above, "They want their families to eat" changes to "They want to feed their families."

You can use a dictionary and a thesaurus to find synonyms. When you use a thesaurus to choose a synonym, look up the word in a dictionary to find the exact definition of the word. Synonyms often have slightly different meanings.

E | Using Synonyms. Read the pairs of sentences below. Rewrite the second sentence in each pair to avoid repetition. (You will need to change the underlined part.) Use your dictionary and thesaurus for help. Share your sentences with a partner.

1. Thomas Thwaites wanted to build a toaster by himself. He found out that it isn't easy to <u>build</u> a toaster.

   _____

2. Thwaites discovered that even a simple toaster has more than 400 separate pieces. He <u>discovered</u> that the <u>pieces</u> came from all over the world.

   _____
   _____

3. Thwaites needed to find instructions for making steel from iron. He <u>found</u> <u>instructions</u> <u>for making</u> steel in an old book.

   _____
   _____

4. Thwaites went to a mine to get the iron he needed. He <u>went</u> somewhere else <u>to get</u> the copper <u>that he needed</u>.

   _____
   _____

F | Using Synonyms. Write three pairs of sentences about three different topics. In the second sentence of each pair, use at least one synonym for a word in the first sentence.

LESSON C | WRITING TASK: Drafting

A | Brainstorming. With a partner, brainstorm a list of pros (good things) and cons (bad things) for the topics in the chart.

Buying Local Food		Buying Non-Local Food	
Pros	Cons	Pros	Cons

B | Planning. Follow the steps to make notes for your sentences. Don't worry about grammar or spelling. Don't write complete sentences.

Step 1 Look at your brainstorming notes. Decide which is better: buying local food or buying non-local food. Write your choice in the chart.

Step 2 Look at your notes again. Circle two reasons (pros) that explain why your choice is better. Note them in the chart.

Step 3 Complete the chart with some details for each pro.

Step 4 Check your list of ideas. Do all the pros and details help explain your opinion? Is there anything that isn't related?

Your opinion:

Pro 1:

Detail 1:

Detail 2:

Pro 2:

Detail 1:

Detail 2:

C | Draft 1. Use the information in the chart in exercise **B** to write a first draft of your sentences.

WRITING TASK: Revising and Editing

D | Peer Evaluation. Exchange your first draft with a partner and follow these steps:

Step 1 Answer the questions below about your partner's sentences.

1. Did the writer express an opinion?   Y   N
2. Do the sentences give reasons that explain the writer's opinion?   Y   N
3. Do all of the sentences give new information?   Y   N
4. Did the writer use synonyms to avoid repetition?   Y   N

Step 2 Tell your partner one thing that you liked about his or her sentences.

Step 3 Share your answers to the questions in Step 1 with your partner.

E | Draft 2. Write a second draft of your sentences. Use what you learned from the peer evaluation activity. Make any other necessary changes.

F | Editing Practice. Read the information in the box. Then find and correct one comparative adjective or noun mistake in each of the sentences (1–8).

> In sentences using comparative adjectives and nouns, remember to:
> - use *more* or *less* with nouns and with most adjectives that have two or more syllables.
> - make spelling changes when necessary, for example, *happy/happier*.
> - use the correct form of irregular adjectives, for example, *good/better, bad/worse*.
> - use *than* between the two things you are comparing.

1. Organic food is usually expensiver than non-organic food.
2. Fast food is more cheap than fresh fruits and vegetables.
3. Corporations use more fuel to local farms.
4. Fresh food is also more good for you than fast food.
5. Corporate farms are usually biger than local farms.
6. I feel healthyer when I eat well.
7. Fresh food has more vitamins and minerals as fast food.
8. The supermarket is more far from my house than the neighborhood grocery store.

LESSON C WRITING TASK: Editing

G | Editing Checklist. Use the checklist to find errors in your second draft.

Editing Checklist	Yes	No
1. Are all the words spelled correctly?		
2. Is the first word of every sentence capitalized?		
3. Does every sentence end with the correct punctuation?		
4. Do your subjects and verbs agree?		
5. Are the comparative forms correct?		

H | Final Draft. Now use your Editing Checklist to write a third draft of your sentences. Make any other necessary changes.

UNIT QUIZ

p.82 1. Rice, wheat, and corn are examples of _____.

p.84 2. A period of 100 years is called a _____.

p.86 3. Thomas Thwaites had to get _____ and _____ from mines to build his toaster.

p.88 4. _____ for details is looking over a reading quickly to find certain information.

p.92 5. People who eat locally grown food are called _____.

p.92 6. Some people believe that corporate farms harm the environment because transporting the food releases _____ into the air.

p.95 7. You can use a _____ adjective or noun to talk about the differences between two people or things.

p.97 8. _____ are words that have the same or similar meanings.

Future Living

UNIT 6

ACADEMIC PATHWAYS
Lesson A: Understanding pronoun reference
Evaluating a writer's attitude
Lesson B: Understanding a multimodal text
Lesson C: Using pronouns to avoid repetition
Writing sentences about the future

Think and Discuss

1. How do you think life will be different 50 years from now? How about in 100 years?
2. Do you think we will live on other planets someday? Why, or why not?

▲ Robovie, a talking robot, helps a 69-year-old woman with her supermarket shopping in Kyoto, Japan.

Exploring the Theme

A. Look at the information in "Making Predictions" and answer the questions.

1. What past predictions were correct?
2. What past predictions were incorrect?

B. Look at the information in "What Will Life Be Like in 2025?" and answer the questions.

1. What predictions for 2025 are likely to happen, in your opinion?
2. What predictions for 2025 are not likely to happen? Why not?

MAKING PREDICTIONS

In 1900, an American engineer, John Watkins, made some predictions about life in 2000. Many of his predictions were correct. Among other things, Watkins predicted television, mobile phones, and digital photographs.

However, predictions are often very difficult to get right. Here are some examples:

"The telephone [cannot] be seriously considered as a means of communication."

— *Western Union memo, 1876*

"I have no faith in [flying machines] other than ballooning."

— *William Thomson, British scientist, 1899*

"All the calculations . . . in this country could be done on three digital computers. No one else would ever need machines of their own, or would be able to afford to buy them."

— *Cambridge University Professor Douglas Hartree, 1951*

▲ A man chats with Bina48, a human-like robotic head.

WHAT WILL LIFE BE LIKE IN 2025?

Here are some experts' predictions for life in 2025:

- Most cars will be electric, and they will drive by themselves.
- Most of our energy will come from the sun, not oil.
- People will be able to record and replay their memories.
- Most families will own a robot.
- Some robots will have rights, such as the right to own property or run a business.

LESSON A — PREPARING TO READ

A | Building Vocabulary. Find the words and phrases in **blue** in the reading passage on pages 105–106. Read the words around them and try to guess their meanings. Then match the sentence parts below to make definitions.

> **Word Partners**
> Use **intelligence** with adjectives:
> **human** intelligence,
> **ambient** intelligence,
> **artificial** intelligence.

_____ 1. If things **adapt to** you,
_____ 2. You use "**entire**"
_____ 3. You say "**for instance**"
_____ 4. If you **suggest** something,
_____ 5. If something has **intelligence**,

a. you tell people what you think they should do.
b. to give an example.
c. it can understand and learn things.
d. to describe all of something.
e. they change in order to deal with you.

B | Building Vocabulary. Find the words and phrases in **blue** in the reading passage on pages 105–106. Read the words around them and try to guess their meanings. Then complete the sentences.

| keep track of | link | network | pattern | temperature |

1. The _____ on Mars is much lower than on Earth.
2. A _____ connects all the computers in a computer lab.
3. Some people use the calendar in their phone to _____ their appointments.
4. Some people prefer a striped _____ on their walls; others prefer plain walls instead.
5. You can _____ your computer with the Internet using a cable, or you can connect wirelessly.

C | Using Vocabulary. Answer the questions. Discuss your ideas with a partner.

1. What do you think the **temperature** outside is today?
2. How do you **keep track of** news events?
3. What **patterns** can you see around you (for example, on people's clothes or on book covers)?

D | Brainstorming. List some technologies that make life easier or more fun today than in the past.

Technologies That Make Life Easier	Technologies That Make Life More Fun
high-speed trains	3-D movies

E | Predicting. Scan the reading passage on pages 105–106 quickly. Underline five sentences with *will*.

What do you think the passage is about?

a. schools in the future
b. offices in the future
c. homes in the future

READING

HOW WILL WE LIVE?

▲ Will the homes of the future be located in tall skyscrapers like these in Dubai? And what will life inside the home really be like?

A **PICTURE THIS**: You wake up in the morning. A soft light turns on in your room. You go into the bathroom and the shower starts. The water is the perfect temperature. After your shower, you go into the kitchen. Your favorite breakfast is already cooked, and it's on the table, ready to eat. Now it's time to go to work. It's a rainy day. You live alone, but you find that your umbrella and hat are already by the door.

How is all this possible? Welcome to your future life!

APPLIANCES THAT TALK

B Technology will allow homes in the future to be "smart." Appliances will communicate with each other—and with you. Your stove, for instance, will tell you when your food is cooked and ready to eat. Refrigerators will suggest recipes based on food items you already have.

C The technology is possible because of tiny information-storing devices called RFID[1] chips. People already use them to keep track of pets and farm animals. Future RFID chips will store information about all the items in your cabinets.[2] For example, they will record the date that you bought each item. Other devices will "read" this information using radio waves. When you need more food, your cabinets will tell you to buy it.

[1] **RFID** is "radio-frequency identification."
[2] A **cabinet** is a type of cupboard used for storing medicine, drinks, and other items.

FUTURE LIVING | 105

LESSON A READING

HOUSES THAT THINK

D Are you tired of the color or pattern of your walls? In a smart home, you won't have to repaint them. The walls will actually be digital screens, like computer or TV screens. The technology is called OLED,[3] and it's here already. OLEDs are tiny devices that use electricity to light things. You can find the same technology in today's thin TV screens. OLED walls will become clear, like windows, or display colors and patterns, like walls.

E A computer network will link these walls with everything else in your house. Called "ambient[4] intelligence," this computer "brain" will control your entire house. It will also adapt to your preferences. Your house will learn about your likes and dislikes. It will then use that knowledge to control the environment. For example, it will set the heat in the house to your favorite temperature. It will turn on the shower at the right temperature. It will also darken the windows at night and lighten them when it's time to wake up.

ROBOTS THAT FEEL?

F But how about your cooked breakfast, and the umbrella and hat you found by the door? For those, you can thank your robot helper. Futurologists predict that many homes will have robots in the future. Robots already do many things such as building cars and vacuuming floors. But scientists today are starting to build friendlier, more intelligent robots—ones that people will feel more comfortable having around in the house.

G Sociable[5] robots will be able to show feelings with their faces, just like humans. They will smile and frown, make eye contact, and speak. These robots will do work around the house such as cooking and cleaning. They will even take care of children and the elderly.

H How soon will this smart home be a reality? There's a good chance it will be a part of your life in 25 or 30 years, perhaps sooner. Much of the technology is already here.

PR2
Developer: Willow Grange, USA
Abilities: cooks breakfast; takes care of elderly people; delivers mail

---

[3] **OLED** means "organic light-emitting diode."
[4] **Ambient** refers to what is around you.
[5] If you are **sociable**, you are friendly.

UNDERSTANDING THE READING

A | Understanding the Gist. Look back at your answer for exercise **E** on page 104. Was your prediction correct?

B | Identifying Main Ideas. Look back at the reading on pages 105–106. Match each main idea below to a paragraph from the reading (A–H).

_____ 1. An electronic system called "ambient intelligence" will control an entire house.
_____ 2. RFID technology will allow parts of the house to communicate with us.
_____ 3. OLED screens will change the way your walls look.
_____ 4. Intelligent homes may be a part of our everyday life within 30 years.
_____ 5. Robots that act like humans will do housework and take care of people.

C | Identifying Key Details. Read each statement below. Then circle **T** for true and **F** for *false*, according to the reading. Correct the false statements.

Appliances That Talk

1. Someday, kitchen cabinets will tell you it's time to buy more food.   T   F
2. RFID chips are already used today for keeping track of children.   T   F

Houses That Think

3. People will change their wall patterns using RFID technology.   T   F
4. Darkening windows at night is an example of ambient intelligence.   T   F

Robots That Feel?

5. Scientists are building robots that can help take care of elderly people.   T   F
6. Robots will soon be more intelligent and sociable than humans.   T   F

D | Critical Thinking: Evaluating Attitude. Work with a partner. First, circle the words to complete this sentence.

The author of the reading passage on pages 105–106 seems **positive (optimistic)** / **negative (pessimistic)** about the future.

Find examples that support your answer. Look for words and phrases the writer uses to describe the scene in the opening paragraph. Does the description make life sound pleasant or unpleasant?

Look at how the writer describes appliances, houses, and robots. Does the writer make these devices sound **practical (useful)** or **impractical (not useful)**?

Now discuss this question with your partner: Do you agree with the writer's attitude about the future? Why, or why not?

> **CT Focus**
>
> **Evaluating a writer's attitude** means thinking about how they feel about the subject. Ask yourself: Is the author generally positive or negative? Do I agree or disagree with his or her attitude?

E | Personalizing. Discuss answers to these questions in a small group.

1. Which future technologies in the reading would you like to have in your home?
2. Are there other household technologies you would like to have?

LESSON A | DEVELOPING READING SKILLS

Reading Skill: *Understanding Pronoun Reference*

Pronouns usually refer to nouns that appear earlier in a text. The pronoun may refer to a noun earlier in the sentence, or in a previous sentence. It's important to understand which noun a pronoun refers to.

Subject pronouns usually refer back to subjects in sentences:

Your favorite <u>breakfast</u> is already cooked, and <u>it's</u> on the table, ready to eat.
            subject   subject pronoun

Object pronouns usually refer back to objects in sentences:

When you need more <u>food</u>, your cabinets will tell you to buy <u>it</u>.
                object   object pronoun

Note: Pronouns always match the nouns they refer to in number and in gender.

A | Matching. Underline the subject and object pronouns in the following paragraph about Wakamaru. Then draw an arrow to the noun that each pronoun refers to.

track 2-02

<u>Engineers</u> in Japan built a sociable robot named Wakamaru. <u>They</u> designed Wakamaru to help and serve people in a friendly, caring, and intelligent way. Wakamaru can recognize faces and use gestures. It knows 10,000 words and can use them to talk to people about the weather and other subjects. Wakamaru can do many tasks for a family. For example, at night, it moves quietly around the house, but it can wake family members up if there is any trouble. During the day, Wakamaru can also send them email and text messages.

B | Understanding Pronoun Reference. Find these sentences in the reading passage on pages 105–106. Write the word(s) that each underlined pronoun refers to.

1. Paragraph C: People already use <u>them</u> to keep track of pets and farm animals.

   them = _____

2. Paragraph C: For example, <u>they</u> will record the date that you bought each item.

   they = _____

3. Paragraph D: The technology is called OLED, and <u>it's</u> here already.

   it = _____

4. Paragraph G: <u>They</u> will smile and frown, make eye contact, and speak.

   They = _____

VIEWING

COLONIZING MARS

Before Viewing

A | Using a Dictionary. Here are some words you will hear in the video. Complete each definition with the correct word. Use your dictionary to help you.

> ambitious   colonize   credible   frontier   mission   restore

1. A _____ is an important job that usually involves travel.
2. If you _____ a place, you go there and control it.
3. If you are _____, you want very much to be successful.
4. If an idea is _____, it is believable.
5. A _____ is an area where people are just starting to live.
6. If you _____ a place, you make it the way it was in the past.

B | Predicting. Do you think humans could live on Mars now? How about in the future? Discuss your ideas with a partner.

While Viewing

A | As you view the video, circle whether statements 1–4 are true (**T**) or false (**F**).

1. Only a few unmanned missions have gone to Mars.   T   F
2. There are some places on Earth that are similar to the surface of Mars.   T   F
3. We are certain that there never was any life on Mars.   T   F
4. Scientists believe that humans could live on Mars in the future.   T   F

After Viewing

A | Discuss the statements (1–4) above with a partner. Correct the false statements.

B | Synthesizing. Which technologies in the reading on pages 105–106 might be useful for living on Mars?

LESSON B | PREPARING TO READ

A | Building Vocabulary. Read the paragraph below. Notice the words in **blue**. These are words that you will see in the reading passage on pages 112–113. Match each word with its definition.

We know that it is very cold on Mars. Scientists recorded the temperature of Mars in several places on the planet. They took these temperatures to discover the **average** temperature on Mars, which is minus 60 degrees Celsius. Because the temperature is so low, there is no **liquid** on Mars, only ice. Carbon dioxide (a gas) is **trapped** in this ice—it cannot get out. However, heat can melt the ice and turn it into water. This can **release** the carbon dioxide and let it into the atmosphere. When the **level** of carbon dioxide increases in the atmosphere, Mars will become warmer.

_____ 1. **average**
_____ 2. **trapped**
_____ 3. **liquid**
_____ 4. **release**
_____ 5. **level**

a. a substance that flows freely, for example, water or oil
b. stop holding; let go
c. the normal, or typical, amount of something
d. a point on a scale, usually showing the amount of something
e. held and kept from moving

B | Building Vocabulary. Find the words in **blue** in the reading passage on pages 112–113. Read the words around them and try to guess their meanings. Then match the sentence parts below to make definitions.

_____ 1. A **survey**
_____ 2. A **goal**
_____ 3. When you **breathe**,
_____ 4. A **factory**
_____ 5. A **plant**

a. is a place where people use machines to make things.
b. is a living thing that grows in the earth with a stem, leaves, and roots.
c. is the aim or purpose of an activity.
d. is an activity in which people try to get information.
e. you take air into your lungs.

> **Word Partners**
>
> **Plant** is both a noun and a verb:
> (n.) I. a living thing that grows in the earth: **a tomato** plant; **a healthy** plant;
> 2. a factory, or a place where power is produced: **an assembly** plant; **a nuclear power** plant;
> (v.) put in the ground: plant **a tree**; plant **a flag**.

C | Using Vocabulary. Answer the questions in complete sentences. Then share your sentences with a partner.

1. What is one of your main **goals** in life? How will you achieve it?

   _____

   _____

2. What is the **average** temperature in your area?

   _____

   _____

3. What kind of **plants** grow well in your area?

   _____

   _____

4. Are there many **factories** in your area? What do they make?

   _____

   _____

5. When was the last time you gave information in a **survey**?

   _____

   _____

> **Word Usage**
>
> **Average** has noun and adjective forms:
>
> (*n.*) 1. In math, the result of adding two or more amounts and then dividing the total by the number of amounts: *The **average** temperature is 70 degrees.* 2. the normal amount or quality for a particular group: *Rainfall was twice the **average** for this time of year.*
>
> (*adj.*) 1. typical, normal: *The **average** adult man burns 1,550 to 2,000 calories a day.* 2. ordinary: *Wakamaru is not an **average** robot.*

D | Predicting. Read the title and look at the pictures and captions of the reading passage on pages 112–113. What do you think the passage is about?

a. the technology we will use to travel to Mars and other planets

b. what an average day on Mars will be like for people in the future

c. how we can make Mars a place where people can live

FUTURE LIVING | 111

LESSON B READING

AT HOME ON MARS

A **WILL HUMANS** someday live and work on Mars? Many scientists think so. In fact, they are already working on plans to turn Mars into a new Earth.

B Humans need three basic things to live: water to drink, air to breathe, and food to eat. Because of the lack of these necessities, it isn't possible to live on Mars right now. For one thing, there is not enough oxygen. There is also no liquid water—just some ice. So how can we make Mars habitable?[1] The answer, say scientists, is a process called *terraforming*.

C Terraforming means changing the environment of a planet so that it is similar to Earth's. On Mars, the average temperature is about minus 60 degrees Celsius. So one of the main goals of terraforming Mars is to warm it up. One idea for warming Mars comes from a problem here on Earth—climate change. Most scientists agree that Earth is becoming warmer due to increased levels of greenhouse gases in our atmosphere. We might create similar conditions on Mars by building factories that release greenhouse gases. The gases will change the atmosphere on Mars. Rain will fall, and it may be possible to grow plants for food. The plants will add more oxygen to the air.

D There will be many difficulties in terraforming Mars. The project could take many centuries, and the cost will be high. We have some of the technology, such as the ability to create greenhouse gases, but not the money. However, life on Mars is a real possibility for future generations.

[1] If a place is **habitable**, you can live there.

TURNING THE RED PLANET GREEN

1. FIRST VISITS

E   Terraforming Mars will probably be a thousand-year project, starting with several survey missions. The flight to Mars will take six months, and each mission might last 18 months.

2. HOMES ON MARS

F   Each new mission will build more habitation modules—places to live. These will allow future visitors to spend more time on Mars and learn more about living on the planet.

3. GLOBAL WARMING

G   To warm up the planet and to make water flow and create an atmosphere, we will need to increase the carbon dioxide level on Mars. Greenhouse gases will melt the ice in Mars's polar regions. When the ice becomes water, the water will release the carbon dioxide that was trapped inside the ice.

4. LIFE UNDER DOMES

H   Enormous domes will provide climate-controlled living spaces, first for plants and later for humans. It will take centuries to improve the rocky surface so that people can grow plants.

5. POWERING THE PLANET

I   Nuclear power[2] and wind turbines[3] are two current technologies that we might be able to use on Mars for power.

6. DON'T FORGET YOUR MASK

J   Even 1,000 years from now, there may still not be enough oxygen for humans to breathe. People on Mars may still need to use equipment similar to scuba gear.[4]

---

[2] **Nuclear power** comes from the energy that is released when the central parts of atoms are split or combined.
[3] **Wind turbines** are engines with blades. They produce power when wind spins the blades.
[4] **Scuba gear** is equipment that helps people breathe underwater.

FUTURE LIVING | 113

LESSON B: UNDERSTANDING THE READING

A | Understanding the Gist. Look back at your answer for exercise **D** on page 111. Was your prediction correct?

B | Identifying Key Details. Complete the following sentences with information from the reading on pages 112-113. Note the paragraphs where you find the information.

Paragraph _____ 1. There is no _____ on Mars—just ice.

Paragraph _____ 2. Terraforming Mars means making it similar to _____.

Paragraph _____ 3. For many years, humans probably won't be able to _____ on Mars without special equipment.

Paragraph _____ 4. The flight to Mars will take _____ months.

Paragraph _____ 5. One way to warm up Mars is to build _____. These will release _____ gases into the air.

Paragraph _____ 6. Two technologies that exist now will probably give us power on Mars: _____ and _____.

C | Sequencing. Put the steps to living on Mars in the correct order. Write the letter of the step in the correct place on the time line.

a. People will build more habitation modules, spend more time on Mars, and learn more about it.
b. People will build domes and start to grow plants in them for food.
c. People will build factories on Mars to warm it up.
d. People will visit Mars on 18-month missions and start to build places to live.

NOW _____ _____ _____ _____ _____ 1,000 years from now

Strategy

To find the noun that a pronoun refers to, remember that:

(1) the pronoun and noun normally have the same relationship to the verb (either subject or object)

(2) the pronoun and noun have the same number and gender (male or female).

D | Understanding Pronoun Reference. Find these sentences in the reading passage on pages 112–113. Then match the underlined pronoun to the noun it refers to. Two nouns will not be used.

_____ 1. Terraforming means changing the environment of a planet so that <u>it</u> is similar to Earth's.

_____ 2. So one of the main goals of terraforming Mars is to warm <u>it</u> up.

_____ 3. <u>These</u> will allow future visitors to spend more time on Mars . . .

a. greenhouse gases
b. the environment
c. terraforming
d. Mars
e. habitation modules

E | Critical Thinking: Synthesizing/Evaluating. Discuss these questions in small groups.

1. Does the information in the reading support the information in the video "Colonizing Mars"? What additional information did you learn?

2. Which predictions from this unit do you think are most likely to happen? Why?

EXPLORING WRITTEN ENGLISH

LESSON C

GOAL: In this lesson, you are going to plan, write, revise, and edit sentences on the following topic: **What will a typical day be like in 2050?**

A | Read the information in the box. Then complete the sentences (1–8) with *and*, *but*, or *so*.

Language for Writing: Using *And*, *But*, and *So*

Writers use the conjunctions *and*, *but*, and *so* to connect information in sentences.

***And* introduces an additional idea . . .**

- to connect words: People will visit Mars and Venus.
- to connect phrases: People will visit Mars and build habitation modules.
- to connect clauses: People will visit Mars, and they will build habitation modules.

***But* introduces a contrasting idea . . .**

- to connect words: It's hot but habitable.
- to connect phrases: People will live on Mars but not on Venus.
- to connect clauses: People will live on Mars, but they won't live on Venus.

***So* introduces results . . .**

- to connect clauses: It's very cold on Mars, so we will need to warm it up.

Remember:

- to use a comma when you connect clauses.
- when you use *and* and *but*, you don't have to use the subject and the auxiliary verb in the second clause, if they are the same in the first clause:

   People will live on Mars. People will work on Mars.
   subject auxiliary verb   subject auxiliary verb

   People will live **and** work on Mars.

For more explanation of conjunctions, see page 213.

Example: In the future, we will use solar energy for fuel, ___but___ we probably won't use oil.

1. Missions to Mars are expensive, _____ we probably won't send people there for many years.

2. Scientists have sent robots to the moon _____ to Mars.

3. In 1900, John Watkins predicted digital photographs _____ mobile phones.

4. We already know how to warm up the Earth, _____ it will probably be possible to warm up Mars.

FUTURE LIVING | 115

LESSON C | EXPLORING WRITTEN ENGLISH

5. There is no liquid water on Mars, _____ no plants can grow there.

6. NASA wanted to send people to Mars 30 years ago, _____ the government didn't have enough money.

7. People have already been to the moon, _____ they haven't been to Mars.

8. Travel to Mars is dangerous, _____ we will send robots instead.

B | Combine the sentences using *and*, *but*, or *so*. Leave out the pronoun and auxiliary verb when possible.

Example: Robots can vacuum houses. They can build cars. (*and*)

<u>Robots can vacuum houses and build cars.</u>

1. PR2 can take care of elderly people. It can deliver mail. (*and*)

   _____

2. PR2 cooks. It doesn't communicate. (*but*)

   _____

3. Wakamaru knows 10,000 Japanese words. It is able to communicate with people. (*so*)

   _____

4. There is not enough oxygen on Mars. Humans cannot breathe there. (*so*)

   _____

C | With a partner, list three items that will be different in the future. Think about what they will look like and how they will work. Note your ideas in the chart. Then write sentences about the items using *and*, *but*, and *so*.

Object	What It Will Look Like / How It Will Work
1.	
2.	
3.	

Writing Skill: *Using Pronouns to Avoid Repetition*

As you saw on page 108, pronouns usually refer to nouns that appear earlier in a text. Writers use pronouns to avoid repetition.

> Example: *Robots will do many things around the house.* ➔ *For example, robots will clean the house and prepare food.*
>
> *Robots will do many things around the house.* ➔ *For example, **they** will clean the house and prepare food.*

Try not to use the same pronoun to refer to more than one thing in a sentence, as this can confuse the reader.

D | Draw a line through the repeated nouns in sentences 1–5 and replace them with pronouns.

1. RFID chips will keep track of the food in your cabinets, and RFID chips will tell you when it's time to go to the store.
2. People on survey missions to Mars will build domes and live in the domes.
3. People will terraform Mars and make Mars more like Earth.
4. Even after a thousand years, people won't be able to breathe on Mars, so people will have to use breathing equipment.
5. Mars doesn't have any oxygen, but plants will slowly add oxygen to the atmosphere over many years.

E | Replace the underlined pronouns with a word or phrase from the box. One item is not needed.

| people | plants | the robots | the domes | the colors |

1. Sociable robots will communicate better with people. <u>They</u> will speak to them and make eye contact with them, so <u>they</u> will feel more comfortable.
2. People will build domes on Mars. They will live in <u>them</u> and grow plants in them.
3. People will use OLED screens to change the colors of their walls. If they don't like <u>them</u>, they will just push a button and change them.

FUTURE LIVING | 117

LESSON C WRITING TASK: Drafting

A | Brainstorming. Imagine a typical day in 2050. What will it be like? Brainstorm some ideas about your typical day. Use these categories or your own ideas.

My home: _____

Study: _____

Work: _____

Family: _____

Travel: _____

Entertainment: _____

Other things: _____

B | Planning. Follow the steps to make notes for your sentences.

Step 1 Choose three categories you want to write about (for example, your home, work, and travel). Write them in the chart below.

Step 2 Use your brainstorming notes above to add two or three details for each category.

On a typical day in 2050 . . .	
Category:	
Details:	
Category:	
Details:	
Category:	
Details:	

C | Draft 1. Use the information in the chart in exercise **B** to write a first draft of your sentences.

WRITING TASK: Revising and Editing

D | Peer Evaluation. Exchange your first draft with a partner and follow these steps:

Step 1 Read your partner's sentences. Then answer the questions below about them.

1. Are the ideas organized in a logical way?   Y   N
2. Does all the information relate to the main idea?   Y   N
3. Does the writer include details for each category?   Y   N
4. Does the writer use pronouns to avoid repetition?   Y   N

Step 2 Tell your partner one thing that you liked about his or her sentences.

Step 3 Share your answers to the questions in Step 1 with your partner

E | Draft 2. Write a second draft of your sentences. Use what you learned from the peer evaluation activity. Make any necessary changes.

F | Editing Practice. Read the information in the box. Then find and correct one mistake with *and*, *but*, or *so* in each of the sentences (1–7).

> In sentences with *and*, *but*, and *so*, remember to:
> - use *and* to introduce an additional idea, *but* to introduce a contrasting idea, and *so* to introduce a result.
> - use a comma when you connect two clauses.
> - leave out repeated subjects and auxiliary verbs with *and* or *but*.

1. People will live on Mars someday, and it is too expensive to travel there now.
2. Mars is too cold for human visitors, but they will need to warm it up.
3. Robots will take care of children, so they will do housework.
4. A trip to Mars sounds amazing, and I would not like to live there!
5. Smart appliances will buy food but cook dinner.
6. We might have flying cars in 2050, and there will probably be fewer cars on our roads.
7. In the future, you will put a language chip in your brain, but you won't have to study foreign languages.

LESSON C   **WRITING TASK: Editing**

G | Editing Checklist. Use the checklist to find errors in your second draft.

Editing Checklist	Yes	No
1. Are all the words spelled correctly?		
2. Do your subjects and verbs agree?		
3. Is the first word of every sentence capitalized?		
4. Does every sentence end with the correct punctuation?		
5. Did you use *and*, *but*, and *so* correctly?		

H | Final Draft. Now use your Editing Checklist to write a third draft of your sentences. Make any other necessary changes.

UNIT QUIZ

p.103   1. One _____ for 2025 is that most of our energy will come from the _____ and not from oil.

p.104   2. You can use *for instance* to give an _____.

p.106   3. We already have _____ that build cars and vacuum floors.

p.108   4. Pronouns usually refer to nouns that appear _____ in a text.

p.109   5. If a human travels into space, the journey is called a manned _____.

p.110   6. A _____ is a living thing that grows in the earth with a stem, leaves, and roots.

p.112   7. Terraforming means changing a planet so it's more similar to _____.

p.115   8. You combine ideas with *but* to show a _____.

Exploration and Discovery

UNIT 7

ACADEMIC PATHWAYS
Lesson A: Understanding prefixes
Evaluating reasons
Lesson B: Understanding an explanatory text and infographic
Lesson C: Linking examples and reasons
Writing sentences to give reasons

▲ A diver makes an unusual discovery—the skull of a cow—in an underwater cave in Yucatán, Mexico.

Think and Discuss

1. Do you know of any famous explorers?
2. What places are people exploring today?

Exploring the Theme

Look at the information on these pages and answer the questions.

1. What happened in 1871?
2. Why were the journeys of Valentina Tereshkova and James Cameron important?
3. Can you think of other important moments of exploration?

Great Moments in Exploration

A Historic Meeting

In 1871, the *New York Herald* newspaper sent journalist Henry Stanley on an important journey. His goal was to find the world's most famous explorer, David Livingstone. Livingstone had disappeared six years earlier while exploring in Africa. After a nine-month journey, Stanley found the missing Livingstone in a village called Ujiji. As they met, Stanley took off his hat and said the famous words, "Dr. Livingstone, I presume?"

1850

1865: Explorer David Livingstone disappears while exploring the Nile River.

1900

1911: Roald Amundsen is the first person to reach the South Pole.

▲ A modern-day explorer crosses the sand dunes of Ash Samat, Oman.

Into Space

In 1963, 26-year-old Valentina Tereshkova of the Soviet Union became the first woman to go into space. She circled the earth 48 times over three days. Her photographs from space helped scientists understand more about the Earth's atmosphere.

Into the Deep

In 2012, explorer and film director James Cameron became the first person to travel alone to the deepest place on Earth. Cameron arrived at the Mariana Trench in the Pacific Ocean after a journey of nearly seven miles (11 kilometers). He used a robotic tool to collect samples that will help scientists learn about deep-sea environments.

1950

2000

1960: Don Walsh and Jacques Piccard dive to the deepest place on Earth—the Mariana Trench.

1961: Yuri Gagarin becomes the first man in space.

1969: Astronauts Neil Armstrong and Buzz Aldrin walk on the moon.

1985: Robert Ballard finds the wreck of the *Titanic*.

EXPLORATION AND DISCOVERY | 123

LESSON A — PREPARING TO READ

A | Building Vocabulary. Find the words in **blue** in the reading passage on pages 125–126. Read the words around them and try to guess their meanings. Then circle the correct word to complete each sentence (1–10).

1. Your **search** / **occupation** is your job or profession.
2. A **journalist** / **source** collects news and writes about it, for example, for a newspaper.
3. You use **finally** / **especially** to show that a fact is truer about one person or thing than any other person or thing.
4. You use the word **finally** / **especially** to suggest that something happens after a long period of time.
5. A **moment** / **search** is an attempt to find someone or something by looking for the person or object carefully.
6. The **camp** / **source** of a river or a stream is the place where it begins.
7. A radio or television **journalist** / **series** is a set of programs or shows.
8. A particular **moment** / **journalist** is the point in time at which something happens.
9. If you **search** / **recreate** something, you make it exist or happen again.
10. If you **camp** / **search** somewhere, you sleep there overnight, usually in a tent.

> **Word Link**
> The prefix **re-** can mean again: **re**create, **re**connect, **re**produce, **re**trace, **re**cycle, **re**organize, **re**do, **re**write, **re**read, **re**turn, **re**place.

B | Using Vocabulary. Answer the questions. Share your ideas with a partner.

1. What **occupations** do you think are the most difficult or dangerous?
2. Have you ever **camped** anywhere? Where did you camp? What was it like?
3. What news **sources** do you use the most? Why?

C | Brainstorming. Look back at the information about Henry Stanley on page 122. What kinds of difficulties do you think explorers had during his time? Make a list.

no modern medicine, _____

_____

D | Predicting. Look at the pictures and the title of the reading passage on pages 125–126. Who do you think is the writer of the passage?

a. the journalist and explorer Henry Stanley

b. the man who discovered the source of the Nile

c. an explorer who followed Henry Stanley's journey

READING

In Stanley's Footsteps

In 1865, the world's most famous explorer disappeared. Nearly 140 years later, I set out in the footsteps of the man who found him.

By Mireya Mayor

track 2-04

A WHEN I TELL PEOPLE I am an explorer, they look at me skeptically.¹ Are there really explorers today? It is a rare occupation now, especially compared to the nineteenth century. The explorers then were as famous as movie stars are today.

B Probably the most famous explorer was the Scotsman David Livingstone. His disappearance in 1865, during a search for the source of the Nile, made news around the globe. For six years no one knew where he was. Finally, a journalist named Henry Stanley found Livingstone—alive but very ill—in a village called Ujiji. At the end of their nine-month journey, most of Stanley's team members were dead.

C Nearly a century and a half later, I traveled in Stanley's footsteps. I was part of a four-member team making a TV series called *Expedition Africa*. Our goal was simple. We wanted to see whether we could survive the same journey, under the same conditions, as Stanley. We had no phones, tents, water filters,² or even matches. With just a compass³ and some basic maps, we set out to recreate one of the most famous expeditions of all time.

¹ If you are **skeptical** about something, you don't really believe that it is true.
² A **filter** is a device through which something such as water is passed, in order to remove certain substances.
³ A **compass** is a device you use for finding direction. It has a needle that always points north.

EXPLORATION AND DISCOVERY | 125

LESSON A — READING

Day 2
After our first day, we are now crossing an area of swamps. There are crocodiles everywhere. Walking through thick mud while carrying heavy backpacks is nearly impossible. Somehow we get through the swamps. In two days we have covered about nine miles. We have more than 900 miles to go!

Day 6
We arrive at the base of the Uluguru Mountains. It's more than 100 degrees Fahrenheit (38 degrees Celsius). We stop to camp at just over 4,200 feet (1,280 meters). That night a strong windstorm blows through. It is so loud and strong that no one can sleep.

Day 7
We complete our climb, another 2,000 feet. We walk through the clouds and into the oldest forest in Africa, 25 million years old. The tallest trees seem to reach the sky. Stanley called Uluguru the "misty mountains." He was right—it's so wet here in the morning that it's impossible to start a fire. But we have to push on. . . .

Day 8
We begin crossing the Makata Plains—lion country. It is very hot and dry, and the bones of dead animals cover the ground. A sharp piece of grass cuts my hand. A team member stops to help me, but I want to keep moving. I don't want to sit there, bleeding, with lions around!

Day 13
We are now in the Segarra Mountains. Near the camp, a team member finds some hairy insect larvae.[4] They're a popular food with local people, he explains. We cook them, and I try one or two. Another team member eats more than a dozen. He is up all night, violently[5] sick.

Day 29
After kayaking on the river, we are in swampland again. There are snakes and crocs around us. I slip and land face first in the mud. My shoe is now missing, and I have lost one of my toenails. The last few weeks are nothing compared to these last two days!

Day 30
Suddenly, we are on dry land and Ujiji is finally within reach! We walk down a mango tree-lined path into the village where Stanley met Livingstone. As we turn the corner, we find thousands of people. They dance and clap to welcome our arrival. All the pain and dangers of the trip are worth the pride and joy I feel at this moment.

---

[4] **Larvae** are insects that have come out of their eggs and are not yet adult.

[5] If you do something **violently**, you do it forcefully in a way that may cause injury.

Raphael, a Maasai warrior

UNDERSTANDING THE READING

A | Understanding the Gist. Look back at your answer for exercise **D** on page 124. Was your prediction correct?

B | Identifying Main Ideas. Look back at the reading on pages 125–126. Write the letter of the paragraph for each main idea below.

1. _____ Mayor and the other team members have some unusual food at their camp.
2. _____ Mayor and three other explorers plan to make the same journey as Henry Stanley.
3. _____ The explorers enter a wet environment near the top of a mountain.
4. _____ The explorers reach the place where Stanley found Livingstone.
5. _____ In the past, explorers were very famous, like movie stars are today.

C | Identifying Key Details. Scan the reading on pages 125–126 to find a word or phrase to complete each sentence.

- [ ] a. The team hikes through a forest that is 25 _____.
- [ ] b. The team enters the Makata Plains and finds _____ _____ on the ground.
- [ ] c. The team sets up camp at _____ feet, but can't sleep because of the wind.
- [1] d. Mayor and her team set out on an expedition without matches, tents _____, or water filters.
- [ ] e. Mayor cuts her hand on a piece of _____.
- [ ] f. The team kayaks down a river and arrives at a swamp full of _____ and crocodiles.
- [ ] g. Mayor falls and tears off a _____.
- [ ] h. Mayor and her team travel _____ miles in two days, but have another _____ miles to travel.

▲ The Expedition Africa explorers had to hike through dangerous swampland before reaching their goal.

D | Sequencing. Now number the sentences in exercise **C** to put the events in the correct order.

E | Critical Thinking: Evaluating Reasons. Work with a partner. Discuss your answers to the questions below.

1. What was the main goal of *Expedition Africa*, according to Mayor?
2. What might be some other reasons for recreating the expedition?
3. Do you think the reasons for the expedition were worth the dangers? Why, or why not?
4. Why do you think Stanley's expedition took nine months, but Mayor's took 30 days?
5. Would you like to join an expedition like this? Explain your reasons.

> **CT Focus**
>
> As you read a personal narrative, **think about the reasons** for a person's actions. Does the writer state his or her reasons or motivations? What else can you infer about the writer's reasons?

LESSON A | DEVELOPING READING SKILLS

Reading Skill: *Understanding Prefixes*

A prefix can sometimes be found at the beginning of a word. If you know the meaning of a word's prefix, this can help you guess the meaning of the word. Here are some common prefixes, with their meanings and some example words:

dis: opposite or negative meaning   *disbelieve, disapprove, disadvantage*

ex: out, away from, upward, completely   *explore, expedition, extremely*

im/in: not, without   *impossible, inappropriate, imperfect*

mis: bad, false   *mislead, misbehave, misjudge*

pre: before   *prehistoric, predict, prepay*   **un:** not   *unexplored, unreal, unhappy*

re: again, back   *recreate, reboot, recycle*   **under:** below   *underwater, underground, underline*

For more examples of common prefixes, see page 211.

A | **Understanding Prefixes.** Find and underline the words with prefixes in the sentences below. Then discuss the meaning of each underlined word with a partner.

track 2-05

1. In 1325, Moroccan traveler Ibn Battuta set out on a journey across unexplored parts of Africa and Asia.
2. He had many misfortunes during the trip, such as losing his boat in a storm near India.
3. After traveling almost 75,000 miles (120,000 kilometers), he returned to Morocco and told people of his travels.
4. No one knows how or when he died—he disappeared from history.
5. Although he traveled so far, Ibn Battuta today is largely unknown in many parts of the world.
6. In 2007, a Scotswoman named Carolyn McIntyre set out to retrace the whole of Ibn Battuta's amazing journey.

▲ Ibn Battuta met the ruler of Delhi during his visit to India.

B | **Identifying Prefixes.** Find one example for each prefix below in the reading on pages 125–126. Then use your dictionary to add two more words for each prefix.

1. dis: _____   _____   _____
2. ex: _____   _____   _____
3. re: _____   _____   _____
4. im: _____   _____   _____

VIEWING

Madagascar Discovery

▲ Primatologist Mireya Mayor holds a newly discovered mouse lemur.

Before Viewing

A | Using a Dictionary. Here are some words you will hear in the video. Complete each definition with the correct word. Use your dictionary to help you.

> identified
> primate
> species
> surroundings

1. A _____ is a class of plants or animals that have the same main characteristics.

2. If something is _____, it is discovered or noticed.

3. A _____ is a member of the group that includes humans, monkeys, and apes.

4. You can describe the place you are now, or the place you live, as your _____.

B | Predicting. Look at the photo, the title of the video, and the vocabulary words in exercise **A**. What do you think the video is about?

a. Mireya Mayor travels through a dangerous jungle.   b. Mireya Mayor tries to save endangered animals.

c. Mireya Mayor finds a new kind of primate.

While Viewing

A | As you view the video, circle whether statements 1–5 are true (**T**) or false (**F**).

1. Mouse lemurs may be the smallest primates in the world.   T   F
2. Mouse lemurs mainly eat leaves and insects.   T   F
3. Mouse lemurs drink water from streams and rivers.   T   F
4. One reason mouse lemurs are considered primates is because they have large brains.   T   F
5. Another primate characteristic is large eyes.   T   F

After Viewing

A | Discuss the statements (1-5) above with a partner. Correct the false statement(s).

B | Synthesizing. Answer the questions with your own ideas.

1. Based on what you learned from reading the passage on pages 125–126 and watching the video, describe Mireya Mayor's personality.

2. Which do you think was the more important achievement—retracing Stanley's journey or discovering a new species? Why?

EXPLORATION AND DISCOVERY | **129**

LESSON B | PREPARING TO READ

A | **Building Vocabulary.** Read the sentences below. Look at the words around the **bold** words to guess their meanings. Then circle the best definition.

1. The mouse lemur is a **creature** that lives only in the jungles of Madagascar. Other animals on the island include the chameleon and the crocodile.

   a. a living thing that is not a plant
   b. a very small animal or plant

2. Scientists wonder if any life forms **exist** on other planets.

   a. live   b. communicate

3. Mayor and her team survived an **extremely** dangerous journey through Africa.

   a. sadly   b. very

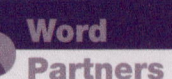

4. The *Expedition Africa* team **followed** the path that Stanley took in the 1870s.

   a. went the same way as someone else
   b. showed someone the way to a place

> Use **follow** with nouns: follow **signs**, follow **a path**, follow **orders**, follow **rules**, follow **advice**, follow **directions**, follow **instructions**, follow **a leader**.

5. Ujiji is **located** in the African country of Tanzania.

   a. discovered by explorers   b. found in a particular place

6. Explorers need to be careful of **poisonous** snakes and insects.

   a. able to kill you or make you ill   b. extremely large and powerful

7. Environmentalists are working to **preserve** rain forests that are in danger of being cut down.

   a. visit an unexplored area in order to study it and do research
   b. make sure that something stays the same and is not changed or destroyed

8. Explorers such as Mireya Mayor sometimes **risk** their lives on dangerous expeditions.

   a. do something knowing that it might have a bad result
   b. do something without knowing what you are really doing

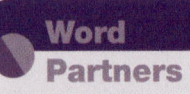

9. It can be very dangerous to **run out** of drinking water during an expedition.

   a. find something that you need   b. have no more left of something

> The word **run** can be used with several prepositions to make phrasal verbs. If you **run across** or **run into** someone, you meet that person by chance. If you **run up against** a problem, you have to face that problem.

10. Our sun is only one of many stars in the **universe**.

    a. the whole of space   b. the planets circling our sun

B | Using Vocabulary. Answer the questions in complete sentences. Then share your sentences with a partner.

1. Do you think that life might **exist** on other planets in the **universe**? If yes, what kind of life do you think exists?

   _____
   _____

2. What parts of the world do you think are **extremely** difficult to live in? Why?

   _____
   _____
   _____

3. In which region or state are your mother's and father's hometowns **located**?

   _____
   _____

4. Why do you think people want to **preserve** rain forests?

   _____
   _____

C | Brainstorming. Can you think of any places on Earth that are still unexplored? Make a list.

   _____
   _____

D | Predicting. You are going to read about a type of underwater cave called a blue hole. Look at the pictures and captions on pages 132–133. Then read the first paragraph. Answer the questions below.

1. Which topics do you think the reading will cover? Check (✓) your prediction(s).

   ☐ where blue holes are located   ☐ how blue holes are formed
   ☐ how to preserve blue holes   ☐ how deep blue holes are
   ☐ what we can learn from blue holes   ☐ what it's like to dive in blue holes

2. Why do you think diving in blue holes is dangerous? Check (✓) your prediction(s).

   ☐ Dangerous animals live there.   ☐ They contain poisonous gas and bacteria.
   ☐ It is easy to get lost.   ☐ They are very dark inside.
   ☐ They are very deep.   ☐ It is very cold inside.

EXPLORATION AND DISCOVERY | 131

LESSON B READING

INTO THE

IN THE DAYS of Stanley and Livingstone, much of the world was still unexplored. Today, most places on the surface of the world have been mapped. Some places, however, are still waiting to be discovered. Some of these are underground, in deep caves called blue holes.

A blue hole is a special kind of inland[1] underwater cave. The cave forms when the earth above it falls in. Some of the world's most spectacular[2] blue holes are located in the Bahamas. The islands there may have more than a thousand blue holes. These caves are very deep—for example, Dean's Blue Hole, the deepest blue hole in the world, is more than 660 feet (200 meters) deep.

Diving into blue holes is extremely dangerous. Near the top of a blue hole, there is a layer of poisonous gas. This gas causes itching, dizziness, and—in large amounts—death. Divers must also be fast. They have to get in and out of a cave before their oxygen runs out. Additionally, it's very dark in these caves, so it is very easy to get lost. Divers therefore have to follow a guideline[3] as they swim through a blue hole. If they lose the guideline, they may not find their way back out of the cave.

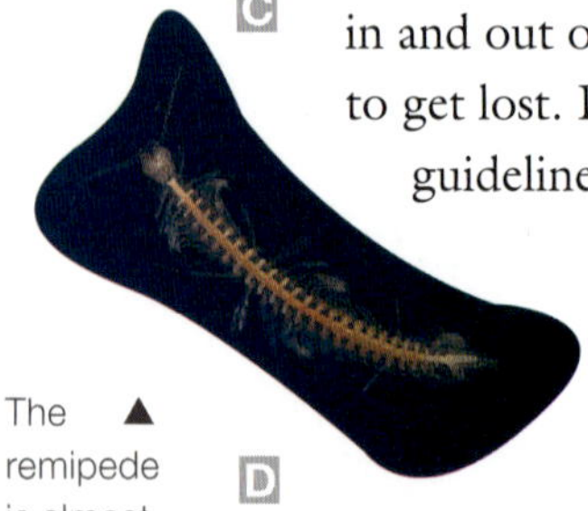

▲ The remipede is almost the same as it was 300 million years ago.

If blue holes are so dangerous, why do explorers and scientists risk their lives to explore them? One reason is that these underwater caves can provide valuable scientific information. They provide clues about geology, archaeology, and even astrobiology—the study of life in the universe. For example, some blue hole creatures, such as the remipede, probably haven't changed for millions of years. Divers have also found bacteria that can live without oxygen. Similar life forms probably existed on Earth billions of years ago.

In addition, the oxygen-free environment of the blue holes preserves bones of humans and animals that fell into the caves long ago. By studying the blue holes, we can understand what life was like in prehistoric[4] times. As cave diver Kenny Broad says, "I can think of no other environment on Earth that is so challenging to explore and gives us back so much scientifically."

UNKNOWN

▲ Divers often risk their lives to explore extreme environments. Photographer Wes C. Skiles, who took this photo of Dan's Cave in the Bahamas, died during a dive on July 21, 2010.

Windows on an Alien World?

An inland blue hole's water is very still and has different layers. A layer of fresh rainwater floats on top of salt water. The fresh water keeps oxygen from the atmosphere from reaching the salt water. Brightly colored bacteria live where the two layers meet. Scientists believe these bacteria could teach us about life in outer space. Astrobiologist Kevin Hand says the bacteria may be similar to forms of life that might exist on Jupiter's fourth largest moon, Europa. "Our study of life's extremes on Earth," says Hand, can help increase "our understanding of habitable environments off Earth."

[1] If something is **inland**, it is away from the ocean.
[2] If something is **spectacular**, it is very impressive or dramatic.
[3] A **guideline** is a line or a rope that someone follows to go from one place to another.
[4] **Prehistoric** people and things existed at a time before information was written down.

EXPLORATION AND DISCOVERY | 133

LESSON B
UNDERSTANDING THE READING

A | Understanding the Gist. Look back at your answers for exercise **D** on page 131. Were your predictions correct?

B | Identifying Key Ideas. Complete the sentences with information from the reading on pages 132–133.

1. A blue hole forms when _____.
2. The deepest blue hole is _____.
   It is _____ deep.
3. The gas near the top of the blue hole can cause _____
   _____.
4. Divers _____ in order not to get lost.

C | Labeling a Diagram. Use information from the reading to label the diagram of a blue hole.

A layer of fresh _____ floats at the top of a blue hole.

Unusual kinds of colored _____ live beneath the top layer. Scientists think similar life forms might exist on a moon of _____.

The lower part of a blue hole is a layer of _____. _____ from the atmosphere does not reach this layer.

D | Critical Thinking: Evaluating Reasons. Work with a partner. Discuss your answers to the questions below.

1. Write two reasons why blue holes are dangerous.
   _____
   _____

2. Write two reasons why divers risk their lives to explore blue holes.
   _____
   _____

E | Synthesizing. Discuss these questions in small groups.

1. In what ways are Mireya Mayor and blue-hole divers similar? How are they different?
2. Do you think the reasons for exploring blue holes are worth the risk? Why, or why not?

EXPLORING WRITTEN ENGLISH

LESSON C

GOAL: In this lesson, you are going to write sentences about the following topic:
Where would you most like to explore? Why would you like to go there?

A | Read the information in the box. Then complete the chart with notes about things you want to do and reasons that you want to do them.

> **Language for Writing:** Giving Reasons with *would like to* + *because*
>
> You can use *would like to*, or *would love to*, to introduce what you want to do. Use the base form of a verb after *would like to*.
>
> Use *because* to introduce the reason why you want to do it. Use a clause after *because*. (A clause includes both a subject and a verb.)
>
> > I **would like to** explore the blue holes of the Bahamas **because** they look very interesting.
> > I **would** also **like to** visit them **because** I want to see the unusual creatures that live there.
> >
> > I **would love to** explore Central America **because** I'm interested in Mayan history.
> > I **would** also **like to** go there because I am learning Spanish and I want to improve my Spanish language skills.

Things you want to do	Two reasons you want to do each one
1.	1. 2.
2.	1. 2.
3.	1. 2.
4.	1. 2.

EXPLORATION AND DISCOVERY | 135

LESSON C — EXPLORING WRITTEN ENGLISH

B | Use your notes in the chart in exercise **A** to write two sentences about each of the things that you want to do.

1. _____

2. _____

3. _____

4. _____

Writing Skill: *Linking Examples and Reasons*

When you write about ideas on the same topic, you can use certain words and phrases to vary your sentences: *also, in addition, another / one other (reason) . . . is, finally*.

Read these reasons to visit the blue holes. Then read the sentences that connect the ideas.

look very beautiful   *want to see unusual creatures*
enjoy scuba diving   *interested in caves*

I would love to go to the Bahamas to see the blue holes because they are probably very beautiful.

I **also** want to explore the caves because I would like to see some of the unusual creatures that live there.

Another reason that I want to visit the blue holes **is** because I really enjoy scuba diving.

In addition, I would like to see the blue holes for myself one day because I am interested in how caves are formed.

Remember to vary the verbs when you list reasons. For example, the sentences above use *go, explore, see,* and *visit*. Using different verbs avoids repetition and makes the sentences more interesting for the reader.

C | Linking Ideas. Read the set of sentences below. Add words and phrases to link the ideas and to avoid repetition.

One place I would like to explore is Australia.

I would love to explore Australia's National Parks because they have many interesting animals.

I enjoy scuba diving, so I would like to see Australia's Great Barrier Reef.

I want to visit Australia to see the famous Sydney Opera House.

I would love to travel around Australia because I really like hot weather!

D | Linking Ideas. Rewrite the second sentence from each pair of sentences you wrote in exercise **B**. Use a linking word or phrase in each one. Then read your sentence pairs aloud to a partner.

1. _____

2. _____

3. _____

4. _____

◀ One of the most popular places to explore in Australia is the Great Barrier Reef, home to many unusual types of fish, such as this potato cod fish.

EXPLORATION AND DISCOVERY | 137

LESSON C   WRITING TASK: Drafting

A | Brainstorming. Make a list of places you would like to explore or learn more about. Discuss with a partner.

_____

_____

_____

B | Planning. Follow the steps to prepare to write your sentences.

Step 1   Look at your brainstorming notes. Circle one place you want to write about.

Step 2   Complete the chart. Don't worry about grammar or spelling. Write four reasons that you want to explore this place.

Place: _____

Reasons:

1. _____

_____

2. _____

_____

3. _____

_____

4. _____

_____

C | Draft 1. Use the information in the chart in exercise **B** to write a first draft of your sentences. Begin with an introductory sentence.

Example: One day, I would like to explore . . .

WRITING TASK: Revising and Editing

D | Peer Evaluation. Exchange your first draft with a partner and follow these steps:

Step 1 Answer the questions below about your partner's sentences.

1. Does the writer include an introductory sentence? Y N
2. Does the writer give reasons for wanting to explore the place? Y N
3. Do all of the sentences give new information? Y N
4. Does the writer use words and phrases to link the ideas? Y N
5. Does the writer vary the verbs in the sentences? Y N

Step 2 Tell your partner one thing that you liked about his or her sentences.

Step 3 Share your answers to the questions in Step 1 with your partner.

E | Draft 2. Write a second draft of your sentences. Use what you learned from the peer evaluation activity. Make any other necessary changes.

F | Editing Practice. Read the information in the box. Then find and correct one mistake in each of the sentences (1–5).

> In sentences using *would like to* + *because*, remember to:
> - use *to* after *would like*.
> - use a clause with a subject and a verb after *because*.

1. I would like visit the rain forests of the Amazon because they are full of different species.
2. I would love to explore New York City because is full of interesting art and culture.
3. My brother and I would like to explore Russia we are interested in Russian history.
4. My sister would like traveling to every continent because she loves to learn about different cultures.
5. My parents like to go to Easter Island one day because they want to see the statues there.

Easter Island is famous for its carved statues, or moai.

LESSON C — WRITING TASK: Editing

G | Editing Checklist. Use the checklist to find errors in your second draft.

Editing Checklist	Yes	No
1. Are all the words spelled correctly?		
2. Is the first word of every sentence capitalized?		
3. Does every sentence end with the correct punctuation?		
4. Do your subjects and verbs agree?		
5. Are all instances of *would like to* + *because* correct?		

H | Final Draft. Now use your Editing Checklist to write a third draft of your sentences. Make any other necessary changes.

UNIT QUIZ

- p.123 1. In 2012, James Cameron went to the Mariana Trench, the _____ place in the world.
- p.125 2. Mireya Mayor wanted to recreate the journey of _____.
- p.128 3. A _____ comes at the beginning of a word and gives the word a specific meaning.
- p.129 4. Mireya Mayor discovered a new species of _____ in Madagascar.
- p.132 5. A blue hole is an inland _____.
- p.133 6. Some bacteria in blue holes may be similar to life forms that could exist on a _____ of Jupiter.
- p.135 7. You can give a reason why you want to do something by using *would like to* and the word _____.
- p.136 8. You can use words and phrases such as *also* and *in* _____ to link examples and reasons.

Musicians with a Message

UNIT 8

ACADEMIC PATHWAYS
Lesson A: Taking notes
Understanding idiomatic language
Lesson B: Reading interviews and profiles
Lesson C: Presenting one main idea in a paragraph
Writing sentences to explain a preference

Think and Discuss

1. Who are some of your favorite musicians? Do you mainly like their music or their song lyrics (words)?
2. Do you think musicians can change the world? In what ways?

▲ Blues musician Keb' Mo, a songwriter for the Playing for Change music project, is one of many performers around the world working for social change.

Exploring the Theme

Look at the information on page 143 and answer the questions.

1. Have you seen or listened to any benefit concerts? What do you remember about them?
2. For what reasons do musicians perform in benefit events?
3. How is Playing for Change different from other benefit events?

▲ Bono, lead singer of the Irish band U2, works to raise awareness of social issues through his music.

Bringing the World Together

For more than 40 years, musicians have helped bring people around the world together. Benefit concerts, for example, raise money and help make people aware of global problems such as poverty and environmental issues.

1971

George Harrison, former member of The Beatles, organized **The Concert for Bangladesh** to raise money for refugees from East Pakistan (now Bangladesh). Forty thousand people attended the concert in New York City, raising almost $250,000. The event inspired many other benefit concerts.

1985

The **Live Aid** concerts took place on the same day in several countries, including the United States, the United Kingdom, Australia, and Germany. The purpose was to raise money to help people experiencing famine (extreme hunger) in Ethiopia. The 18-hour event raised more than $280 million.

2005

Like Live Aid, **Live 8** included several concerts on the same day. More than a thousand musicians performed in 10 countries, including France, Japan, and South Africa. The goal was to raise money for poor countries.

2007

The purpose of **Live Earth** was to help make people aware of climate change. One hundred and fifty performers appeared in concerts on every continent, including Antarctica. People in over 130 countries watched the concerts on TV.

Today, musicians are raising money and awareness in new ways. **Playing for Change** (http://playingforchange.com/) records musicians around the world performing the same song. The recordings are edited to make online videos. The goal of the project is to promote peace through music.

LESSON A | **PREPARING TO READ**

A | Building Vocabulary. Find the words in **blue** in the reading passage on page 145. Read the words around them and try to guess their meanings. Then match the sentence parts below to make definitions.

> **Word Link**
> **dis** = *not*:
> **dis**abled, **dis**agree, **dis**organized, **dis**appear, **dis**ease.

_____ 1. Your **appearance**
_____ 2. An **audience**
_____ 3. Your **circumstances**
_____ 4. If you are a **composer**,
_____ 5. If you are physically **disabled**,

a. are the conditions of your life, for example, how much money you have.
b. you have a condition that makes it difficult to move around.
c. is a group of people watching a concert or other event.
d. is the way you look.
e. you write music.

B | Building Vocabulary. Find the words in **blue** in the reading passage on page 145. Read the words around them and try to guess their meanings. Then complete the definitions.

> encourage   energetic   founder   instrument   perform

1. A musical _____ is an object you use to make music.
2. If you _____ someone, you give them hope or confidence.
3. If you _____ music, you play it in front of a group of people.
4. The _____ of a group is the person who started it.
5. An _____ person is very active and does not feel tired.

C | Using Vocabulary. Answer the questions. Share your ideas with a partner.

1. Which famous **composers** do you know? What do you think of their music?
2. Where in your town can you go to listen to musicians **performing** live music?

D | Brainstorming. Why is music important? How can music help people? List your ideas in the word web.

E | Predicting. Read the title, subheads, and first paragraph of the reading passage on pages 145-146. What do you think the passage is about?

a. a concert to raise money for disabled people
b. disabled musicians who became famous

144 | UNIT 8

READING

The Power of Music

track 2-07

A TWO FRENCH FILMMAKERS were working in Kinshasa, the capital of the Democratic Republic of the Congo (DRC). One day, they found a group of musicians performing on the streets. But these were not ordinary street musicians. Most of the band members were disabled, and they made music with homemade instruments.

The Message in the Music

B The band is called Staff Benda Bilili. Its members are Ricky, one of the founders of the band; Coco, the band's composer, who helped Ricky start the band; Junana, the group's choreographer;[1] and Coude, a bass player and singer. A nondisabled teenager, Roger, plays the satongé, a one-string guitar he designed and built himself out of a tin can, a fish basket, and an electrical wire.

C The band's name, Benda Bilili, means "look beyond appearances" in the local language, and it describes the group's mission. Staff Benda Bilili's audience was at first made up of poor street people, just like the band members themselves. The band wanted to tell its audience to be positive and strong, even in difficult circumstances.

D "Our songs encourage kids to go to school, encourage people to work hard," says Ricky. "The message of our music is that if you want to do something with your life, you need to take things in your own hands."

E The band members themselves are examples of their message. They don't see themselves as disabled. Instead, they see themselves as rock musicians. Their energetic performances show this. For example, when the group is playing, Junana sometimes jumps out of his wheelchair and dances around the stage on his hands.

[1] A **choreographer** creates dances.

LESSON A   READING

▲ Today, Staff Benda Bilili are one of the most exciting bands anywhere in the world.

From the Streets to the World

F   The filmmakers, Florent de la Tullaye and Renaud Barret, were amazed by Staff Benda Bilili's music and their life stories. So the filmmakers decided to make a documentary about the band. The film follows them as they play their music in Kinshasa, the capital of a country that had many wars in its recent past.[2] These wars affected millions of people in Kinshasa and elsewhere in the DRC. The documentary illustrates how Staff Benda Bilili's music helped them survive in this very difficult environment.

G   The film also shows the power of their music: Staff Benda Bilili members experience problems in their lives, and the problems become songs. Many of the songs offer solutions to the problems. For example, "Polio" is about living with polio[3] and getting around the city on crutches. The song also tells parents to have their children vaccinated against[4] the disease.

H   The documentary follows Staff Benda Bilili as they go from playing in the streets of Kinshasa to playing in large European cities. Because of the film, the band is now well known, and today their music gives hope to people around the world.

---

[2] The **Second Congo War** (1996–2003) caused the deaths of as many as 5.4 million people, more than any other war since World War II.
[3] **Polio** is a disease. It sometimes makes people unable to use their legs.
[4] If you are **vaccinated against** a disease, you receive an injection so you will not get the disease.

UNDERSTANDING THE READING

A | Understanding the Gist. Look back at your answer for exercise **E** on page 144. Was your prediction correct?

B | Understanding the Main Ideas. Circle the main idea of each of these sections of the reading passage on pages 145–146.

The Message in the Music

a. At first, the members of Staff Benda Bilili were similar to the people in their audience.

b. Staff Benda Bilili's music encourages people who live in difficult circumstances.

From the Streets to the World

a. A film about Staff Benda Bilili brought the band's message to people around the world.

b. A film about Staff Benda Bilili showed how life is difficult for people with polio.

C | Identifying Key Details. Read each statement below. Circle **T** for *true* and **F** for *false*. Then change the false statements to make them true.

1. All members of Staff Benda Bilili are disabled.   T   F
2. The band's name means "difficult circumstances."   T   F
3. Roger's satongé is a homemade instrument.   T   F
4. Junana uses his wheelchair to dance around the stage.   T   F
5. Two French filmmakers made a movie about the band.   T   F
6. One of the group's songs is about the importance of vaccination.   T   F

D | Critical Thinking: Interpreting Idioms. Write answers to these questions. Then share your ideas with a partner.

1. The band's name, Benda Bilili, means "look beyond appearances." What does "look beyond appearances" mean? Why do you think the band chose this name?

   _____

   _____

2. Ricky says, "The message of our music is that . . . you need to take things in your own hands." What do you think he means?

   _____

   _____

3. Do you have phrases in your own language that are similar to these expressions?

   _____

   _____

CT Focus

Use context clues to **interpret idiomatic language**. Look at the information around it to help you understand what it means.

LESSON A: DEVELOPING READING SKILLS

Reading Skill: Taking Notes

> **Strategy**
>
> **When you take notes**, remember to note only the key points. Don't write complete sentences. Try to use your own words as much as possible.

Taking notes helps you understand not only the main ideas of a reading passage, but also how supporting details in the passage relate to the main ideas. It also helps you to collect important information for writing assignments and for tests.

One way to take notes is to identify the main idea and the supporting details of each paragraph, or section, as you read.

It is often helpful to use some kind of graphic organizer when you take notes. A simple chart or grid is a good way to take notes on main ideas and supporting ideas.

It is also helpful to use abbreviations and symbols when you take notes. You can abbreviate (shorten) words any way you want (as long as you understand them). For example, *abbreviation* can become *abbr.* Some common abbreviations and symbols include:

& or + — and	w/ — with	e.g./ex. — example
→ — leads to/causes	= — is/means	b/c — because

See page 211 for a list of common abbreviations and symbols.

A | Taking Notes. Complete the following chart with notes on "The Power of Music."

Paragraph	Main Idea	Supporting Details
B	5 members of Staff Benda Bilili	Ricky: co-founder. Junana: choreo. Coco: comp. Coude: bass player, singer Roger: not disabled, plays _____
C	group's mission = _____	band's name = "_____" audience incl's _____
E	band members = exs. of their message	see themselves as _____ energetic performances —e.g., Junana _____
F	film shows how they survive in diff. circum.	wars affected mil. of people in _____
G	film shows insp. for their music	band exper. a problem + the problem becomes _____ e.g., song "Polio" = _____

B | Analyzing. Use your notes to write answers to these questions about "The Power of Music."

1. What is Staff Benda Bilili's mission?
2. How do the members of Staff Benda Bilili see themselves?
3. What does the movie show about Staff Benda Bilili's life in Kinshasa?
4. Where do the members of Staff Benda Bilili get ideas for their songs?

VIEWING

World Music

Before Viewing

A | Using a Dictionary. Here are some words you will hear in the video. Complete each definition with the correct word. Use your dictionary to help you.

> fan   open-minded
> stunning   traditional

1. If something is _____, it is very beautiful.
2. If you are a _____ of something, you like it a lot.
3. If something is _____, it has existed for a long time.
4. If you are _____, you like to experience things you have never tried.

B | Brainstorming. Which types of music do musicians sometimes combine? (For example, folk + rock = folk rock.) Make a list with a partner.

While Viewing

A | Think about the statements as you view the video. Then circle **T** for *true* and **F** for *false*.

1. WOMAD is a festival of traditional music and dance.   T   F
2. Spaccanapoli plays traditional music from England.   T   F
3. Marcello Collasurdo says the group's music is like rock.   T   F
4. People in Naples often sing in the street.   T   F

After Viewing

A | Discuss the statements (1–4) above with a partner. Correct the false statement(s).

B | Synthesizing. Discuss answers to these questions with a partner.

1. Where do Staff Benda Bilili and Spaccanapoli get inspiration for their music? In what ways are the groups' inspirations similar and different?
2. How is WOMAD similar to and different from the events described on page 143?

▲ Thousands of people attend WOMAD festivals around the world, such as this concert in New Zealand in 2005.

LESSON B PREPARING TO READ

A | Building Vocabulary. Read the definitions below. Then complete the sentences with the correct words.

> If you **escape** from something, you get away from it.
> If you **improve** something, you make it better.
> An **issue** is an important topic that people have different views on.
> You take **medicine** if you are ill or injured so that you can feel better.
> If you do something **regularly**, you do it often.

1. If you exercise _____, you can stay healthy. Some experts recommend exercising three to five times a week.

2. One _____ that people talk about a lot today is the environment.

3. Education and training can _____ the lives of people in poor countries. When people receive an education, they can get jobs or start businesses. In this way, they are able to _____ from a life of poverty.

4. _____ for AIDS patients in Africa is expensive. There also aren't enough of these drugs for all the people who need them.

B | Building Vocabulary. Find the words in **blue** in the reading passage on pages 152–153. Read the words around them and try to guess their meanings. Then match the sentence parts below to make definitions.

_____ 1. A **bond** between people
_____ 2. If you **rescue** someone,
_____ 3. A **responsibility**
_____ 4. A **situation**
_____ 5. If doctors or nurses **treat** someone with an illness,

a. you save the person from danger.
b. is what is happening at a particular time.
c. they make the person well again.
d. is a strong connection or a feeling of friendship.
e. is a job you have to do.

Members of Staff Benda Bilili ▶ developed a strong bond with the people in their audience.

C | Using Vocabulary. Answer the questions in complete sentences. Then share your sentences with a partner.

1. What **issues** in the news are you interested in?

   _____

   _____

2. Which members of your family do you have the strongest **bond** with?

   _____

   _____

3. What **responsibilities** does a teacher have?

   _____

   _____

4. Which activities do you do **regularly**?

   _____

   _____

> **Word Partners**
>
> Use **issue** with verbs and adjectives:
> (v.) **become** an issue, **discuss** an issue, **vote on** an issue; (adj.) **difficult** issue, **important** issue, **legal** issue, **serious** issue.

D | Scanning. Scan the reading passage on pages 152–153. Find the names and nationalities of the three main people described. Write the information in the chart. Then scan for the issues they are working on. Match the person with the issue (a–c).

| a. HIV/AIDS | b. teaching music to children | c. child slavery |

Issue	Name	Nationality
1. _____		
2. _____		
3. _____		

MUSICIANS WITH A MESSAGE | 151

LESSON B   READING

Music for Change

track 2-08

A From ending child slavery[1] to teaching people about AIDS and world peace, musicians around the world are spreading a message of hope.

Jason Mraz: Singing for Freedom

B "If my music can contribute to happiness, then that's my main responsibility," says American singer and songwriter Jason Mraz. But Mraz does more than make people happy. He wants to use his music to make a positive change and improve people's lives.

C Mraz is working with an organization called Free the Slaves. Their goal is to stop child slavery, a serious issue in many parts of the world. In Ghana, for example, parents who are very poor sometimes sell their own children into slavery.

What inspired you to visit Ghana?

D **Mraz:** It started with "Freedom Song," written by musician Luc Reynaud.... I loved it, performed it, and passed it on to my friends at Free the Slaves. Later they sent me photos of kids in Ghana dancing and singing the song.

Tell us about your trip.

E **Mraz:** I went to work with James Kofi Anan, a former child slave who has spent his adult life liberating[2] slaves.... He works to rescue children, [and] get them back to health. [He also] works with their parents to make sure they can make a living so the children aren't vulnerable[3] to traffickers.[4] I wrote several songs during my time in Ghana. I went back to my room every night [to compose] new songs about what I was seeing.

---

[1] A **slave** is someone who is owned by other people and works for them without being paid.
[2] **Liberating** people means freeing them from the control of other people.
[3] Someone who is **vulnerable** is weak and without protection.
[4] A **trafficker** is someone who illegally buys or sells something.

▶ "Music helps us to express our feelings," says Chorn-Pond. "[It is a] basic human right, to express yourself."

Zinhle Thabethe: Bringing Hope

◀ The Zulu word *Sinikithemba* means "we bring hope."

Zinhle "Zinny" Thabethe is a lead singer of a South African group called the Sinikithemba Choir. The members of this choir have a strong bond: They are all HIV positive. Thabethe first learned she had HIV in 2002. A doctor told her he could not treat her condition because medicine was not widely available. Without treatment, she would probably die in less than a year, he said. But Thabethe did not give up, and she finally found a clinic[5] that was able to help HIV/AIDS patients.

Today, Thabethe and other members of the Sinikithemba Choir send a message of hope to people with HIV/AIDS. She feels that she understands their situation. "I know what they are going through, and can help support and guide them," she says. "Only by being open and asking for help will we know that we are not alone. If you have someone who will walk the journey with you, it is always easier."

[5] A **clinic** is a place where people receive care or advice from doctors and nurses.

Arn Chorn-Pond: Healing with Music

As a child, Arn Chorn-Pond worked in a prison camp in Cambodia during the Khmer Rouge period.[6] Life in the camp was terrifying. Guards regularly killed camp workers, including children. Chorn-Pond stayed alive mainly because of his skills as a musician. The camp guards liked listening to him as he played his flute. Chorn-Pond closed his eyes when he played. He said, "I escaped with the music. I played it, and my mind would be somewhere else."

Chorn-Pond finally escaped into the jungle, where he lived alone for many months. Later, an American aid worker[7] met him and took him to the United States. When Chorn-Pond grew up, he went back to Cambodia. He learned that many traditional musicians and dancers died during the Khmer Rouge period. So Chorn-Pond is working with older musicians to teach young Cambodians to play traditional music. In this way, he is helping a new generation keep their musical traditions alive.

[6] During the **Khmer Rouge period** (1975–1979), a political organization called the Khmer Rouge governed Cambodia. Almost two million Cambodians died during this period.
[7] An **aid worker** goes to dangerous parts of the world and gives people things they need, such as education, food, and medical treatment.

MUSICIANS WITH A MESSAGE | **153**

LESSON B
UNDERSTANDING THE READING

A | Understanding the Gist. Look back at your answers for exercise **D** on page 151. Were your answers correct?

B | Identifying Main Ideas. Match the main ideas (1–4) to the paragraphs in the chart below.

1. Zinny Thabethe did not give up even though she learned she had HIV/AIDS.
2. When Chorn-Pond grew up, he helped other Cambodians with music.
3. Music saved Chorn-Pond's life during the Khmer Rouge period.
4. Mraz works with James Kofi Anan to stop child slavery.

C | Taking Notes. Complete the following chart with supporting details from the reading passage on pages 152–153.

Paragraph	Main Idea	Supporting Details
D	a song inspired Mraz to go to Ghana	Mraz gave 'Freedom Song' to Free the Slaves / FTS sent him photos of kids dancing to song
E		Anan works w/ parents so _____ / Mraz wrote many songs about _____
F		learned she had HIV in _____ / found a _____ that could help her
H		played flute for _____ / playing music helped C-P to think about other things
I		went to U.S. / grew up and then went back to _____ / encourages _____ to learn trad. music

D | Using Your Notes. Discuss your answers to the questions with a partner.

1. How does James Kofi Anan help to stop child slavery?
2. In what ways might the Sinikithemba Choir bring hope to people?
3. How did Arn Chorn-Pond survive in a prison camp?

E | Critical Thinking: Making Inferences. Zinny Thabethe says, "If you have someone who will walk the journey with you, it is always easier." What do you think "walk the journey" means? What are some other ways to say this?

F | Critical Thinking: Evaluating. Think about the issues the musicians in this unit are working on. Discuss in a small group. Which one is the most important, in your opinion? Why?

EXPLORING WRITTEN ENGLISH

LESSON C

> **GOAL:** In this lesson, you are going to plan, write, revise, and edit a paragraph on the following topic: **Choose your favorite musician, band, or song and explain the reasons for your choice.**

A | Read the information in the box. Then read the pairs of sentences (1–4). Decide which sentence expresses a cause or a reason and which sentence expresses a result. Then connect the sentences using the word in parentheses.

> **Language for Writing:** Using *therefore* and *since*
>
> In Units 6 and 7, you saw that writers use *so* and *because* to connect reasons or causes with results. Writers also use *therefore* and *since* to connect reasons or causes with results.
>
> *Therefore* introduces a result. It can begin a new sentence, and it follows the reason or cause. Use a comma after *therefore* if it is at the start of a sentence.
>
> Zinhle Thabethe has HIV. **Therefore**, she understands other people who have the disease.
>   reason   result
>
> Or: She **therefore** understands other people who have the disease.
>
> *Since* introduces a reason. It can appear at the beginning of a sentence or where the two clauses connect.
>
> Use a comma after the first clause when *since* begins the sentence.
>
> **Since** she also has the disease, Zinhle Thabethe understands people who have HIV / AIDS.
>   reason   result
>
> Zinhle Thabethe understands people who have HIV / AIDS **since** she also has the disease.
>   result   reason

Example: Many dentists play recordings of music for their patients. / Music can make people feel relaxed. (*therefore*)

Music can make people feel relaxed. Therefore, many dentists play recordings of music for their patients.

1. Jason Mraz has traveled around the world playing music. / He has met a lot of people from different cultures. (*therefore*)

   _____
   _____

2. It is very peaceful and relaxing. / I listen to classical music before I go to sleep. (*since*)

   _____
   _____

LESSON C   EXPLORING WRITTEN ENGLISH

3. Music helped Arn Chorn-Pond survive as a child. / He wants to use music to help other children. (*since*)

   _____
   _____

4. Peter Gabriel loves world music. / He decided to start a world music festival. (*therefore*)

   _____
   _____

B | Discuss these questions with a partner: In what situations do you usually listen to music (for example, when you are exercising)? Why do you listen to music in these situations?

Now write about the situations in which you listen to music. Write two sentences using *therefore* and two sentences using *since*.

Example:

Since hip-hop is fast and energetic, I like to listen to it when I exercise.

_____
_____
_____
_____
_____

Writing Skill: *Presenting One Main Idea in a Paragraph*

A paragraph is a group of sentences about one topic. All the sentences in a paragraph should relate in some way to the same topic. The sentences may give examples, facts, or reasons to help the reader clearly understand the main idea.

Remember to include only sentences that directly relate to the main idea of your paragraph.

C | Here are some sentences for a paragraph about a person's favorite composer. Check the one(s) that do not belong.

_____ A. R. Rahman is my favorite composer.

_____ Rahman was born in Madras, India, in 1966.

_____ When he was 11 years old, he dropped out of school and became a professional musician.

_____ He played music with some very famous Indian musicians, including Zakir Hussain.

_____ Rahman became an excellent musician and received a scholarship to study music at Oxford University in England.

_____ The conductor Adrian Boult also studied at Oxford University.

_____ When Rahman came back to India, he became a composer.

_____ He wrote music for many films, and in 2009, he won an Academy Award for his music for the movie *Slumdog Millionaire*.

_____ The film *Man on Wire* won the Academy Award for Best Documentary in 2009.

▼ A. R. Rahman is an Indian composer, musician, singer-songwriter, and music producer.

D | Cross out three sentences that do not belong in this paragraph about a musical group from Thailand.

One of my favorite musical groups is Fong Naam. Fong Naam plays a traditional type of music from Thailand. The population of Thailand is about 70 million. Classical Thai music began to lose popularity in the mid-20th century, as modern types of music became more popular. Before 1939, Thailand was called "Siam." In the 1980s, two musicians—Buyong Ketkhong and an American named Bruce Gaston—decided to try to keep traditional Thai music alive. So Buyong and Gaston started a group, which they named Fong Naam. Fong Naam performs classical Thai music, and the group also writes new music using the classical style. I think people should visit Thailand, as it is a very interesting country. Fong Naam performs for both Thai audiences and international audiences. Therefore, they are saving a musical style from the past for future generations of Thai people, and also introducing it to people around the world.

LESSON C — WRITING TASK: Drafting

A | Brainstorming. Work with a partner. Brainstorm a list of your favorite musicians, bands, and songs. Note some reasons why you like them.

B | Planning. Follow the steps to make notes for your sentences. Don't worry about grammar or spelling. Don't write complete sentences.

Step 1 Decide on the topic of your paragraph—a favorite musician, band, or song—and complete the first sentence in the chart below.

Step 2 Choose three reasons for your choice and write them in the chart.

Step 3 Now write one or two details about each reason.

Who/What is your favorite musician/band/song?

My favorite _____ is _____

Reason 1 _____
Details:

_____

_____

_____

Reason 2 _____
Details:

_____

_____

_____

Reason 3 _____
Details:

_____

_____

_____

C | Draft 1. Use the information in the chart in exercise **B** to write a first draft of your paragraph.

WRITING TASK: Revising and Editing

D | Peer Evaluation. Exchange your first draft with a partner and follow these steps:

Step 1 Answer the questions below about your partner's sentences.

1. Does the paragraph have one main idea?   T   F
2. Do all the reasons relate to the main idea?   T   F
3. Are the reasons presented in a logical order?   T   F
4. Do the reasons have facts, examples, or details?   T   F
5. Are the reasons connected using linking words or phrases?   T   F

Step 2 Tell your partner one thing that you liked about his or her sentences.

Step 3 Share your answers to the questions in Step 1 with your partner.

E | Draft 2. Write a second draft of your paragraph. Use what you learned from the peer evaluation activity. Make any other necessary changes.

F | Editing Practice. Read the information in the box. Then find and correct one mistake with *because*, *so*, *therefore*, or *since* in each of the sentences (1–6).

> In sentences with *because*, *so*, *therefore*, and *since*, remember to:
> - use *so* and *therefore* before a result.
> - use *since* and *because* before a cause or a reason.
> - use a comma after *therefore* when it begins a sentence.
> - use a comma after a clause with *since* or *because* when it's at the beginning of a sentence.

1. Therefore, he played music in the camps, Chorn-Pond survived in a difficult situation.
2. Since he wanted to help keep traditional Cambodian music alive Chorn-Pond went back to Cambodia to teach music.
3. Because music is important in Naples people there often sing in the streets.
4. Celine Dion was born in Canada. Therefore some of her songs are in French.
5. Because their instruments are homemade Staff Benda Bilili's music has a special sound.
6. Marcello Collasurdo's father played the tambourine since Marcello wanted to learn how to play it, too.

LESSON C WRITING TASK: Editing

G | Editing Checklist. Use the checklist to find errors in your second draft.

Editing Checklist	Yes	No
1. Are all the words spelled correctly?		
2. Is the first word of every sentence capitalized?		
3. Does every sentence end with the correct punctuation?		
4. Do your subjects and verbs agree?		
5. Did you use *because*, *so*, *therefore*, and *since* correctly?		

H | Final Draft. Now use your Editing Checklist to write a third draft of your paragraph. Make any other necessary changes.

UNIT QUIZ

p.143 1. _____ concerts raise money and help make people aware of important problems.

p.144 2. A _____ of a group is a person who started it.

p.145 3. The meaning of Benda Bilili is "look beyond _____."

p.148 4. _____ on a reading passage helps you to understand the information better.

p.150 5. Your _____ are the things you have to do because of your job or position.

p.152 6. James Kofi Anan helps to rescue _____ so they don't have to live as slaves.

p.153 7. Arn Chorn-Pond played the _____ to help him survive a very difficult situation.

p.155 8. *Therefore* is a way to introduce a **result / reason**.

160 | UNIT 8

Behavior

ACADEMIC PATHWAYS
Lesson A: Recognizing noun clauses
Making inferences from an interview
Lesson B: Reading news articles about science
Lesson C: Writing a topic sentence
Writing a paragraph to compare animals

UNIT 9

Think and Discuss

1. What types of animals do you see in your everyday life? Give some examples of their behavior.
2. What can humans do that animals cannot do? What can some animals do that humans cannot do?

▲ Mother and baby orangutan in Lowery Park Zoo, Tampa, Florida

Exploring the Theme

Read the information below and discuss the questions.

1. What are some skills that chimpanzees have?
2. What are some skills that dogs have?
3. What other animals are close to humans? In what ways?

Close to us

Nonhuman primates such as great apes and monkeys are the closest animals to human beings in terms of biology. The chimpanzee (pictured above) is our closest relative—we share much of the same genetic material. Scientists say that humans and chimpanzees share 96 percent of their DNA. Chimpanzees and humans also share several behavioral characteristics, such as living in social groups and using tools.

However, nonhuman primates are wild animals and rarely live with or near people. Dogs, on the other hand, have lived and worked closely with humans for over 10,000 years. Dogs are more than just companions and pets. Many dogs also have jobs such as guarding homes, performing police and rescue work, and helping people with disabilities. Dogs cannot think like humans or use tools like some primates, but they are an important part of many people's everyday lives. In some ways, perhaps, they are "closer" to us than our nearest relatives.

LESSON A PREPARING TO READ

A | Building Vocabulary. Find the words and phrases in **blue** in the reading passage on pages 165–166. Read the words around them and try to guess their meanings. Then match the sentence parts below to make definitions.

_____ 1. If you are the **owner** of something,
_____ 2. When you **work out** a problem,
_____ 3. Your **approach to** something
_____ 4. A **companion**
_____ 5. If you are **confused**,

a. is the way you deal with it.
b. you do not know what is happening, or you do not know what to do.
c. you solve it.
d. you have the legal right to have or use it.
e. is someone who spends time with you, such as a friend.

> **Word Usage**
> **Approach** is both a noun and a verb.
> Noun: an **approach to** a problem, an **approach to** a situation
> Verb: **approach** the door, **approach** the end.

B | Building Vocabulary. Find the words in **blue** in the reading passage on pages 165–166. Read the words around them and try to guess their meanings. Then complete the sentences.

> angry   integrity   powerful   professional   trainer

1. A _____ is a person who teaches people or animals certain skills.
2. A _____ has the skills to do a certain kind of job, such as a lawyer or a doctor.
3. If you are _____, you are very annoyed or feel a strong dislike about something.
4. If you have _____, you are honest and you have strong moral values.
5. If you are _____, you are able to control people and events.

C | Using Vocabulary. Answer the questions. Share your ideas with a partner.

1. What people in your country do you think are very **powerful**? Why?
2. How do you deal with people who are **angry**?
3. Would you like to be a **professional** someday? If so, what kind?

D | Skimming/Predicting. Skim the interview with Cesar Millan on pages 165–166. Which topic(s) do you think the interview covers?

☐ some reasons that people have certain dogs as pets

☐ some differences between human and dog behavior

☐ some things that dogs can teach us

☐ how and why Millan became a dog trainer

☐ Millan's parents' views about his job

☐ what a normal day is like for Millan

READING

Meet the Dog Whisperer

▲ "I train people. I rehabilitate dogs," Millan says.

1 **MEXICAN-BORN** animal trainer Cesar Millan is known around the world for his TV show *Dog Whisperer*. On the show, Millan helps dogs and dog owners deal with their problems. He helps angry and scared dogs become good companions. He also helps confused humans become confident, happy dog owners.

5 *What is the biggest mistake we make with dogs?*

We humanize dogs. We hold conversations with them as if they were people. . . . A dog doesn't know it lives in Beverly Hills¹ or how much we spend on it.

Why do people like certain kinds of dogs?

It's about what they want from another human but can't get, so they get it from a dog.

10 *So a person gets a pit bull because . . . ?*

Because it represents power, strength, masculinity²—like driving a Ferrari.

And a small poodle?

Because it's feminine. Decorative.³

---

¹ **Beverly Hills** is a city in Los Angeles, California, where many rich and famous people live.
² **Masculinity** means the characteristics thought to be typical of being a man. The opposite of masculinity is **femininity**.
³ Something that is **decorative** is designed to look pretty or attractive.

BEHAVIOR | 165

LESSON A   READING

So people get dogs that are like them?

15 I walk into a home, and I don't have to hear much. I see the dog, and I know who you are. It's a mirror.

What is your approach to helping owners with their dog problems?

If you don't tell a dog what to do, it will tell you what to do. My clients[4] are powerful, they have Harvard[5] degrees, they run
20 [big corporations], but they can't control a dog. You don't ask a dog if it would like to go for a walk. You put on the leash[6] and go.

Is there any creature you can't rehabilitate?[7]

My father.... I want him to tell my mother, "I appreciate you.
25 Thank you. I love you." But he can't, not in the machismo[8] culture of Mexico.

Can't you take your father for a walk and work out the issues?

No. He'd just run away.

How did your parents feel about your choice of profession?

30 They wanted me to become a professional, [like a] doctor [or] lawyer.

How does your father feel now that you've made it?

He still can't understand why Americans pay me for walking their dogs.

35 *What are the lessons we learn from dogs?*

To live in the moment. Also honesty ... [and] integrity. They will never stab you in the back or lie to you.

Do dogs think and feel?

They feel—they are instinctual.[9] They don't think.

40 *So which animal behaves better—humans or dogs?*

Oh, dogs.

▲ From poodles (above) to pit bulls (top), the biggest mistake we make with dogs is trying to humanize them, says Millan: "A dog is first an animal, then a dog, then a breed, and then its name."

[4] A **client** receives a professional service in return for payment.
[5] **Harvard University** is a high-ranking American university.
[6] A **leash** is a long, thin piece of material used to keep a dog under control.
[7] To **rehabilitate** someone means to help that person to live a normal life again, for example, following an illness.
[8] **Machismo** refers to a man's behavior when he is very proud of his masculinity.
[9] **Instinctual** actions are made according to feelings, rather than opinions or ideas.

UNDERSTANDING THE READING

A | Understanding the Gist. Look back at your answer for exercise **D** on page 164. Were your predictions correct?

B | Identifying Key Details. Scan the interview on pages 165–166 to find information to complete each sentence.

1. Millan says that many dog owners make the mistake of _____ dogs.
2. According to Millan, a poodle is more _____ and decorative than a pit bull.
3. Many of Millan's clients are _____ people, but they _____ their dogs.
4. Millan's father can't understand why Americans pay him to _____.
5. According to Millan, two lessons we can learn from dogs are _____ and _____.

C | Critical Thinking: Making Inferences. First, read the statements in the chart. Then write who Millan is talking about.

	What Millan says directly in the reading	Who he is talking about
1.	They have Harvard degrees, but they can't control a dog.	
2.	They wanted me to be a professional, like a doctor or lawyer.	
3.	They will never stab you in the back or lie to you.	

Now read three possible inferences based on what Millan says above. Write *1*, *2*, or *3* from the chart above to match the statements and inferences.

_____ a. They don't really like his job.
_____ b. They aren't so smart or powerful.
_____ c. In some ways, he likes them better than humans.

 D | Critical Thinking: Making Inferences. Read again some of Millan's answers. What can we infer about Millan's beliefs, or assumptions? Discuss your ideas in small groups.

1. Q. *So a person gets a pit bull because . . . ?* A. Because it represents power, strength, masculinity—like driving a Ferrari.
   Q. *And a small poodle?* A. Because it's feminine. Decorative.
2. Q. *Is there any creature you can't rehabilitate?* A. My father. . . . I want him to tell my mother, "I appreciate you. Thank you. I love you." But he can't, not in the machismo culture of Mexico.

> **Strategy**
>
> When you make an **inference**, you conclude something based on things a person suggests *indirectly*, not what the person states *directly*.

LESSON A — DEVELOPING READING SKILLS

Reading Skill: *Recognizing Noun Clauses*

A noun clause is a type of dependent, or subordinate, clause. Dependent clauses cannot stand alone as sentences; they are always part of a sentence.

A noun clause has a subject and a verb and acts like a noun in a sentence.

                              subject   verb

   A dog doesn't know **how much we spend on it**.
    main clause   noun clause

One type of noun clause is the *wh-* clause. These noun clauses start with a question word:

   Do you know **who** Cesar Millan is?   I don't know **how** old the dog is.
   Millan understands **why** dogs behave in certain ways.   I wonder **where** Beverly Hills is.

Noun clauses can also come at the beginning of a sentence: **What** Millan says makes sense to me.

                                                 For more explanation and examples, see page 217.

A | Identifying Noun Clauses. Underline the noun clause in each sentence.

1. A good dog trainer knows a lot about what dogs need.
2. Many people do not understand why pet owners have trouble with their dogs.
3. One of Millan's specialties is teaching people how to control their dogs.
4. I don't know how many dog owners there are in the United States.
5. Statistics show where most pet owners get their dogs.

B | Matching. Match the noun clauses (a–d) to complete each sentence (1-4). Then scan the interview to check your answers.

1. A dog doesn't know it lives in Beverly Hills or _____
2. I see the dog, and I know _____
3. If you don't tell a dog what to do, it will tell you _____
4. [My father] still can't understand _____

a. what to do.
b. why Americans pay me for walking their dogs.
c. how much we spend on it.
d. who you are.

C | Applying. Read the paragraph below. Find and underline the noun clauses. Then discuss answers to the questions with a partner.

track 2-10

    Some people think that your preference for dogs or cats says a lot about who you are. Sam Gosling, a psychologist at the University of Texas in Austin, decided to find out if this is true. In particular, Gosling wanted to learn what the characteristics of certain types of pet owners are. In the study, Gosling first found out how people classify themselves: as dog people, cat people, neither, or both. Then he gave the same people a standard personality test. The results showed what Gosling expected: dog people and cat people are different. For example, Gosling learned that dog people are more outgoing than cat people, and cat people are generally more imaginative than dog people. Why these differences exist, however, is still a mystery.

                                                  Source: http://www.psychologytoday.com/

1. What did Gosling want to learn in his study?
2. What did Gosling find out first?
3. What were some of the results of Gosling's study?

VIEWING

Gorilla Toolmakers

Before Viewing

A | Using a Dictionary. Here are some words and phrases you will hear in the video. Complete each definition with the correct word or phrase. Use your dictionary to help you.

> evidence
> invent
> measure the depth of
> think through

▲ Scientists are discovering that gorillas, such as this silverback in the Democratic Republic of the Congo, may have more skills than we previously knew about.

1. If you _____ something such as water, you find out how far down it goes.
2. When you _____ something, you consider it carefully until you understand it.
3. If people or animals _____ something, they create it for the first time.
4. _____ is information that shows that something is true.

B | Brainstorming. Discuss this question with a partner: What can people do that gorillas cannot do?

While Viewing

A | As you view the video, choose the correct option (a–o) to complete each sentence.

1. Evidence shows that gorillas can ____
2. One female gorilla used a stick to measure ____
3. Another female gorilla used a tool to ____
4. Gorillas' tool use shows that ____
5. Understanding animals' tool use can help us ____

a. avoid falling into water.
b. some animals can plan and solve problems.
c. make and use tools.
d. understand how we developed as humans.
e. the depth of water before she walked over it.

After Viewing

A | Discuss your answers to the items (1–5) above with a partner.

B | Synthesizing. Think about the behavior of dogs and gorillas. How are these animals similar and different? In what ways is each animal's behavior similar to, and different from, human's?

BEHAVIOR | 169

LESSON B | PREPARING TO READ

A | **Building Vocabulary.** Find the words and phrases in **blue** in the reading passage on pages 172–173. Read the words around them and try to guess their meanings. Then match the sentence parts below to make definitions.

1. If you **pay attention**, _____
2. If you **break down** something, _____
3. A **reward** _____
4. Your **response** to something _____
5. If you **share** something with someone, _____

a. is your reaction to it.
b. you both have it.
c. you destroy it or make it weaker.
d. you watch and listen carefully.
e. is something you get for doing a good job.

B | **Building Vocabulary.** Read the definitions below. Then complete each sentence with the correct word in **blue**.

> If you **continue** to do something, you keep doing it without stopping.
> **Cooperation** is working with or helping other people.
> Someone who is **fair** treats everyone the same way.
> An academic **field** is a particular subject of study.
> **Research** involves studying something and trying to discover facts about it.

Word Partners
Use **research** with adjectives and nouns.
Adjectives: **biological** research, **recent** research, **scientific** research
Nouns: **animal** research, research **findings**, research **results**

1. Pet owners should give the same amount of food to each of their dogs. Otherwise, they are not being _____.

2. Animal behavior has become a more popular _____ of study partly because of shows such as *Dog Whisperer*.

3. Dogs sometimes don't know when to stop eating. They often _____ to eat as long as they have food in front of them.

4. _____ is a normal part of human behavior. For example, in many jobs people need to work together on projects.

5. Recent _____ on gorilla behavior shows that gorillas may be able to use tools.

170 | UNIT 9

C | Using Vocabulary. Answer the questions in complete sentences. Then share your sentences with a partner.

1. What **field** do you want to study or work in someday?

   _____

   _____

2. What are three things you usually **share** with other people?

   _____

   _____

3. In what ways do people in your class **cooperate** with each other?

   _____

   _____

4. Can you think of any times when you received **unfair** treatment?

   _____

   _____

5. When was the last time you did some **research**? What was it for?

   _____

   _____

> **Word Partners**
>
> Use **field** (meaning "subject") with nouns: field of **study**, the field of **biology**, the field of **genetics**. **Field** can also mean an area for playing games or growing plants: a **soccer** field, a **wheat** field.

D | Skimming/Predicting. Read the main title and the headings on pages 172-173. What kind of reading passage is this?

a. a pair of interviews   b. factual stories   c. personal stories

What do you think the reading is about?

a. how monkeys are helping humans
b. recent studies of monkey behavior
c. a comparison of monkeys and humans

BEHAVIOR | 171

LESSON B READING

SCIENCE In the News

▲ Research suggests capuchin monkeys, such as this one in Costa Rica, care about fair treatment.

track 2-11

Monkeys Show a Sense of Fairness

A Most humans expect to receive fair treatment. A recent study shows that brown capuchin monkeys may feel the same way. This is the first time scientists have seen this kind of behavior in a species other than humans.

B Scientists chose brown capuchin monkeys for the research because capuchins are known to have strong social bonds. In other words, they have close relationships with other capuchins. They also cooperate; for example, they share responsibilities for food-gathering activities such as finding fruit trees.

C Sarah Brosnan, the leader of the study, put female monkeys in pairs. A different researcher worked with each pair of capuchin partners. The researchers trained the monkeys to exchange a small rock with them. "That may sound simple, but not very many species are willing to [give things away]," says Brosnan. When a monkey exchanged a rock with the researcher within 60 seconds, she received a reward. Usually, the reward was a piece of cucumber.

D The partner of each capuchin who made an exchange also received a reward. Sometimes the partner got the same reward (a cucumber slice), but other times the partner received a better reward (a grape). Brosnan said the response to the unequal treatment was astonishing.[1] When a capuchin saw its partner get better treatment, it was unhappy. Some capuchins did not want to continue the test or eat the cucumbers they received. Some threw their food at the researchers.

E Brosnan's research suggests there is a connection between animal cooperation and a dislike of unfair treatment. However, as Brosnan explains, "We don't know whether [monkeys] become cooperative and then learn to not like being treated unfairly, or the other way around. But that opens up a whole new research field."

"Love Drug" Results in Kinder Monkeys

F Scientists studying monkeys recently found some surprising results using a chemical called oxytocin. Oxytocin is a hormone[2] produced by humans and other mammals. It is sometimes called the "love hormone," because it is related to bonding and maternal[3] behavior. Women produce large amounts of oxytocin during and after childbirth. Scientists believe this makes mothers feel more connected to their children.

▲ Aside from humans, macaques are the most widespread type of primate. They live in places ranging from Japan (pictured) to North Africa.

G The scientists at Duke University, in North Carolina, USA, studied a monkey species called macaques. They wanted to see how the macaques responded to larger-than-normal amounts of oxytocin. In the experiment, some of the monkeys inhaled[4] the hormone. Then they had to make a choice: drink a serving of fruit juice, give the fruit juice to another monkey, or do neither.

H The monkeys who inhaled the oxytocin were more likely to give the juice to other monkeys. The researchers think that oxytocin made the monkeys pay more attention to other monkeys. "If that's true," says researcher Michael Platt, "it's really cool because it suggests that oxytocin breaks down normal social barriers."[5]

I Scientists think the hormone might help people with conditions such as autism.[6] People with autism are often not interested in other people. Oxytocin might help because it seems to increase trust. It may also improve social skills and make people more aware of others. However, scientists need to do further research before oxytocin can be used as a medication.

[1] Something that is **astonishing** is very surprising.
[2] A **hormone** is a chemical that makes an organ in the body perform a certain action.
[3] **Maternal** relates to the feelings or actions of a mother toward her child.
[4] When you **inhale**, you breathe in.
[5] A **barrier** is something that makes it difficult or impossible to do something.
[6] **Autism** is a mental condition that can make someone less able to respond to other people.

LESSON B | UNDERSTANDING THE READING

A | Understanding the Gist. Look back at your answers for exercise **D** on page 171. Were your predictions correct?

B | Identifying Main Ideas. Match the key ideas (a–e) from "Monkeys Show a Sense of Fairness" with the correct category (1–5).

a. The monkeys got angry when they noticed unfair treatment.
b. Scientists gave unequal rewards to pairs of monkeys.
c. Whether cooperation occurs before or after monkeys develop a sense of fairness.
d. To find out if capuchin monkeys value fair treatment.
e. There is a link between animal cooperation and their dislike of unfair treatment.

1. The purpose of the study: _____
2. How researchers did the study: _____
3. What they noticed: _____
4. What they concluded: _____
5. Question for further research: _____

C | Identifying Main Ideas. Complete the key ideas for "Love Drug Results in Kinder Monkeys."

1. The purpose of the study: To find out _how a hormone affects monkey behavior_.

2. How researchers did the study: They gave _____ to some macaques and none to others. Then the macaques chose to drink some juice, give the juice to _____, or do neither.

3. What they noticed: Macaques with more oxytocin were more likely to _____.

4. What they concluded: Oxytocin made the monkeys _____.

5. Question for further research: Whether oxytocin can be used as a medication for _____.

D | Understanding Pronoun Reference. Find these sentences on pages 172–173. Then circle the noun that each underlined pronoun refers to. Check your answers with a partner.

Monkeys Show a Sense of Fairness

1. In other words, they have close relationships with other capuchins.
   a. capuchins   b. scientists
2. The researchers trained the monkeys to exchange a small rock with them.
   a. the monkeys   b. the researchers
3. Some threw their food at the researchers.   a. cucumbers   b. capuchins

"Love Drug" Results in Kinder Monkeys

1. They wanted to see how the macaques responded to larger-than-normal amounts of oxytocin.
   a. the scientists   b. the macaques
2. It may also improve social skills . . .   a. trust   b. oxytocin
3. . . . and make people more aware of others.   a. other people   b. other social skills

EXPLORING WRITTEN ENGLISH

LESSON C

> **GOAL:** In this lesson, you are going to write a paragraph about the following topic:
> **Choose two kinds of animals and compare their behavior.**

A | Read the information in the box. Then use the words and expressions in parentheses to combine or link each pair of sentences (1–5).

Language for Writing: Making Comparisons

As you saw in Unit 5, we use the comparative form of adjectives to talk about similarities and differences between two things. We also use other words and expressions for making comparisons.

Showing Similarities

> **Both** gorillas **and** chimpanzees use tools.
> **Like** gorillas, chimpanzees are endangered.
> Gorillas mainly eat plants. **Similarly**, monkeys are mostly herbivores.

- Use the plural form of the verb with the expression **both . . . and . . .** .
- Use a comma after the word **similarly**, and after an expression with **Like . . .** .

Showing Differences

> **Unlike** gorillas, monkeys have tails.
> Monkeys live about 30 years. **In contrast**, apes can live almost 60 years.
> Dogs are easily trained. **However**, it is very difficult to train a cat.
> OR: Dogs are easily trained. It is very difficult, **however**, to train a cat.

Use a comma after the word **however**, and after expressions with **Unlike . . .** and **In contrast . . .** .

For more explanation and examples, see page 218.

1. Gorillas can make tools. Dogs cannot make tools. (*unlike*)
   _____

2. Apes eat insects. Monkeys eat insects. (*both . . . and*)
   _____

3. Reptiles lay eggs. Mammals give birth to live babies. (*in contrast*)
   _____

4. Old World monkeys, such as capuchins, live in the Eastern Hemisphere. New World monkeys, such as macaques, live in the Western Hemisphere. (*however*)
   _____
   _____

5. German shepherds can become guide dogs. Capuchin monkeys can be trained to help people. (*similarly*)
   _____

LESSON C — EXPLORING WRITTEN ENGLISH

B | Look at the Venn diagram comparison of two dog breeds. Use your dictionary to look up any words you don't know.

Discuss with a partner: How are Australian terriers and basenjis similar? How are they different?

Write sentences about the information using the words and phrases below.

Both . . . and . . .   Unlike . . . ,

Like . . . ,   However, . . .

Similarly, . . .   In contrast, . . .

Australian Terrier
- can be aggressive
- courageous
- lives 12–14 years
- barks a lot
- can breed twice a year

Both
- alert
- social
- normally good with children
- easy to train

Basenji
- independent
- intelligent
- lives 10–12 years
- doesn't bark much
- can only breed once a year

◀ Australian terrier

▲ Basenji

Writing Skill: *Writing a Topic Sentence*

As you saw in Unit 8, a paragraph normally has one main idea, or topic. A topic sentence states the main idea of a paragraph. Topic sentences normally begin a paragraph, but they can also appear later in a paragraph.

A topic sentence states what a paragraph is about. It also includes enough details to give the reader a clear picture of what the paragraph will discuss. For example:

Cats make good pets because they are independent and clean.

C | Identifying a Topic Sentence. The paragraph below is missing a topic sentence. Write the letter (a-c) of the best topic sentence to begin the paragraph. Discuss why it is the best topic sentence.

a. I believe that Basenjis are the safest type of pet dog.
b. Basenjis are good pets because they are easy to train and are good with children.
c. There are a lot of things that you need to think about when you get a new pet.

_____ Basenjis are intelligent, so they are easy to train. If a dog is easy to train, then its owner does not need to spend much time and money helping it adapt to its new environment. Basenjis also make good pets because they are not normally dangerous to children. Children are very energetic and can sometimes be aggressive with dogs. Nervous or antisocial dogs may react angrily to aggressive treatment, so they are not good choices for families with children. Since basenjis are normally calm animals, however, they are safe to have around children.

D | Writing a Topic Sentence. Write a topic sentence for the paragraph below.

_____

_____

Studies of gorillas in the wild show that they can invent and use tools. One example is a female gorilla who used a stick to measure the depth of water before she walked through it. In addition, gorillas are capable of learning languages. Michael, for example, is a lowland gorilla that learned to communicate with humans using American Sign Language. He can also understand spoken English.

LESSON C

WRITING TASK: Drafting

A | Brainstorming. Make a list of animals that you are most familiar with. Use the ones you read about in this unit and your own ideas. Next to each one, make notes on what you know about the behavior of that animal.

Example: Gorilla:　　*uses tools*　　*can walk on two legs*　　*uses instinct*　　*uses thumbs*

B | Planning. Follow the steps below to make notes for your paragraph. Don't worry about grammar or spelling. Don't write complete sentences.

Step 1　Look at your brainstorming notes from exercise **A**. Choose two animals that you want to compare. Note them in the Venn diagram below.

Step 2　List at least two types of behavior in each part of the diagram. Include some details for each one.

Step 3　Write a topic sentence for your paragraph that tells the reader what you are going to discuss in the paragraph.

Topic sentence: _____

_____

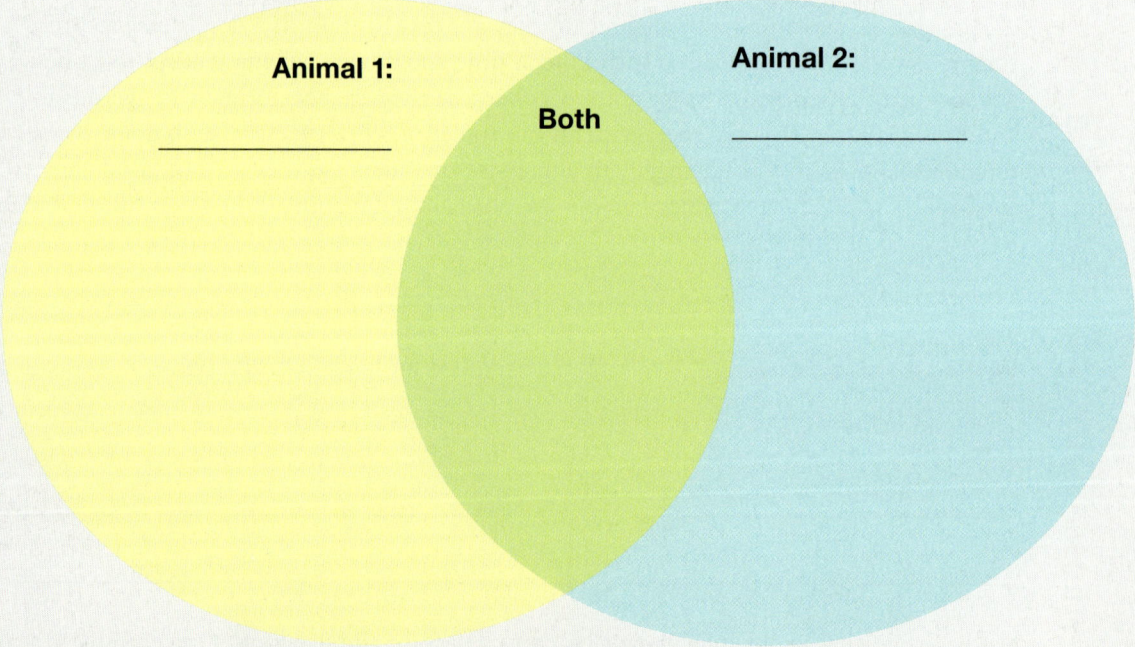

C | Draft 1. Use the information you noted above to write a first draft of your paragraph.

WRITING TASK: Revising and Editing

D | Peer Evaluation. Exchange your first draft with a partner and follow these steps:

Step 1 Answer the questions below about your partner's paragraph.

	Y	N
1. Does the paragraph have one main idea?	Y	N
2. Does the topic sentence tell the reader what the paragraph is about?	Y	N
3. Does all the information relate to the main idea?	Y	N
4. Does the writer include points of similarity and difference?	Y	N
5. Are the points of comparison in a logical order?	Y	N
6. Does the writer include examples, facts, or details?	Y	N

Step 2 Tell your partner one thing that you liked about his or her paragraph.

Step 3 Share your answers to the questions in Step 1 with your partner.

E | Draft 2. Write a second draft of your paragraph. Use what you learned from the peer evaluation activity. Make any other necessary changes.

F | Editing Practice. Read the information in the box. Then find and correct one mistake with comparison words and expressions in each of the sentences (1–8).

> In sentences with comparison words and expressions, remember to:
> - use the plural form of the verb with *both . . . and*.
> - use *similarly* and *in contrast* at the start of a sentence, and follow them with a comma.
> - use *like* and *unlike* with a noun or a noun phrase followed by a comma.
> - use a comma after *However* when it is at the start of a sentence.
> - use a comma before and after *however* when it is in the middle of a sentence.

1. Like humans do, chimpanzees make tools to solve problems.
2. Both female capuchins and humans values fairness.
3. Some chimpanzees make tools in zoos, in contrast, gorillas rarely make tools in captivity.
4. Unlike cats need, dogs need a lot of attention from their owners.
5. Some dog trainers believe in punishing bad behavior. However other trainers believe in rewarding good behavior.
6. Both a basenji and an Australian terrier makes good pets for children.
7. Scientists often use monkeys in behavioral studies. Similarly rats are useful in scientific research on behavior.
8. Like children dogs need a lot of training and attention.

LESSON C — WRITING TASK: Editing

G | Editing Checklist. Use the checklist to find errors in your second draft.

Editing Checklist	Yes	No
1. Are all the words spelled correctly?		
2. Is the first word of every sentence capitalized?		
3. Does every sentence end with the correct punctuation?		
4. Do your subjects and verbs agree?		
5. Are the comparative forms correct?		

H | Final Draft. Now use your Editing Checklist to write a third draft of your paragraph. Make any other necessary changes.

UNIT QUIZ

p.163 1. The _____ is our closest relative.

p.164 2. Your _____ something is the way you deal with it.

p.166 3. According to Cesar Millan, if you don't tell a dog what to do, it will _____.

p.168 4. A noun clause acts like a _____ in a sentence.

p.169 5. We now know that gorillas can make and use _____.

p.170 6. _____ means working with or helping someone.

p.172 7. Recent research shows that capuchin monkeys value _____.

p.177 8. A _____ tells you what a paragraph is about.

The Power of Image

UNIT 10

ACADEMIC PATHWAYS

Lesson A: Recognizing subordinating conjunctions
Understanding mood
Lesson B: Reading a personal narrative
Lesson C: Using supporting ideas in a descriptive paragraph
Writing a paragraph to describe a photograph

Think and Discuss

1. In your opinion, what makes a photograph powerful?
2. Describe a photograph you like. Why do you like it?

▲ This photo of a 32-year-old migrant mother and three of her children became a powerful symbol of the Great Depression, a period of economic hardship during the 1930s. The photographer, Dorothea Lange, worked as a photojournalist for *Life*, *National Geographic*, and several other magazines.

Exploring the Theme

A. Look at the information on page 183 and answer the questions.

1. According to Annie Griffiths, what makes a great photograph?
2. What do you think are some other elements of a great photograph?

B. Look at the captions for the photos and answer this question:
Which photo do you think is the best example of each element?

One day, photographer David Doubilet was diving off the coast of South Australia. He saw some sea lions playing in the water and he took this photo. Doubilet liked the way the light was shining on the sea lions' fur. ▼

BOTTOM RIGHT As Jim Blair was walking across a bridge over a river in Dacca, Nigeria, he ▶ heard laughter. He looked down and saw children playing with the water buffaloes that they take care of. He was able to record a moment of joy at the end of a workday, as one boy jumped off the back of a water buffalo.

Light, Action, . . . Camera!

What makes a great photograph? According to Annie Griffiths, a photographer for *National Geographic*, there are three basic elements of any great photo: **composition**—the way objects are arranged in a scene, "**moment**"—the way a picture shows a moment in time, and **light**. Some other elements add to the beauty of an image: **color**, **motion** (a sense of movement), and **wonder**—something unusual or amazing in a photo.

▲ **TOP RIGHT** Danish photographer Sisse Brimberg took this picture of a baby and mother in a park in St. Petersburg, Russia. The composition is unusual—the baby is the middle of the scene, slightly behind and to the left of the mother. The smiling mother is turning her head to look back at her baby. Brimberg feels the picture shows a universal experience—a mother's pride in her child.

THE POWER OF IMAGE | 183

LESSON A — PREPARING TO READ

A | Building Vocabulary. Find the words in **blue** in the reading passage on pages 185–188. Read the words around them and try to guess their meanings. Then circle the correct word or phrase to complete each sentence (1–10).

1. If something is **sudden / illegal**, it is not allowed by law.
2. A(n) **element / ceremony** is a formal event, such as a wedding.
3. A(n) **emotion / quality** of a thing is a particular characteristic.
4. If something happens **visually / suddenly**, it happens quickly and unexpectedly.
5. A(n) **emotion / ceremony** is a feeling, such as fear or love.
6. A(n) **adult / quality** is a person who is fully grown.
7. When someone **points out / reminds you of** something, they show it to you or tell you about it.
8. If something is **visual / illegal**, you can see it.
9. When things or people **point out / remind you of** a fact or event you already know about, they make you think about it again.
10. A(n) **ceremony / element** of something is a part of it.

Word Link
vis = seeing
visual, **vis**ualize, tele**vis**ion, **vis**ion, **vis**ible, **vis**it

B | Using Vocabulary. Answer the questions. Share your ideas with a partner.

1. Describe a **ceremony** you have been to. What was its purpose?
2. At what age do you think a person becomes an **adult**? Why?
3. What things are **illegal** in your country?

C | Brainstorming. Look at the photos on pages 185–188. How does each photo make you feel? List words that describe your emotions, such as *sadness*, *happiness*, and *fear*. Share your ideas with a partner.

_____
_____
_____

D | Predicting. Skim the first page of the reading passage (page 185). Look for information about David Griffin. Then answer these questions.

1. Who is David Griffin?
2. What links him to the photographs on pages 186–188?

184 | UNIT 10

READING

How Photography Connects Us

▲ Jou Jou, a chimpanzee, reaches out its hand to Dr. Jane Goodall. The moment was captured by *National Geographic* photographer Michael "Nick" Nichols.

track 2-12

A **ONE DAY SOME YEARS AGO,** David Griffin was at a beach watching his son swimming in the water. Suddenly, a big wave caught the boy and started to pull him out to sea. As Griffin ran to help his son, time seemed to slow down. The scene froze. Griffin can still remember what the moment felt like. "I can see the rocks are over here," he says. "There's a wave about to crash onto him. I can see his hands reaching out, and I can see his face in terror, looking at me, saying, 'Help me, Dad.'"

B Griffin was able to help his son out of the water and both were fine. But Griffin will never forget the details of the event. For Griffin, it is an example of a "flashbulb[1] memory." In a flashbulb memory, all the elements of an event come together. These elements include both the event and the viewer's emotions as the event is happening. In these situations, time slows down and details become very clear, he says.

C Today, Griffin is as an award-winning photography director. He believes that a great photograph is like a flashbulb memory. It copies the way the mind works when something important is happening. It shows the event, and also the story and feelings behind the event. "I believe that photography can make a real connection to people," says Griffin. In other words, we do not just see the event in a photo. We also feel an emotional connection with it.

D On the following pages are some examples of how photographers make an emotional connection by capturing moments in time.

[1] A **flashbulb** is a lightbulb attached to camera. It lights up a scene for a very short period of time.

THE POWER OF IMAGE | 185

LESSON A READING

E   In India, more and more people are leaving the countryside to live in cities. Many of these migrants live in poor city areas called slums. Photographer Jonas Bendiksen traveled to India to record life in Mumbai's Dharavi slum. Although life in the slum is hard, Bendiksen was able to show the spirit and strength of this community. In this photo, he shows a Dharavi street coming alive for a Hindu festival.

F   The image below is by amateur[2] photographer Elmar Rubio. As a storm approached, he caught his two daughters throwing their coats into the strong wind. Griffin points out that amateur photographers, not just professionals, can capture a special moment. "The quality of amateur photographs can at times be amazing," he says. "Everyone has at least one, maybe two, great photos in them."

The best professional photojournalists, says Griffin, "create a visual narrative."³ That is, they know how to use pictures to tell a story. Two examples are shown here. The top photograph, by Brent Stirton, shows villagers carrying a 500-pound (225-kilogram) silverback gorilla from Virunga Park in 2007. The gorilla, called Senkwekwe, was one of several gorillas illegally shot by unknown gunmen that year. The bottom photo is by underwater photographer Brian Skerry. It shows a thresher shark caught in a fishing net near Baja California. A recent study found that up to 73 million sharks are caught each year, mostly for their fins. After they saw these photographs, people around the world became more aware of the dangers facing these wild animals.

² If you are an **amateur**, you do something as a hobby and not as a job.
³ A **narrative** is a story.

THE POWER OF IMAGE | 187

LESSON A READING

In 2005, Randy Olson traveled to central Africa's Ituri Forest for a photo story. His goal was to photograph a pygmy tribe called the Mbuti. Pygmies are some of the shortest people in the world—most adult males are less than 4 feet 11 inches (150 centimeters) tall. They are also very difficult to reach, as they live deep inside the forest. In the foreground of this image[4] is a blind, young Mbuti boy. He is getting ready for a ceremony to mark the beginning of his life as an adult. Behind him is a young Mbuti girl. "I love this photograph because it reminds me of Degas's bronze sculptures of a little dancer," says Griffin.

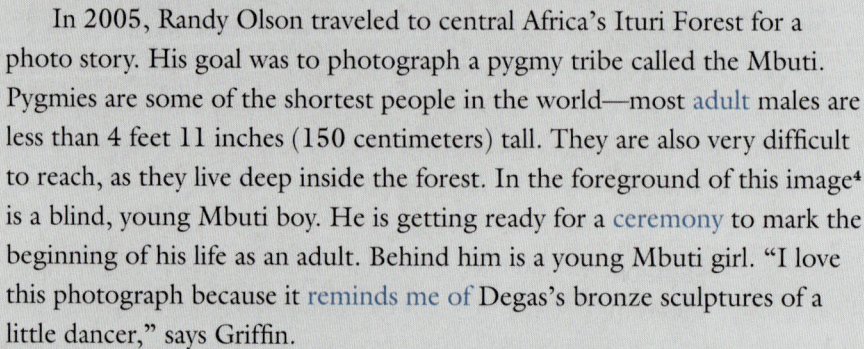

◀ Statue of a ballet dancer, by Edgar Degas (1834–1917)

[4] The **foreground of an image** is the area in the front of the picture.

To see more of Griffin's favorite photos, see "David Griffin on how photography connects us" at http://www.ted.com.

UNDERSTANDING THE READING

A | Understanding the Gist. Look back at your answers for exercise **D** on page 184. Were your answers correct?

B | Understanding the Main Ideas. Look back at page 185 to answer these questions.

1. What happened to Griffin's son? _____
2. What is a "flashbulb memory"? _____
3. According to Griffin, what does a great photograph do? _____

C | Identifying Key Details. Read each description below. Then match each one to the photograph(s) it describes.

1. helped people become aware of a serious wildlife problem
2. is similar to a famous work of art
3. shows that amateurs can also take good photos
4. shows the spirit of a community
5. makes an emotional connection

D | Critical Thinking: Understanding Mood. What kind of emotion, or mood, is created by the first paragraph on page 185? What words and phrases help to create this mood? Share your ideas with a partner.

E | Critical Thinking: Analyzing. Discuss your answers to these questions with a partner.

1. Why does Griffin tell the story of his son at the beach? What idea does it explain?
2. Does the story help you to understand the idea? Why, or why not?

CT Focus

To **understand the mood of a piece of writing**, look for how writers describe what they see, hear, and feel.

LESSON A DEVELOPING READING SKILLS

Reading Skill: *Recognizing Subordinating Conjunctions*

Subordinating conjunctions show relationships between ideas in clauses. Some subordinating conjunctions show time and contrast.

The subordinating conjunctions *after*, *before*, *until*, *while*, and *as* can show **time relationships**:

<u>I decided to study photography</u> **after** <u>I saw Brent Stirton's photographs</u>.
      independent clause   dependent clause

The subordinating conjunctions *although, even though, though,* and *while* can show **contrast**:

Although <u>the camera was old</u>, <u>it took excellent pictures</u>.
      dependent clause   independent clause

Remember to use a comma before **while** if you are making a contrast.

A | Recognizing subordinating conjunctions. Match the underlined subordinating conjunctions with their meanings. Write **T** for *time* and **C** for *contrast*.

1. _____ Elmar Rubio got his equipment ready <u>before</u> the storm started.
2. _____ Rubio is an amateur photographer, <u>while</u> Brent Stirton is a professional.
3. _____ David Griffin spoke about the photographs <u>while</u> he showed them to the audience.
4. _____ You usually cannot become a professional photographer <u>until</u> you have many years of experience.
5. _____ <u>Although</u> the photo of the dead gorilla is very sad, it made more people aware of an environmental issue.

B | Scanning/Analyzing. Find four sentences on pages 185–188 with subordinating conjunctions. Write the sentences and underline the conjunction. Does each one show contrast or a time relationship? Circle **Time** or **Contrast**. Discuss your answers with a partner.

1. Paragraph A: _____
   _____ **Time / Contrast**

2. Paragraph E: _____
   _____ **Time / Contrast**

3. Paragraph F: _____
   _____ **Time / Contrast**

4. Paragraph G: _____
   _____ **Time / Contrast**

C | Applying. Choose two of the photographs from pages 185–188. Write a sentence about each one using a subordinating conjunction.

VIEWING

Photo Camp

Before Viewing

▲ "Tent cities" provide a short-term home for refugees in the central African nation of Uganda.

A | Using a Dictionary. Complete each definition with the correct word. Use your dictionary to help you.

> document
> exhibition
> portrait
> reflection
> refugees

1. A(n) _____ is an event where people come to see art.
2. A(n) _____ is a picture of a person.
3. _____ are people who have to leave their home, usually due to war or a natural disaster.
4. A(n) _____ is an image that you can see in a mirror or in a body of water.
5. When you _____ something, you make a record of it.

B | Brainstorming. The video is about refugee children in Uganda. Some professional photographers are teaching them how to take good pictures. How might photography help the children? Share your ideas with a partner.

While Viewing

A | Watch the video about the Ugandan photo camp. As you watch, circle whether each statement is true (**T**) or false (**F**).

1. The young people in the video have all used cameras before.   T   F
2. Reza thinks that photos can communicate like language.   T   F
3. The young people are learning to use cameras to tell stories about themselves.   T   F
4. One goal of the camp is to learn more about the lives of professional photographers.   T   F

After Viewing

A | Discuss the statements (1–4) above with a partner. Correct the false statement(s).

B | Critical Thinking: Evaluating. Discuss this question with a partner: What do you think the photographers learned from the children at the camp?

THE POWER OF IMAGE | 191

LESSON B | PREPARING TO READ

A | Building Vocabulary. Read the definitions of the words and phrases in **blue** below. Then complete each sentence with the correct word.

> If something is true **according to** a particular person, the information comes from that person.
> If something is **incredible**, it is very good or very surprising.
> A **calm** person does not show any worry, fear, or excitement.
> If you are **disappointed**, you are sad because something is not as good as you hoped.
> A **frightened** person is afraid, anxious, or nervous.

1. Some of the pictures the young refugees took at photo camp are _____. They're very good quality for amateurs.

2. David Griffin was probably very _____ when he saw his son caught in a big wave.

3. Amateur photographers are often _____ when their pictures are not as good as they hoped.

4. _____ David Griffin, the best photographs make an emotional connection.

5. Wildlife photographers need to stay very _____ if they want to take pictures of dangerous animals.

B | Building Vocabulary. Find the words and phrases in **blue** in the reading passage on pages 194–195. Read the words around them and try to guess their meanings. Then complete the sentences.

> belong to   gear   immediately   intelligent   protect

1. Photographers such as Brent Stirton and Brian Skerry want to use their photographs to help _____ wild animals.

2. Scientists believe that chimps are very _____. They are smart enough to use tools, for example.

3. Underwater photographers need to use diving _____ when they take images of sea animals.

4. The cameras at a photo camp usually _____ the photographers, but the students are allowed to use them, too.

5. It's a good idea to have your camera ready at all times, so you can _____ take a photo!

Word Usage

The verb **belong** has several meanings:
1. If something **belongs to** you, you own it.
2. If people **belong to** a group or an organization, they are members of it.
3. If something **belongs** somewhere, that is the right place for it.

C | Using Vocabulary. Answer the questions in complete sentences. Then share your sentences with a partner.

1. When you feel nervous, what do you do to feel **calm**?

   _____

   _____

2. In what kinds of situations do you feel **frightened**?

   _____

   _____

3. Do you know an **incredible** true story that happened recently? Describe it.

   _____

   _____

4. When did you last feel **disappointed**? Why?

   _____

   _____

5. Which animals do you think need the most **protection**? Why?

   _____

   _____

> **Word Partners**
> Use **protect** with nouns: protect **children**, protect **citizens**, protect **the environment**, protect **property**, protect (**yourself**) against **something**.

D | Predicting. Look at the pictures and captions in the reading passage on pages 194–195. What do you think the reading is about?

I think the reading passage is about _____.

Read Paragraphs **A** and **B** on page 194. Underline a kind of animal, a man's name, a type of job, and a region. Then answer this question: What do you think the man did?

_____.

Now skim Paragraphs **C–H** and circle the best choice to complete this sentence.

This part of the reading passage is a _____.

a. personal narrative (a story about a personal experience)
b. factual description (like an encyclopedia entry)

THE POWER OF IMAGE | 193

LESSON B   **READING**

A VERY CLOSE ENCOUNTER

A   **IMAGINE LOOKING** straight into these jaws! They belong to a leopard seal, one of the top predators[1] in the waters of the Antarctic. A leopard seal's front teeth are sharp enough to tear apart its prey[2] in seconds. Usually, the seal hunts fish, squid, and penguins. Sometimes, according to some reports, it attacks people.

B   The man behind the camera is wildlife photographer Paul Nicklen. Nicklen has spent much of his life exploring the Arctic. He is passionate about[3] protecting the region and the animals that live there. He is especially interested in leopard seals. "Are they really so dangerous?" Nicklen wondered. The photographer decided to travel to the Antarctic to find out. Here is his story:

C   One day, I was standing on the boat when a very large female leopard seal swam by. I put on my diving gear and got my camera. I was frightened. My mouth was dry. At first, I couldn't even move. But I knew it was time to get closer to this mysterious creature.

D   I jumped into the freezing water. Immediately, the seal swam toward me. Then she put my entire camera—and much of my head—into her mouth. Thinking this must be a threat,[4] I decided to stay very calm. "Was I going to be her next meal?" I wondered.

E Although the seal was threatening me, I tried not to show any fear. After a few seconds, she let go of my head. She threatened me a few more times and swam away. Then she came back with a live penguin. The penguin was for me. Of course, I didn't eat the penguin, and I think the seal was very disappointed.

F The seal thought I was just another large predator, I realized. The two most important things in a leopard seal's life are eating and breeding.⁵ So perhaps this seal was worried about me—she didn't want me to starve. She brought me several penguins. She even tried to show me how to eat them. The seal tried to push penguins into my camera—she thought the camera was my mouth!

▲ One time, the seal brought Nicklen a penguin and placed it on top of his head.

G As a biologist, I understood that she was trying to feed me. But I think that she was really trying to communicate with me. By now, she didn't seem very dangerous. She stayed by me and tried to feed me for four days. One time, she noticed another leopard seal come up behind me. She made a deep, threatening sound and scared the other seal away. She then took that seal's penguin and gave it to me.

H Those four days were the most incredible experience I ever had as a wildlife photographer. I got some amazing pictures. I also learned that animals do not always behave the way we expect. My relationship with this powerful and intelligent animal will stay with me forever.

▼ Adult leopard seals can grow to a length of 12 feet (3.6 meters) and weigh as much as 1,000 pounds (450 kilograms).

¹ **Predators** are animals that kill and eat other animals.
² An animal's **prey** are the animals that it hunts and eats.
³ If a person **is passionate about** something, he or she has very strong feelings about it.
⁴ A **threat** is a statement by someone that they will harm you in some way.
⁵ **Breeding** means having babies.

THE POWER OF IMAGE | 195

LESSON B | UNDERSTANDING THE READING

A | Understanding the Gist. Look back at your answers for exercise **D** on page 193. Were your predictions correct?

B | Identifying Sequence. Number the events in Nicklen's story from 1 to 9 to show the order in which they happened. Then take turns retelling Nicklen's story to a partner using your own words.

☐ The seal put Nicklen's camera and head into her mouth.
☐ Nicklen felt frightened.
☐ The seal swam toward Nicklen as soon as he got into the water.
☐ Nicklen went to the Antarctic to photograph leopard seals.
☐ The seal stayed with Nicklen, and she protected him for four days.
☐ Nicklen put on his gear and got into the water.
☐ A leopard seal swam by Nicklen's boat.
☐ The seal tried to give Nicklen a penguin to eat.
☐ Nicklen didn't eat the penguin, and the seal seemed disappointed.

C | Critical Thinking: Understanding Mood. What emotions did Nicklen experience before and after his encounter? List words and phrases from the reading that describe these emotions. Then discuss your answers with your partner.

Before _____
After _____

D | Critical Thinking: Synthesizing/Evaluating. Evaluate the photos in the reading using the elements of photography described on page 183. Choose three elements that each photo is an example of. Discuss the reasons for your choices in small groups.

1. light   2. composition   3. moment   4. color   5. motion   6. wonder

EXPLORING WRITTEN ENGLISH

LESSON C

GOAL: In this lesson, you are going to plan, write, revise, and edit a paragraph on the following topic:
Describe a photograph from this book and explain why you think it is a good photograph.

A | Analyzing. Read the information in the box. Then look at the photo at the top of page 183 and circle the best word or phrase to complete each sentence (1–8).

Language for Writing: Describing Spatial Relationships

Writers use certain phrases to describe images, for example:

The image shows . . .   *In this image, we [can] see . . .*

In this image, we see a mother proudly looking at her baby.

Other phrases show where things in the image are located:

behind	next to	beside
on the left	in the middle (of)	on the right
to the left (of)	between X and Y	to the right (of)
in the foreground/background	in front/back of	

In the foreground, we can see a boy getting ready for a ceremony. **Behind** him, there is a little girl in a grass skirt.

In the photo, the girl is standing to the right of the boy. We can see her standing **between** the boy and a tree.

Example: There is a hole in the ground **in front** / **in the middle** of the trees.

1. In the **background** / **foreground** of the image, there are several trees.
2. The mother is **behind** / **next to** her baby.
3. The baby is in **front** / **back** of the scene.
4. The mother is sitting to the **right** / **left** of the baby in this photo.
5. The baby is **to the left** / **in front** of the mother.
6. We see two trees **between** / **behind** the baby and the mother.
7. A man is sitting to the **right** / **left** of the two trees.
8. The mother is in the **foreground** / **background** of the scene.

LESSON C: EXPLORING WRITTEN ENGLISH

Language for Writing: Describing Emotions

When you describe a picture, you can use adjectives to express sensory experiences—how people or things in the image look and feel:

The people in the photo seem joyful.
The scene feels very sad.
The man looks bored.

In these cases, the adjectives follow the verbs *seem*, *feel*, and *look*.

You can also describe how an image makes you feel, or what it makes you think about:

The image makes us/me/people/the viewer feel . . .

It reminds us/me/people/the viewer of . . .   *It makes us/me/people think of . . .*

The girl in the Mbuti ceremony photo reminds Griffin *of a Degas sculpture.*

Notice that an object follows *remind* and *make*.

B | Unscramble the words to make sentences that describe feelings and thoughts.

Example: of / me / light / the / water / the / on / think / makes / diamonds

The light on the water makes me think of diamonds.

1. and / happy / the / seems / relaxed / boy

   _____

2. angry / the / me / dead / and / sad / makes / gorilla / feel

   _____

3. looks / water / the / cool / refreshing / and

   _____

4. of / reminds / problems / this / people / image / environmental

   _____

5. us / girl / of / young / the / famous / makes / sculpture / think / a

   _____

C | Describe a photo in this unit using words and phrases for describing locations and feelings. Write your sentences below. Then read them to your partner. Can your partner guess which photo you are describing?

Description: _____

How it makes me feel / What it makes me think of: _____

_____

> **Writing Skill:** *Using Supporting Ideas in a Descriptive Paragraph*
>
> When you describe a photograph, you describe what you see and how it makes you feel. First, state your main idea in your topic sentence. Tell the reader which photo you are going to describe and your opinion of it (in other words, why you like it). Then explain the reasons that support your main idea. Why is it a great photo? Give specific details and examples of what you see and how you feel.

D | **Describing a Photograph.** Read the paragraph about a photograph. Then find and label the paragraph with the following items:

a. the topic sentence
b. a concluding sentence
c. the first reason for the main idea
d. another reason for the main idea
e. details or explanation for the first reason
f. details or explanation for the second reason

The Moment ▶
by Peter Essick

☐ → This picture of trees in a snowstorm is a great photo. One reason the photo is great is because it ← ☐ has the element of motion. This makes the scene look very real. For example, a heavy wind is blowing, ☐ and the trees are bending to the right. The wind is moving so fast that some of the tree branches are blurred. This blurring really gives the feeling of motion. Another thing that makes this photo great is ← ☐ the way it shows a moment in time. It makes a moving scene in nature stand still for a second, so we ☐ → can see how powerful the storm is. In fact, the moment is so powerful that you feel you are also in the storm! ← ☐

LESSON C | **WRITING TASK: Drafting**

A | **Brainstorming.** Make a list of your six favorite photographs in this book. With a partner, discuss what makes each one a great photograph.

B | **Planning.** Follow the steps to make notes for your paragraph. Don't worry about grammar or spelling. Don't write complete sentences.

Step 1   Look at your brainstorming list in exercise **A**. Choose the best photo from your list. Note its page number and write a short description in the chart.

Step 2   Now choose two reasons for your choice. Think about the elements of a great photo that you read about in this unit. Note them in the chart.

Step 3   Write some details in the chart to explain each reason.

What is the best photo in this book? Describe it.	
What is one reason or element that makes it great?	
Explain how this makes the photo great.	
What is another reason or element in the photo that makes it great?	
Explain how this makes the photo great.	

C | **Draft 1.** Use the information in the chart in exercise **B** to write a first draft of your paragraph.

WRITING TASK: Revising and Editing

D | Peer Evaluation. Exchange your first draft with a partner and follow these steps:

Step 1 Answer the questions below about your partner's paragraph.

1. Does the paragraph have one main idea? — Y N
2. Does all the information relate to the main idea? — Y N
3. Are the supporting ideas arranged in a logical order? — Y N
4. Do the supporting ideas have examples, facts, or details? — Y N
5. Are the ideas in the paragraph connected? — Y N

Step 2 Tell your partner one thing that you liked about his or her paragraph.

Step 3 Share your answers to the questions in Step 1 with your partner.

E | Draft 2. Write a second draft of your paragraph. Use what you learned from the peer evaluation activity. Make any other necessary changes.

F | Editing Practice. Read the information in the box. Then find and correct one mistake with prepositions of location in each of the descriptive sentences (1–8).

In sentences with phrases that describe location, remember to:
- use the correct words, for example, *between x* **and** *y* (not *between x* **to** *y*).
- be careful with words that have similar spelling, for example, *behind* and *beside*.

---

1. Next of the boys is a large group of elephants.
2. In this photo, a mother is sitting between her son to her daughter.
3. A young girl in a pink coat is standing behind of her brother.
4. At the middle of the scene, there is a small yellow fish.
5. Of the foreground, we see a small dog in a green sweater.
6. There is a large tree at behind the little boy.
7. There is a baby the right of her mother.
8. The children are beside to the water buffaloes.

LESSON C — WRITING TASK: Editing

G | Editing Checklist. Use the checklist to find errors in your second draft.

Editing Checklist	Yes	No
1. Are all the words spelled correctly?		
2. Is the first word of every sentence capitalized?		
3. Does every sentence end with the correct punctuation?		
4. Do your subjects and verbs agree?		
5. Did you use location phrases correctly?		

H | Final Draft. Now use your Editing Checklist to write a third draft of your paragraph. Make any other necessary changes.

UNIT QUIZ

p.183 1. According to Annie Griffiths, the six elements of a beautiful photo are light, composition, _____, color, motion, and wonder.

p.184 2. If something is _____, you can see it.

p.185 3. Griffin used his son's frightening experience at the beach as an example of a _____.

p.190 4. The subordinating conjunction *while* can show both a contrast and a _____ relationship.

p.191 5. The photographer Reza says that photos can communicate like _____.

p.192 6. If you are _____, you are not worried, angry, or excited.

p.195 7. The leopard seal scared another seal away and gave Nicklen a _____.

p.199 8. A good paragraph has _____ ideas, for example, reasons and examples.

Video Scripts

UNIT 1: BioBlitz: Life in 24 Hours

Narrator: Welcome to Rock Creek Park. It's a big park in the middle of Washington, DC.

Today, this park is going to be the site of a big research project. Dozens of scientists from around the United States, along with hundreds of volunteers are here for something called a BioBlitz. In a BioBlitz, teams of scientists, parents, kids, and volunteers all go to a park and look for examples of everything that's alive there. They work in teams to count every living thing that they find—from the big animals like deer and rabbits to tiny plants. But they only have 24 hours to do it.

Boyd Matson: I'm taking credit for the first species. Here's one that's easy to spot! A luna moth that blends right into my shirt. I found the first species of the BioBlitz, and it's a beautiful one!

Narrator: National Geographic explorer-in-residence, oceanographer Sylvia Earle, is at the BioBlitz.

Sylvia Earle: The thing about the BioBlitz is that it brings out the kid in everybody.

Narrator: Sylvia Earle likes the BioBlitz because people discover and appreciate the living things in their own community.

Dr. Stuart Pimm, an ecologist from Duke University, is certainly excited about the event. He studies biodiversity.

Dr. Pimm: The extraordinary thing about this BioBlitz is just how much stuff there is here! This is really where the wild things are. There really is a huge amount of stuff in this city park!

Narrator: Park rangers are there to help. Here, they are helping a group to catch caterpillars, spiders, and butterflies.

Insects are an important part of the BioBlitz. One reason is there are a lot of them. They also come in a great variety of color, shapes, and behaviors. It's easier to see how special they are when you look at them close up.

Photographer David Littschwager usually takes photos of endangered species, but at the BioBlitz he's taking photos of insects.

David Littschwager: We see a lot of pictures of lions and tigers and bears, but you don't often see a portrait of a spider nice and close. Some people don't like spiders, but I have great affection for them. But I like them to stay on the glass.

Narrator: Littschwager worked all night taking pictures, but he wasn't the only one who didn't sleep. People had only 24 hours to find all the living things in the park, so all the participants worked hard until the final minute. And even at the end, there were a lot of plants and creatures that they couldn't identify.

The official count after 24 hours showed 666 different species in Rock Creek Park. But as searchers continue to identify species, that number is going to increase.

The real purpose of the BioBlitz is to get people interested in the biodiversity that's all around them, even in their own back yards.

Just ask Gary Hevel, who lives in Maryland, a state next to Washington, D.C. In four years, Hevel has identified over 4,000 different species of living things in his backyard.

So what are you waiting for? The clock is ticking. Isn't it time to start counting the living things in *your* backyard?

UNIT 2: Alex the Parrot

Parrots: Buongiorno. Hi! Hi! Hello. Hello. Aloha.

Narrator: Cognitive biologist Dr. Irene Pepperberg worked with Alex, an African gray parrot, on a project that showed some surprising results.

Dr. Pepperberg: Now once more. How many green wooden blocks?

Alex: Four.

Dr. Pepperberg: Good birdy. On the tray, what sound is yellow? What sound is yellow?

Alex: Or. Or.

Dr. Pepperberg: Very good.

Narrator: Many parrots can talk, but Alex amazed scientists. Why? Alex knew what he was talking about.

Narrator: Pepperberg designed special tests for Alex because she did not want him to simply repeat, or mimic, information. She wanted him to answer specific questions.

Dr. Pepperberg: He can tell me how many, he can tell me what's same, what's different, what color bigger, what color smaller, or what matter bigger or what matter smaller.

Dr. Pepperberg: How many?

Alex: Two.

Dr. Pepperberg: Two is right. Good boy. What color bigger? What color bigger?

Alex: None.

Dr. Pepperberg: None. Very good. OK. Good boy.

Alex: Treat!

Narrator: Alex was able to identify an object many ways—by color, size, and so on. This shows cognitive abilities similar to those of four- to five-year-old humans.

Dr. Pepperberg: What number is green?

Alex: Four.

Dr. Pepperberg: That's right. Good boy.

Narrator: Alex showed that parrots might be able to communicate and to use basic reasoning. Alex died in 2007. During his life, he learned about 150 words. His last words to Irene were reportedly, "I love you."

UNIT 3 The World in a Station

Narrator: There are seven billion people around the globe, from many different backgrounds. But we're more similar and more connected than you might think.

Who were our ancestors? Where do we come from? And how did we get here?

In April 2005, National Geographic and IBM worked together on a joint project to find out.

Dr. Spencer Wells: I wanted to draw people together to make people realize that we're all part of an extended family and that our DNA connects all of us.

Narrator: National Geographic and IBM wanted to conduct a study to show that, as a human species, we're all part of one big family—and that our DNA connects all of us. So they started the Genographic Project. The goal was to trace our human DNA back tens of thousands of years to our first ancestors in East Africa.

National Geographic and IBM are working with hundreds of thousands of people around the world and gathering DNA samples so they can learn about our human history. They need to create the world's largest database of DNA. To do this, they have to get samples from hundreds of thousands of people around the world.

There's no better place to show that we're all connected than here at Grand Central Station, a huge train station in the middle of New York City. Here, you can find people from all over the world.

Dr. Wells: My name is Spencer Wells.

Dee Dee: Hello, Spencer.

Dr. Wells: I work with National Geographic. I direct a project for them called the Genographic Project.

Frank: Yeah?

Dr. Wells: And we're using DNA as a tool to study how people all over the world are related to each other. Would you be interested in maybe giving us a sample?

Cecile: Oh, definitely. Yes, I'd love to contribute my DNA.

J. W.: Absolutely.

Dr. Wells: Maybe getting yourself tested?

J. W.: 100 percent.

Dr. Wells: What do you think you might find out? What is your family history?

Cecile: I have a lot of questions. My last name is not common in the country where I was born.

Frank: We have Aztec Indian in our . . . Because my basic heritage is Mexican, as far as I'm concerned, but we traced it back to Spain.

Dr. Wells: Fascinating. So you'd be interested in maybe getting yourself tested . . .

Narrator: Wells explains that the test is very simple. People swab the inside of their cheek to get some DNA cells. Then they send the cells to a lab anonymously. The lab analyzes the DNA and puts the results on a website in a few weeks.

Dr. Wells: Well, let's get you started swabbing.

Dee Dee: Don't look at any of my fillings.

Dr. Wells: Up and down. Perfect.

Narrator: Wells explains that the DNA research shows all people are related. Humans all started out in Africa about 50,000 years ago. They only started separating and moving to other parts of the world about 2000 generations ago.

Dr. Wells: What do you know about your family history?

J. W.: I know a lot of my relatives. Some of them look as you do. Then I have, for example, my mother's father was very dark.

Dr. Wells: We all started off in Africa around 60,000 years ago. So you're African, I'm African . . .

Dee Dee: So like, you and I are related?

Dr. Wells: We could be related. How do you feel about that?

Dee Dee: Oh, fantastic. I can't wait for my Christmas present.

Narrator: In just a few weeks, Cecile, J. W., Frank, and Dee Dee will get the results of their DNA tests and learn about the mysteries of their past. So far, the Genographic Project has collected over 200,000 samples. Dr. Ajay Royyuru is computational director at IBM. He is helping analyze the results.

Dr. Royyuru: This is our first chance in the history of human civilization to look within and learn something that actually was not knowable before.

Narrator: Analyzing this DNA helps us understand how we're all connected, like our four participants from Grand Central Station. They are about to learn about their distant past. Dee Dee lives near Minneapolis, Minnesota.

Dee Dee: Well, hi, Spencer, the scientist from National Geographic!

Dr. Wells: Hi, Dee Dee. How's it going?

Dee Dee: Nice to see you. Great. How are you?

Dr. Wells: It's good to see you again. You start off in Africa . . .

Narrator: Wells explains that Dee Dee's ancestors, like all other humans, started out in Africa. Around 45,000 years ago, a small group of her ancestors left Africa. They moved north to the Middle East. It was very cold and dangerous there.

Dr. Wells: Suddenly you're living in this icy wasteland with things like that walking around, and you've got to figure out a way to kill them to make a living and survive. What would you have done?

Dee Dee: Well, I would have killed him. No—I would have found a guy to do it for me.

Narrator: Frank lives in Southern California. He discovers that his ancient relatives were the first humans in the Americas. He might really have Aztec ancestors.

Frank: It's quite interesting. Up to the last 15 to 20,000 years, our ancestors were extremely adaptable, who survived by hunting large mammals . . . It kind of makes me understand why I feel that I'm such a survivor, 'cause I am. I can create, you know, things out of nothing. I've always been that way.

Narrator: Cecile Nepal's results show that her ancestors were some of the first humans to live in Southeast Asia. Now Cecile lives and works in New York City, but she still feels connected to her Philippine roots.

Cecile: There is something that we still have that we carry on, and it's something to be proud about.

Narrator: J. W. is a police officer in New York City. He lives there with his wife and son. His DNA results show that he has Puerto Rican, Spanish, and ancient African ancestors. But that isn't all. J. W. finds that some of his early ancestors were probably the first farmers.

J. W.: Coming from grandparents who were farmers themselves, I kind of see the relation there, so pretty interesting.

Dr. Wells: Everybody that we met at Grand Central that day ultimately traces back to an ancestor in Africa.

J. W.: I feel connected because we all have one common place of origin—East Africa.

Dr. Wells: The cool thing that comes out of this research is, obviously, that we're all connected to each other and that we scattered to the wind, if you will, to populate the world over the last 60,000 years.

Trash People

Narrator: When garbage collectors take our trash away, we usually don't think about it again. But a German artist, H. A. Schult, is transforming trash into something very familiar. And he's giving us the chance to think about trash in a new way.

Schult: I made a thousand sculptures from garbage. And these sculptures are people like us.

Narrator: H. A. sculpted the trash people out of materials from a German landfill, but you can find these materials anywhere in the world.

Schult: The garbage today is an international garbage. We know that the garbage of China comes to Europe, the garbage of Europe goes to Russia, the Russian garbage goes to South Africa. We are in a time where the world may be garbage. We're on the garbage planet.

Narrator: H. A. shows his art around the world. He wants people to see that garbage is a problem everywhere.

Schult: Everywhere, in Giza, in Egypt, or in China, on the Great Wall, people have known that I show the problems of our time. And these problems are in every country the same.

Narrator: H. A. first set up 1,000 trash people in Xanten, Germany. Then they went to Red Square in Moscow, along the Great Wall of China, to the foot of the Matterhorn in Switzerland, and then to the Egyptian pyramids. Now the trash people are at National Geographic headquarters in Washington, D.C.

H. A. watches as workers set the trash people up, but he lets the sculptures tell their own story to the visitors.

Schult: I think the answer to the future will come from the children of today. And the children are traveling also around the world now because we are living in a global village.

Narrator: What does our garbage say about us? The trash people don't talk, but they clearly have a lot to say.

Earth University

Narrator: Class is in session. But this isn't a typical college campus. This is Earth University. Earth University is a unique agricultural school in Guacimo, Costa Rica.

According to university president Jose Zaglul, the school's goals are to give poor students an education and to teach them skills to protect the environment.

Video Scripts

Here, students learn sustainable farming methods. These methods have little or no negative impact on the environment.

Gaspari Cordova: They teach us here how to be very respectful to our environment. Not only to the people that we're working with, but also to our environment.

Narrator: Most of the university's 400 students are from Latin America, but some come from as far away as Africa to study here.

Robert Lechipan: Where we come from, the northern part of Kenya, Marsabit, is one of the poorest places we have in Kenya.

Narrator: Lechipan says that Earth University teaches many useful skills. When he returns to Kenya, he can use these skills to make farming more sustainable there.

Students work six days a week, 11 months a year in the classroom and in the fields. There's even a banana farm on campus. At the farm, students and professors can try out new sustainable methods. The farm sells most of its bananas to the United States. Money from banana sales is used for scholarships to students from poor areas.

Mathew Rogers: The profits of the banana business support scholarships for students from poor communities.

Narrator: In addition to farming, Earth University students learn about ecology, business management, and leadership.

According to university president Jose Zaglul, Earth University students will do more than learn about sustainable farming. He believes that they will learn how to be leaders so they can help change their own communities.

UNIT 6: Colonizing Mars

Narrator: Scientists around the world are interested in exploring Mars. Over the past 30 years, there have been dozens of unmanned missions to the red planet. However, traveling to Mars is not easy: about two-thirds of these missions were failures.

Because missions to Mars are dangerous and expensive, plans for a manned mission to Mars have been delayed for decades. The international space community is still not ready to send humans there. However, a manned mission to Mars is a goal that Dr. Bob Zubrin really believes in.

Dr. Zubrin: NASA had plans to send people to Mars by 1981. Those plans were credible. We should have been on Mars a quarter century ago.

Narrator: Bob Zubrin is president of the Mars Society, an international organization he helped start in 1998. The Mars Society supports the goal of having humans explore and live on Mars. Its members talk to government agencies and private companies to get money to explore Mars.

Zubrin is also doing research to prepare for a manned mission to Mars. The Mars Society set up living spaces designed for Mars in the deserts of Utah in the western United States, and on Devon Island in northern Canada. These remote areas are similar in some ways to the surface of Mars.

Dr. Zubrin: We're trying to find out what field tactics and techniques would be most usefully applied on Mars, what technologies would be most useful to the crew.

Narrator: Zubrin has ambitious ideas. He plans to colonize the planet.

Dr. Zubrin: We're going to Mars because Mars is the planet that has on it the resources needed to support life and therefore, potentially someday, human civilization.

Narrator: For Zubrin, Mars is the new frontier.

Dr. Zubrin: Whether or not there has been life on Mars, whether or not there is life on Mars, there will be life on Mars. And it will be us.

Narrator: Zubrin isn't the only one with plans for the red planet. Dr. Chris McKay has another idea: he wants to create an atmosphere on Mars so humans can live there.

Dr. McKay: If we go to Mars and find that there is no life, then I say we might as well move in.

Narrator: McKay believes that for humans to eventually live on Mars, they need to start by warming up its atmosphere.

Dr. McKay: Well, we know how to warm up planets. We're doing it on Earth.

Narrator: The first step to warming up the planet is putting greenhouse gases into the Martian atmosphere.

Dr. McKay: The effect of these gases would be to melt the ice, bring back the atmosphere, and restore Mars to the conditions it was billions of years ago.

Narrator: But if humans are going to live on Mars, they're going to need oxygen. Chris McKay has an idea about how to create oxygen on Mars, using tiny organisms called cyano bacteria.

Dr. McKay: These organisms are known as cyano bacteria. It's a type of algae, a single-cell type of algae, that has a very long history on Earth. These were the organisms that first made the oxygen. These organisms could do the same thing on Mars. Send them to Mars and ask them to change the world.

Narrator: Cyano bacteria—the planet changers! Scientists continue to study Mars, so that one day humans will travel to the red planet. And perhaps someday in the future, humans will live there.

Madagascar Discovery

Narrator: Biologist Mireya Mayor is in Madagascar. She and her team are looking for a specific type of mouse lemur.

Mireya Mayor: What's going on now is that the team has cleared this area by pulling all the trees from the mouse lemur's surroundings so that it can't jump to them.

Narrator: This is it. It may be the smallest primate in the world. It's a new species of primate only found in Madagascar. Scientists haven't identified it yet.

Mireya Mayor: Whew, yeah! We got it. Hey, hey. It's so cute. Huge eyes—they are incredibly alert and wide right now.

Narrator: Biologists don't have a lot of information about mouse lemurs, but they do know a few things. For example, they are the smallest primates in the world. At night, they eat fruit and insects, and find water on leaves and branches.

They are classified as primates for a few reasons. They have 10 fingers and 10 toes—with nails, not claws. They also have opposable thumbs, like humans. Their eyes face forward, not sideways. They also have large brains. These are all features of primates.

The scientists take photos of their new lemur and do some tests before they release it.

Mireya Mayor: It's really difficult to take blood from an animal this small just because its veins are so tiny, but we were able to get enough out to get DNA to confirm the uniqueness of the species.

And there she is. She's free!

World Music

Narrator: Hundreds of people from around the world are arriving in the English countryside. They are coming for a music festival called WOMAD. Womad means "world of music, arts, and dance." The artists come to Womad to perform traditional music and dance from their cultures in a celebration of world music. One fan of world music is singer and songwriter Peter Gabriel. He co-founded Womad in 1982.

Peter Gabriel: I had a very personal, practical attraction to what is now "world music." And I would hear all these fantastic things from all over the world, and there were these really stunning voices doing much better than I ever could have. So that was really inspiring for me. What I love to see when I go to Womad now is so many people being open-minded and listening to music from all over the world.

Narrator: Spaccanapoli, an eight-piece band, is coming from Naples, Italy, to perform at Womad. The head of the group, Marcello Collasurdo, sings and plays the tambourine.

Marcello Collasurdo: Spaccanapoli! Ciao!

Narrator: He is getting the group ready for its first performance at WOMAD.

Marcello Collasurdo (translated): My name is Marcello Collasurdo, and I am from Naples. My father taught me to love the tambourine when I was just a young boy.

Narrator: The band's music is a combination of folk rock and the music from two traditional Italian dances, the tarantella and tamurriata.

Marcello Collasurdo (translated): Tamurriata music is like rap. It's a mountain rap, a country rap— it's part of our culture.

Narrator: Marcello gets the inspiration for his music from the streets of Naples, where he lives. People here often sing in the street. It can happen at any time and in any place.

Cartman (translated): My dear horse, if you climb this mountain, . . . I'll buy you a new harness with bells.

Narrator: For Marcello, everyone on the street is a neighbor, and every street is a stage in his neighborhood in Naples.

Man singing (translated): I passed my note under the door. Get up, beautiful eyes, and take it! And I place it under your . . . door, and I placed it under your door. And I am pacing back and forth . . . and I am pacing back and forth . . . Come take it!

Marcello Collasurdi: OK, grazie.

Gorilla Toolmakers

Narrator: In some ways, gorillas look and act a lot like us. Now there is new evidence that gorillas may also think like us.

These incredible photographs show something that some researchers thought was impossible: proof that wild gorillas can think through problems. And like humans, they can make and use tools to solve those problems.

Wildlife Conservation Society scientists Emma Stokes and Thomas Breuer believe this discovery teaches us a lot about the mind of the great ape.

Thomas Breuer first observed gorillas using tools. It was a fantastic discovery. The discovery happened here, in Mbeli Bai, in northern Congo. One morning Breuer saw

Video Scripts

something amazing, and he took a picture of it. A female gorilla named Leah took a stick and used it as a tool. She used the stick to measure the depth of the water before she walked over it. This was an amazing and scientifically important moment.

Thomas Breuer: When I cross the swamp, I always use a kind of stick to test the water deepness. And what's fascinating is that these gorillas found exactly the same solution to this problem.

Narrator: These are the first photographs that show wild gorillas using tools—something no one has ever seen before.

Thomas Breuer: We know that in the past, we claim that tool use is a unique feature of our own species. But we know that it's not the case any longer. Animals are able to plan. They think and they find a solution to a problem.

Narrator: For years now, we've known that some animals use tools. They often use tools to get food. These chimpanzees use clubs to crack open nuts. Then they teach their skills to the next generation. They use sticks to get insects . . . and they use leaves like cups to scoop up water.

But, until now, scientists did not know that wild gorillas also used tools. Some gorillas in zoos use sticks to find bugs. But scientists never saw them do this in the wild.

And there was more. One month later, Breuer was lucky again. He saw a second gorilla inventing a tool. A female named Efi put a branch into the ground. She held onto it as she reached into the water. Apes at Mbeli Bai often hang onto trees in order to pull themselves up from the water. But this gorilla created a tool to stay out of the water. This incredible new evidence shows that gorillas can create and use tools to solve problems, like humans do.

Discoveries like this may help us understand our own evolution, how our earliest ancestors learned to solve more difficult problems.

Emma Stokes: It just goes to show the kinds of benefits you can see from a long-term research presence in somewhere like Mbeli Bai. We could be here for hundreds of years and still not truly uncover all of the secrets the forests have to offer.

UNIT 10 Photo Camp

Chris Rainier: Get down low on the ground and photograph. Get up high, like up here, and shoot down.

Narrator: These are some of the best photographers in the world.

Reza Deghati: Don't move, don't move.

Narrator: They are working with young people who haven't used cameras before.

Reza Deghati: She's so happy to see how it's working.

Student: Yeah! So happy.

Woman: Take one of Justin.

Narrator: These young people are refugees. They live in Uganda. They are from many parts of Africa, but right now, this camp is their only home. They don't know what will happen to them in the future. They speak many different languages. But award-winning National Geographic photographer Reza Deghati believes they can all understand the meaning of powerful images.

Reza Deghati: Now, I don't speak your language, but I use photography like language, and this is the pictures I take.

Narrator: Reza, and National Geographic photographers Ed Kashi and Chris Rainier . . .

Chris Rainier: That's a very good shot.

Narrator: . . . have joined South African photographer Neo Ntsoma. They are teaching 60 young refugees how to tell the stories of their lives in photographs.

Reza Deghati: This is the way that we say, "telling the stories by picture." What is important for me? What is the good, what is the bad around me? That's how I use the photography.

Narrator: The photographers call this photo camp.

Reza Deghati: Photography is more than just having pictures of your friends standing together.

Narrator: In small groups, the young people learn to use cameras and to compose pictures.

Reza Deghati: This is more reflections off the trees and this . . . What you can get.

Narrator: Photo camp is an inspiration for many of the camp residents. Aganze Grace, for example, wants to become a professional photographer. He hopes to take portraits and passport pictures to help support his family.

Reza Deghati: You are great! You can be a good photographer.

Narrator: Life is difficult in the refugee camp. But Reza and the other photographers are showing these young adults how to see their temporary home in a new way, and perhaps to create something meaningful while they are here.

Near the end of the program, the students have an exhibition. They are excited to show their work. As Reza explained to them at the beginning, their pictures tell stories that everyone can understand, no matter where they are from or what language they speak.

These students received more than just a certificate and a new skill at photo camp.

Neo Ntsoma: Wave your certificates!

Narrator: They also learned how to document their world and to see themselves and their lives in new ways.

Independent Student Handbook

Contents

Tips for Reading and Note Taking

Reading fluently	210
Thinking critically	210
Note taking	210
Learning vocabulary	211
Common affixes	211

Tips for Writing and Research

Features of academic writing	212
Proofreading tips	212
Common signal phrases	213
Coordinating conjunctions	213
Subordinating conjunctions	214

Grammar Reference   214–218

Independent Student Handbook

Tips for Reading and Note Taking

Reading fluently

Why develop your reading speed?

Reading slowly, one word at a time, makes it difficult to get an overall sense of the meaning of a text. As a result, reading becomes more challenging and less interesting than if you read at a faster pace. In general, it is a good idea to first skim a text for the gist, and then read it again more closely so that you can focus on the most relevant details.

Strategies for improving reading speed:

- Try to read groups of words rather than individual words.
- Keep your eyes moving forward. Read through to the end of each sentence or paragraph instead of going back to reread words or phrases within the sentence or paragraph.
- Read selectively. Skip functional words (articles, prepositions, etc.) and focus on words and phrases carrying meaning—the content words. See page 8 for an example.
- Use clues in the text—such as highlighted text (**bold** words, words in *italics*, etc.)—to help you know which parts might be important and worth focusing on.
- Use section headings, as well as the first and last lines of paragraphs, to help you understand how the text is organized.
- Use context and other clues such as affixes and part of speech to guess the meaning of unfamiliar words and phrases. Try to avoid using a dictionary if you are reading quickly for overall meaning.

Thinking critically

As you read, ask yourself questions about what the writer is saying, and how and why the writer is presenting the information at hand.

Important critical thinking skills for academic reading and writing:

- Analyzing: Examining a text in close detail in order to identify key points, similarities, and differences.
- Evaluating: Using evidence to decide how relevant, important, or useful something is. This often involves looking at reasons for and against something.
- Inferring: "Reading between the lines;" in other words, identifying what a writer is saying indirectly, or *implicitly*, rather than directly, or *explicitly*.
- Synthesizing: Gathering appropriate information and ideas from more than one source and making a judgment, summary, or conclusion based on the evidence.
- Reflecting: Relating ideas and information in a text to your own personal experience and preconceptions (i.e., the opinions or beliefs you had before reading the text).

Note taking

Taking notes on key points and the connections between them will help you better understand the overall meaning and organization of a text. Note taking also enables you to record the most important ideas and information for future use such as when you are preparing for an exam or completing a writing assignment.

Techniques for effective note taking:

- As you read, underline or highlight important information such as dates, names, places, and other facts.
- Take notes in the margin—as you read, note the main idea and supporting details next to each paragraph. Also note your own ideas or questions about the paragraph.
- On paper or on a computer, paraphrase the key points of the text in your own words.
- Keep your notes brief—include short headings to organize the information, key words and phrases (not full sentences), and abbreviations and symbols. (See next page for examples.)
- Note sources of information precisely. Be sure to include page numbers, names of relevant people and places, and quotations.
- Make connections between key points with techniques such as using arrows and colors to connect ideas and drawing circles or squares around related information.
- Use a graphic organizer to summarize a text, particularly if it follows a pattern such as cause–effect, comparison–contrast, or chronological sequence. See page 150 for more information.
- Use your notes to write a summary of the passage in order to remember what you learned.

Independent Student Handbook

Useful abbreviations

approx.	approximately	incl.	including	
ca.	about, around (date / year)	info	information	
cd	could	p. (pp.)	page (pages)	
Ch.	Chapter	para.	paragraph	
devt	development	re:	regarding, concerning	
e.g./ex.	example	wd	would	
etc.	and others / and the rest	yr(s)	years(s)	
excl.	excluding	C20	20th century	
govt	government			
i.e.	that is; in other words			
impt	important			

Useful symbols

→	leads to / causes
↑	increases / increased
↓	decreases / decreased
& or +	and
∴	therefore
b/c	because
w/	with
=	is the same as
>	is more than
<	is less than
~	is approximately / about

Learning vocabulary

More than likely, you will not remember a new word or phrase after reading or hearing it once. You need to use the word several times before it enters your long-term memory.

Strategies for learning vocabulary:

- Use flash cards. Write the words you want to learn on one side of an index card. Write the definition and/or an example sentence that uses the word on the other side. Use your flash cards to test your knowledge of new vocabulary.
- Keep a vocabulary journal. When you come across a new word or phrase, write a short definition of the word (in English, if possible) and the sentence or situation where you found it (its context). Write another sentence of your own that uses the word. Include any common collocations. (See the Word Partners boxes in this book for examples of collocations.)
- Make word webs (or "word maps"). See an example of a word web on page 4.
- Use memory aids. It may be easier to remember a word or phrase if you use a memory aid, or *mnemonic*. For example, if you want to learn the idiom *keep an eye on someone*, which means to "watch someone carefully," you might picture yourself putting your eyeball on someone's shoulder so that you can watch the person carefully. The stranger the picture is, the more you will remember it!

Common affixes

Some words contain an affix at the start of the word (*prefix*) and/or at the end (*suffix*). These affixes can be useful for guessing the meaning of unfamiliar words and for expanding your vocabulary. In general, a prefix affects the meaning of a word, whereas a suffix affects its part of speech. See the Word Link boxes in this book for specific examples.

Prefix	Meaning	Example
commun-	sharing	communicate
con-	together, with	connected
dis-	not	disabled
en-	making, putting	encourage
ex-	away, from, out	export
il-	not	illegal
in-	not	independent
pre-	before	preserve
re-	back, again	recreate
un-	not	unexpected

Suffix	Part of Speech	Example
-able / -ible	adjective	available, credible
-al	adjective	local
-ance /-ence	noun	appearance, intelligence
-ate	verb	appreciate
-ed	adjective	connected
-ent	adjective	intelligent
-er	noun	trainer
-ful	adjective	harmful
-ity	noun	responsibility
-ize	verb	realize
-ly	adverb	regularly
-ment	noun	govenment
-tion	noun	information

Independent Student Handbook

Tips for Writing and Research

Features of academic writing

There are many types of academic writing (descriptive, argumentative/persuasive, narrative, etc.), but most types share similar characteristics.

Generally, in academic writing you should:

- write in full sentences.
- use formal English. (Avoid slang or conversational expressions such as *kind of*.)
- be clear and coherent—keep to your main point; avoid technical words that the reader may not know.
- use signal words and phrases to connect your ideas. (See examples on page 213.)
- have a clear point (main idea) for each paragraph.
- be objective—most academic writing uses a neutral, impersonal point of view, so avoid overuse of personal pronouns (*I*, *we*, *you*) and subjective language such as *nice* or *terrible*.
- use facts, examples, and expert opinions to support your argument.

Generally, in academic writing you should not:

- use abbreviations or language used in texting. (Use *that is* rather than *i.e.*, and *in my opinion*, not *IMO*.)
- use contractions. (Use *is not* rather than *isn't*.)
- be vague. (*Two men found a group of musicians playing on the streets. -> Two French filmmakers found a group of musicians playing on the streets of Kinshasa.*)
- include several pronoun references in a single sentence.
- start sentences with *or*, *and*, or *but*.
- apologize to the reader. (*I'm sorry I don't know much about this, but . . .*) In academic writing, it is important to sound confident about what you are saying!

Proofreading tips

Capitalization

Remember to capitalize:

- the first letter of the word at the beginning of every sentence.
- proper names such as names of people, geographical names, company names, and names of organizations.
- days, months, and holidays.
- the word *I*.
- the first letter of a title such as the title of a movie or a book.
- the words in titles that have meaning (content words). Don't capitalize *a*, *an*, *the*, *and*, or prepositions such as *to*, *for*, *of*, *from*, *at*, *in*, and *on*, unless they are the first word of a title (e.g., *The First Grader*).

Punctuation

Keep the following rules in mind:

- Use a question mark (?) at the end of every question. Use a period (.) at the end of any sentence that is not a question.
- Exclamation marks (!), which indicate strong feelings such as surprise or joy, are generally not used in academic writing.
- Use commas (,) to separate a list of three or more things (*She speaks German, English, and Spanish.*).
- Use a comma after an introductory word or phrase. (*However, it is very difficult to train a cat. / In contrast, apes can live almost 60 years.*).
- Use a comma before a combining word (coordinating conjunction)—*and*, *but*, *so*, *yet*, *or*, and *nor*—that joins two sentences (*People will visit Mars, and they will build habitation modules.*).
- Use an apostrophe (') for showing possession (*People were fighting and burning houses in Maruge's village.*).
- Use quotation marks (" ") to indicate the exact words used by someone else. (*"I saw more stars than I could count," says Martinez.*).
- Use quotation marks to show when a word or phrase is being used in a special way, such as a definition. (*The name of the band means "look beyond appearances".*).

Independent Student Handbook

Other Proofreading Tips:

- Print out your draft instead of reading it on your computer screen.
- Read your draft out loud. Use your finger or a pen to point to each word as you read it.
- Don't be afraid to mark up your draft. Use a colored pen to make corrections so you can see them easily when you write your next draft.
- Read your draft backwards—starting with the last word—to check your spelling. That way, you won't be distracted by the meaning.
- Have someone else read your draft and give you comments or ask you questions.
- Don't depend on a computer's spell-check. When the spell-check suggests a correction, make sure you agree with it before you accept the change.
- Remember to pay attention to the following items:
  - Short words such as *is*, *and*, *but*, *or*, *it*, *to*, *for*, *from*, and *so*.
  - Spelling of proper nouns.
  - Numbers and dates.
- Keep a list of spelling and grammar mistakes that you commonly make so that you can be aware of them as you edit your draft.

Watch out for frequently confused words:

- *there*, *their*, and *they're*
- *its* and *it's*
- *by*, *buy*, and *bye*
- *your* and *you're*
- *to*, *too*, and *two*
- *whose* and *who's*
- *where*, *wear*, *we're*, and *were*
- *then* and *than*
- *quit*, *quiet*, and *quite*
- *write* and *right*
- *affect* and *effect*
- *through* and *threw*
- *week* and *weak*

Common signal phrases

Giving supporting details and examples

One / an example of this is . . .

For example, . . . / For instance, . . .

Giving reasons

This is because (of) . . .

One reason (for this) is . . .

Describing cause and effect

Therefore, . . .

As a result, . . .

Because of this, . . .

Describing a process

First (of all), . . .

Then / Next / After that, . . .

As soon as . . . / When . . .

Finally, . . .

Presenting contrasting ideas

However, . . .

In contrast, . . .

Giving an opinion

In my opinion, . . .

I think / feel that . . .

I believe (that) . . .

Coordinating conjunctions

Coordinating conjunctions connect independent clauses.

Purpose	Coordinating Conjunction	Example
to add information	and	People will visit Mars, **and** they will build habitation modules.
to show contrast	but	Stirton is a professional photographer, **but** Rubio is an amateur.
to give a choice	or	You can throw away plastic bottles, **or** you can reuse them.
to show result	so	Education in Kenya was free, **so** Maruge decided to attend school.

Independent Student Handbook

Subordinating conjunctions

Subordinating conjunctions connect a dependent clause and an independent clause.

Purpose	Subordinating Conjunction	Example
to show reason or cause	because since	**because** he was old. **Since** education was free, Maruge decided to attend school.
to show contrast	although even though though while	**Although** Rubio is an amateur, he takes great photos. **Even though** it isn't in color, the image is beautiful. **Though** he is disabled, Junana likes to dance. **While** cats are independent, dogs are very dependent on their owners.
to show a time relationship	after before until while as	**After** Nicklen put on his gear, he jumped into the water. **Before** he jumped into the water, Nicklen saw the seal. Nicklen didn't know how cold the water was **until** he jumped in. **While** Nicklen was in the water, the seal brought him food. **As** Jim Blair was crossing the bridge, he saw children playing in the water.

Grammar Reference

Unit 1

Language for Writing: Simple Present of *Be* and Other Verbs

Affirmative and Negative Statements with *Be*						
Affirmative Statements			**Negative Statements**			
Subject	*Am/Are/Is*		Subject	*Am/Are/Is*		
I	am	happy. sad. here. at work.	I	am not	happy. sad. here. at work.	
You We They	are		You We They	are not aren't		
He She It	is		He She It	is not isn't		

Affirmative and Negative Statements : Other Verbs				
Affirmative Statements		**Negative Statements**		
Subject	Verb	Subject	*Do/Does Not*	Verb (Base Form)
I You We They	**work** in an office.	I You We They	do not don't	**work** in a laboratory.
He She It	**works** in an office.	He She It	does not doesn't	

Independent Student Handbook

Unit 3

Language for Writing: Simple Past of *Be* and Other Verbs

Affirmative and Negative Statements with *Be*

Affirmative Statements

Subject	Was/Were	
I He She It	was	happy. sad. here. at work.
You We They	were	

Negative Statements

Subject	Was/Were Not	
I He She It	was not wasn't	happy. sad. here. at work.
You We They	were not weren't	

Affirmative and Negative Statements: Other Verbs

Affirmative Statements

Subject	Verb (Past Form)
I You We They He She It	**started** a project. **walked** home. **studied**. **went** to school.

Negative Statements

Subject	Did Not	Verb (Base Form)
I You We They He She It	did not didn't	**start** a project. **walk** home. **study**. **go** to school.

Spelling Rules for Regular Verbs

1. Add *-ed* to most verbs.
2. If a verb ends in *e*, add *-d*.
3. If a verb ends in a consonant + vowel + consonant (not *w*, *x*, or *y*), double the consonant and add *-ed*.
4. If a two-syllable word ends in consonant + vowel + consonant, double the vowel if the stress is on the last syllable.
5. If a verb ends in consonant + *-y*, drop the *-y* and add *-ied*.

talk—talked
like—liked

stop—stopped
prefer—preferred
edit—edited
study—studied

Past Forms of Commonly Used Irregular Verbs

become—became
begin—began
build—built
break—broke
bring—brought
buy—bought
choose—chose
come—came
do—did
draw—drew
eat—ate

fall—fell
find—found
forget—forgot
get—got
give—gave
go—went
have—had
hear—heard
know—knew
lose—lost
make—made

read—read
say—said
see—saw
speak—spoke
spend—spent
take—took
teach—taught
tell—told
think—thought
understand—understood
write—wrote

Independent Student Handbook

Unit 4

Language for Writing: Giving Advice and Making Suggestions (*should*, *ought to*, and *could*)

Modals for Giving Advice and Making Suggestions		
Use modals with the base form of a verb.		
Affirmative Statements		
Subject	**Modal**	**Verb**
I You We They He She	**should** **ought to** **could**	drive less.
Negative Statements		
Subject	**Modal + *not***	**Verb**
I You We They He She	**shouldn't** **ought not to**	waste fuel.

Note: We do not use the negative form of *could* to make suggestions.

Unit 5

Language for Writing: The Comparative Forms of Adjectives and Nouns

Comparative Adjectives		
1. With one-syllable adjectives, add –*er*. Add –*r* if the adjective ends in –*e*.		
Adjective	**Comparative Form**	**Example**
cheap	cheaper	Non-organic produce is **cheaper** than organic produce.
fresh	fresher	Farm produce is **fresher** than supermarket produce.
large	larger	Corporate farms are **larger** than local farms.
2. With two-syllable adjectives ending in –*y*, change the –*y* to –*i* and add –*er*:		
Adjective	**Comparative Form**	**Example**
healthy	healthier	Home-cooked food is **healthier** than restaurant food.
busy	busier	The farmer's market is **busier** than the supermarket.
3. With most adjectives of two or more syllables, not ending in -*y*, use *more*:		
Adjective	**Comparative Form**	**Example**
attractive	more attractive	Farm produce is **more attractive** than supermarket produce.
sustainable	more sustainable	Organic farming is **more sustainable** than corporate farming.

Independent Student Handbook

4. Some adjectives have irregular comparative forms:

good → better   bad → worse

I think buying local food is **better** than buying imported food.
Processed food is **worse** for your health than fresh fruits and vegetables.

5. You can also make comparisons with *as . . . as* to describe things that are equal, or *not as . . . as* to describe things that are not equal:

Some people think organic produce is **as healthy as** non-organic produce.
However, non-organic produce **is not as expensive as** organic produce.

Comparing Nouns

1. You can show similarities between nouns with *the same* + noun + *as* and *as* + *many/much* + noun + *as*. Use *much* with noncount nouns and *many* with count nouns.

   The eggs come from **the same farm as** the milk.
   We produce **as much milk as** a corporate farm.
   Fujimoto's Farm sells **as many types** of tomatoes **as** Henry's Farm.

2. You can show differences between nouns with *not* + *as much/many* + noun + *as*:

   Local farms don't use **as much fuel as** corporate farms.
   Supermarkets don't sell **as many varieties** of tomatoes **as** farmer's markets.

3. You can show differences between nouns with *more* + noun + *than* and *less/fewer* + noun + *than*. Use *less* with noncount nouns and *fewer* with count nouns.

   Corporate farms produce **more waste than** local farms.
   Local farms use **less fuel than** corporate farms.
   Supermarkets sell **fewer types** of tomatoes **than** farmer's markets.

Unit 9

Reading Skills: Understanding Noun Clauses

Noun Clauses

Noun clauses appear in sentences where nouns or noun phrases appear. They include *wh* clauses, *it/whether* clauses, and *that* clauses.

Wh clauses are sometimes called indirect questions; they turn *wh* questions (questions that ask for information such as *who*, *when*, *where*, *why*, and *how*) into statements:

Why did he become a dog trainer? → We don't know **why** he became a dog trainer.

When did dogs first become pets? → Scientists want to know **when** dogs first became pets.

If/whether clauses are also sometimes called indirect questions; they turn *yes/no* questions into statements:

Does your dog want to go for a walk? → You don't ask **if** your dog wants to go for a walk.
Does the dog have a phobia? → I don't know **whether** the dog has a phobia.

That clauses often show what someone says, knows, thinks, or believes.

Millan believes something. The owner is not in control of the dog.
Millan believes **that** the owner is not in control of the dog.

Primate specialists know something. Chimpanzees teach tool use to their children.
Primate specialists know **that** chimpanzees teach tool use to their children.

Independent Student Handbook

Language for Writing: Making Comparisons

Making Comparisons	
Use the following words and phrases to show similarities within sentences. Notice that we use a comma after the phrase with *like*.	
Both . . . and	**Both** gorillas **and** humans are primates.
Like	**Like** humans, chimpanzees show their offspring how to use tools.
Neither . . . nor	**Neither** basenjis **nor** Australian terriers are difficult to train.
Use *similarly* and *likewise* to show similarities between sentences. Notice that we use a comma after these words.	
Similarly	Washoe the chimpanzee learned sign language. **Similarly**, Alex the parrot learned to communicate with humans.
Likewise	Cats can live in small apartments. **Likewise**, some dog breeds do well in small spaces.
Use the following words and phrases to show differences within sentences. Notice that we use a comma after the phrases.	
Unlike	**Unlike** cats, dogs are very dependent on their owners.
Whereas	**Whereas** dogs will eat anything, cats are very particular about their diet.
While	**While** dogs need to be bathed, cats can clean themselves.
Use the following words and phrases to show differences between sentences. Notice that we use a comma after each one.	
However	Gorillas can weigh up to 400 pounds (181 kg). **However**, chimpanzees only weigh about 100 pounds (45 kg).
In contrast	Domesticated animals make good pets. **In contrast**, wild animals are dangerous around people.
On the other hand	Cat people tend to be shy. **On the other hand**, dog people tend to be extroverted.

Vocabulary Index

according to	192
adapt (to)*	104
adult*	184
aid*	30
alive	50
ancestor	44
ancient	44
angry	164
appearance	144
appreciate*	84
approach*	164
area*	50
arrive	4
attend	24
audience	144
available*	30
average	110
aware*	64
balance	10
basic	84
believe	24
belong (to)	192
bond*	150
break down	170
breathe	110
calm	192
camp	124
cause	64
century	84
ceremony	184
chemical*	90
circumstance*	144
clean up	64
collect	64
combine	70
common	50
communicate*	4
companion	164
company	70
composer	144
concerned	90
confused	164
connect	4
consider	84
consumer*	90
continue	170
cooperation	170
corporate*	90
create*	70
creature	130
deal with	70
decide (to)	24
depend (on)	10
descendant	50
despite*	70
disabled	144
disappointed	192
discover	44
during	10
economy	90
electric	84
element*	184
emotion	184
encourage	144
energetic	144
entire	104
environment*	10

Vocabulary Index

escape 150	medicine 150	response* 170
especially 124	melt 84	responsibility 150
exchange 30	migrate* 44	result 4
exist 130	mobile 30	reward 170
export* 90	moment 124	risk 130
extremely 130	motivated 24	run out 130
factory 110	network* 104	schedule* 10
fair 170	normal* 4	search 124
field 170	notice 64	section* 44
finally* 124	object 50	series* 124
follow 130	occupation 124	share 170
(for) instance* 104	ordinary 24	similar (to)* 30
found(er)* 144	organization 70	situation 150
frightened 192	owner 164	skill 30
gear 192	pattern 104	solution 64
globe* 4	pay attention 170	solve 30
goal* 110	perform 144	source* 124
government 24	plant 110	spend time 10
harmful 90	point out 184	sudden 184
honest 84	poisonous 130	suggest 104
hunter 50	powerful 164	surprise 10
illegal 184	preserve 130	survey* 110
image* 70	primary* 24	take action 64
immediately 192	principal* 24	take care (of) 4
immigrant* 44	probably 50	task* 84
import 90	produce 4	team* 4
improve 150	professional* 164	temperature 104
incredible 192	program 30	threat 192
independent 24	project* 4	throw away 64
information 44	protect 192	trace* 44
instruction* 84	proud 70	trainer 164
instrument 144	quality 184	trap 110
Integrity* 164	reach 50	treat 150
intelligence* 104	realize 10	trend* 91
issue 150	receive 70	trip 30
item* 84	recent 44	trust 91
journalist* 124	record 30	unexpected 10
journey 50	recreate 124	universe 130
keep track (of) 104	recycle 64	visual* 184
level 110	regular 150	work out 164
link* 104	release* 110	
liquid 110	remains 50	
located* 130	remind 184	
major* 44	report 64	
material 70	rescue 150	
measure 10	research* 170	
	resident 24	

*These words are on the Academic Word List (AWL). The AWL is a list of the 570 most frequent word families in academic texts. The list does not include words that are among the most frequent 2,000 words of English. For more information on the AWL, see http://www.victoria.ac.nz/lals/resources/academicwordlist/.

Academic Literacy Skills Index

Critical Thinking

Analyzing 7, 27, 67, 74, 189, 190, 197

Applying 169, 190

Brainstorming 4, 9, 18, 24, 38, 44, 49, 58, 64, 69, 71, 78, 99, 104, 118, 124, 131, 138, 144, 149, 169, 178, 184, 200

Evaluating 17, 94, 107, 114, 127, 134, 154, 191, 196

Fact vs. speculation 47

Guessing meaning from context 7, 8, 14

Interpreting idioms 147

Making inferences 27, 34, 154, 167

Peer-Evaluating 19, 39, 59, 79, 99, 119, 139, 159, 179, 201

Personalizing/Reflecting 2, 7, 21, 27, 41, 42, 47, 49, 62, 81, 87, 89, 94, 101, 102, 107, 111, 121, 141, 142, 181

Predicting 4, 11, 24, 31, 44, 51, 64, 71, 84, 89, 91, 104, 109, 111, 124, 129, 131, 144, 164, 171, 184, 193

Speculating 54

Synthesizing 9, 14, 29, 34, 49, 54, 69, 74, 94, 109, 114, 129, 134, 149, 169, 196

Understanding mood 189, 196

Grammar

Comparative adjectives and nouns 95, 99

Describing emotions 198

Describing spatial relationships 197, 201

Giving reasons 135, 139

Giving advice and making suggestions 75, 79

Making comparisons 175, 176, 179

Simple past tense 55, 59

Simple present tense 15, 19

Using *and*, *but*, and *so* 115, 116, 119

Using *therefore* and *since* 155, 156, 159

Using *want* and *need* 35, 36, 39

Reading Skills/Strategies

Finding the right meaning 48

Identifying:

  fact and speculation 54

  key details 7, 14, 27, 34, 47, 54, 67, 74, 87, 107, 114, 127, 134, 147, 167, 189

  main idea 28, 34, 47, 54, 67, 94, 107, 127, 147, 154, 174, 189

  sequence 87, 114, 127, 196

  supporting ideas/details 68, 74

Recognizing noun clauses 168

Recognizing subordinating conjunctions 190

Scanning for key details 24, 88, 151

Skimming for gist 8, 164, 171, 190

Taking notes 148, 154

Understanding the gist 7, 14, 27, 34, 47, 54, 67, 74, 87, 94, 107, 114, 127, 134, 147, 154, 167, 174, 189, 196

Understanding prefixes 128

Understanding pronoun reference 108, 114, 174

Visual Literacy

Interpreting graphic information

  graphs/charts 18, 73, 74, 82

  infographics 46, 52, 53, 73, 83, 122, 124, 134

  maps 22, 23, 46, 52, 53, 83

Using graphic organizers

Venn diagrams 9, 14, 176, 178

T-charts 54, 94, 104

time lines/flow charts 52, 53, 114, 122, 123, 143

mind maps 4, 18, 88, 126, 144

Vocabulary Skills

Building vocabulary 4, 10, 24, 30, 44, 50, 64, 70, 84, 90, 104, 110, 124, 130, 144, 150, 164, 170, 184, 192

Using a dictionary 9, 29, 48, 49, 69, 89, 109, 128, 129, 149, 169, 191

Using vocabulary 4, 11, 24, 31, 44, 51, 64, 71, 84, 91, 104, 111, 124, 131, 144, 164, 171, 184, 193

Word Link 4, 10, 24, 44, 124, 184

Word Partners 11, 31, 50, 64, 70, 84, 91, 104, 110, 130, 151, 170, 193

Word Usage 30, 111, 171, 192

Writing Skills

Drafting 18, 38, 58, 78, 98, 118, 138, 158, 178, 200

Editing 19, 20, 39, 40, 59, 60, 79, 80, 99, 100, 119, 120, 139, 140, 159, 160, 179, 180, 201, 202

Having one main idea in a paragraph 156

Linking examples and reasons 136, 137

Planning 18, 37, 38, 58, 78, 98, 118, 138, 158, 178, 200

Speculating 56

Taking notes 76

Understanding the writing process 17

Using details 77

Using pronouns to avoid repetition 117

Using supporting details 199

Using synonyms 97

Writing a topic sentence 177

Test-Taking Skills

Categorizing and classifying 9, 14, 36, 38, 74, 94, 176, 178

Chart/diagram completion 4, 9, 14, 18, 36, 54, 58, 67, 74, 76, 95, 98, 104, 116, 134, 135, 144, 167, 178, 200

Choosing correct options 4, 9, 10, 15, 17, 29, 30, 31, 36, 47, 48, 50, 51, 55, 64, 69, 74, 84, 89, 90, 96, 104, 115, 117, 124, 127, 130, 144, 149, 150, 155, 169, 170, 175, 190, 192, 197

Error Identification 19, 39, 59, 76, 79, 99, 119, 139, 157, 159, 179, 201

Filling in missing details 18, 27, 38, 54, 74, 76, 77, 78, 88, 98, 114, 118, 127, 148, 154, 158, 167, 200

Matching questions 7, 8, 14, 24, 28, 44, 50, 68, 70, 77, 84, 87, 89, 104, 108, 110, 114, 144, 150, 151, 167, 168, 170, 174, 189, 191, 199

Notes/summary completion 18, 36, 38, 54, 58, 76, 78, 116, 138, 148

Sequencing and ordering 35, 37, 54, 75, 87, 114, 127, 196, 198

Short answer questions 4, 7, 11, 16, 17, 18, 20, 24, 27, 29, 31, 34, 44, 47, 49, 51, 56, 57, 68, 71, 74, 91, 114, 128, 134, 184, 189,

True-false questions and Yes-no questions 7, 19, 29, 34, 39, 49, 58, 59, 79, 99, 107, 109, 119, 129, 139, 149, 159, 179, 191

Acknowledgments

The authors and publisher would like to thank the following reviewers for their help during the development of this series:

UNITED STATES AND CANADA

Gokhan Alkanat, Auburn University at Montgomery, AL; Nikki Ashcraft, Shenandoah University, VA; Karin Avila-John, University of Dayton, OH; John Baker, Oakland Community College, MI; Shirley Baker, Alliant International University, CA; Michelle Bell, University of South Florida, FL; Nancy Boyer, Golden West College, CA; Kathy Brenner, BU/CELOP, Mattapan, MA; Janna Brink, Mt. San Antonio College, Chino Hills, CA; Carol Brutza, Gateway Community College, CT; Sarah Camp, University of Kentucky, Center for ESL, KY; Maria Caratini, Eastfield College, TX; Ana Maria Cepero, Miami Dade College, Miami, FL; Daniel Chaboya, Tulsa Community College, OK; Patricia Chukwueke, English Language Institute – UCSD Extension, CA; Julia A. Correia, Henderson State University, CT; Suzanne Crisci, Bunker Hill Community College, MA; Lina Crocker, University of Kentucky, Lexington, KY; Katie Crowder, University of North Texas, TX; Joe Cunningham, Park University, Kansas City, MO; Lynda Dalgish, Concordia College, NY; Jeffrey Diluglio, Center for English Language and Orientation Programs: Boston University, MA; Scott Dirks, Kaplan International Center at Harvard Square, MA; Kathleen Dixon, SUNY Stony Brook - Intensive English Center, Stony Brook, NY; Margo Downey, Boston University, Boston, MA; John Drezek, Richland College, TX; Qian Du, Ohio State University, Columbus, OH; Leslie Kosel Eckstein, Hillsborough Community College, FL; Anwar El-Issa, Antelope Valley College, CA; Beth Kozbial Ernst, University of Wisconsin-Eau Claire, WI; Anrisa Fannin, The International Education Center at Diablo Valley College, CA; Jennie Farnell, Greenwich Japanese School, Greenwich, CT; Rosa Vasquez Fernandez, John F. Kennedy, Institute Of Languages, Inc., Boston, MA; Mark Fisher, Lone Star College, TX; Celeste Flowers, University of Central Arkansas, AR; John Fox, English Language Institute, GA; Pradel R. Frank, Miami Dade College, FL; Sherri Fujita, Hawaii Community College, Hilo, HI; Sally Gearheart, Santa Rosa Jr. College, CA; Elizabeth Gillstrom, The University of Pennsylvania, Philadelphia, PA; Sheila Goldstein, Rockland Community College, Brentwood, NY; Karen Grubbs, ELS Language Centers, FL; Sudeepa Gulati, long beach city college, Torrance, CA; Joni Hagigeorges, Salem State University, MA; Marcia Peoples Halio, English Language Institute, University of Delaware, DE; Kara Hanson, Oregon State University, Corvallis, OR; Suha Hattab, Triton College, Chicago, IL; Marla Heath, Sacred Heart Univiversity and Norwalk Community College, Stamford, CT; Valerie Heming, University of Central Missouri, MO; Mary Hill, North Shore Community College, MA; Harry Holden, North Lake College, Dallas, TX; Ingrid Holm, University of Massachusetts Amherst, MA; Katie Hurter, Lone Star College – North Harris, TX; Barbara Inerfeld, Program in American Language Studies (PALS) Rutgers University/New Brunswick, Piscataway, NJ; Justin Jernigan, Georgia Gwinnett College, GA; Barbara Jonckheere, ALI/CSULB, Long Beach, CA; Susan Jordan, Fisher College, MA; Maria Kasparova, Bergen Community College, NJ; Maureen Kelbert, Vancouver Community College, Surrey, BC, Canada; Gail Kellersberger, University of Houston-Downtown, TX; David Kent, Troy University, Goshen, AL; Daryl Kinney, Los Angeles City College, CA; Jennifer Lacroix, Center for English Language and Orientation Programs: Boston University, MA; Stuart Landers, Misouri State University, Springfield, MO; Mary Jo Fletcher LaRocco, Ph.D., Salve Regina University, Newport, RI; Bea Lawn, Gavilan College, Gilroy, CA; Margaret V. Layton, University of Nevada, Reno Intensive English Language Center, NV; Alice Lee, Richland College, Mesquite, TX; Heidi Lieb, Bergen Community College, NJ; Kerry Linder, Language Studies International New York, NY; Jenifer Lucas-Uygun, Passaic County Community College, Paterson, NJ; Alison MacAdams, Approach International Student Center, MA; Julia MacDonald, Brock University, Saint Catharines, ON, Canada; Craig Machado, Norwalk Community College, CT; Andrew J. MacNeill, Southwestern College, CA; Melanie A. Majeski, Naugatuck Valley Community College, CT; Wendy Maloney, College of DuPage, Aurora, IL; Chris Mares, University of Maine – Intensive English Institute, Maine; Josefina Mark, Union County College, NJ; Connie Mathews, Nashville State Community College, TN; Bette Matthews, Mid-Pacific Institute, HI; Richard McDorman, inlingua Language Centers (Miami, FL) and Pennsylvania State University, Pompano Beach, FL; Sara McKinnon, College of Marin, CA; Christine Mekkaoui, Pittsburg State University, KS; Holly A. Milkowart, Johnson County Community College, KS; Donna Moore, Hawaii Community College, Hilo, HI; Ruth W. Moore, International English Center, University of Colorado at Boulder, CO; Kimberly McGrath Moreira, University of Miami, FL; Warren Mosher, University of Miami, FL; Sarah Moyer, California State University Long Beach, CA; Lukas Murphy, Westchester Community College, NY; Elena Nehrebecki, Hudson Community College, NJ; Bjarne Nielsen, Central Piedmont Community College, North Carolina; David Nippoldt, Reedley College, CA; Nancy Nystrom, University Of Texas At San Antonio, Austin, TX; Jane O'Connor, Emory College, Atlanta, GA; Daniel E. Opacki, SIT Graduate Institute, Brattleboro, VT; Lucia Parsley, Virginia Commonwealth University, VA; Wendy Patriquin, Parkland College, IL; Nancy Pendleton, Cape Cod Community College, Attleboro, MA; Marion Piccolomini, Communicate With Ease, LTD, PA; Barbara Pijan, Portland State University, Portland, OR; Marjorie Pitts, Ohio Northern University, Ada, OH; Carolyn Prager, Spanish-American Institute, NY; Eileen Prince, Prince Language Associates Incorporated, MA; Sema Pulak, Texas A & M University, TX; Mary Kay Purcell, University of Evansville, Evansville, IN; Christina Quartararo, St. John's University, Jamaica, NY; James T. Raby, Clark University, MA; Anouchka Rachelson, Miami-Dade College, FL; Sherry Rasmussen, DePaul University, IL; Amy Renehan, University of Washington, WA; Daniel Rivas, Irvine Valley College, Irvine, CA; Esther Robbins, Prince George's Community College, PA; Bruce Rogers, Spring International Language Center at Arapahoe College, Littleton, CO; Helen Roland, Miami Dade College, FL; Linda Roth, Vanderbilt University English Language Center, TN; Janine Rudnick, El Paso Community College, TX; Paula Sanchez, Miami Dade College – Kendall Campus, FL; Deborah Sandstrom, Tutorium in Intensive English at University of Illinois at Chicago, Elmhurst, IL; Marianne Hsu Santelli, Middlesex County College, NJ; Elena Sapp, INTO Oregon State University, Corvallis, OR; Alice Savage, Lone Star College System: North Harris, TX; Jitana Schaefer, Pensacola State College, Pensacola, FL; Lynn Ramage Schaefer, University of Central Arkansas, AR; Ann Schroth, Johnson & Wales University, Dayville, CT;

Margaret Shippey, Miami Dade College, FL; Lisa Sieg, Murray State University, KY; Samanthia Slaight, North Lake College, Richardson, TX; Ann Snider, UNK University of NE Kearney, Kearney, NE; Alison Stamps, ESL Center at Mississippi State University, Mississippi; Peggy Street, ELS Language Centers, Miami, FL; Lydia Streiter, York College Adult Learning Center, NY; Steve Strizver, Miami Beach, FL; Nicholas Taggart, Arkansas State University, AR; Marcia Takacs, Coastline Community College, CA; Tamara Teffeteller, University of California Los Angeles, American Language Center, CA; Adrianne Aiko Thompson, Miami Dade College, Miami, FL; Rebecca Toner, English Language Programs, University of Pennsylvania, PA; Evina Baquiran Torres, Zoni Language Centers, NY; William G. Trudeau, Missouri Southern State University, MO; Troy Tucker, Edison State College, FL; Maria Vargas-O'Neel, Miami Dade College, FL; Amerca Vazquez, Miami Dade College, FL; Alison Vinande, Modesto Junior College, CA; Christie Ward, IELP, Central CT State University, Hartford, CT; Colin Ward, Lone Star College - North Harris, Houston, TX; Denise Warner, Lansing Community College, Lansing, MI; Rita Rutkowski Weber, University of Wisconsin – Milwaukee, WI; James Wilson, Cosumnes River College, Sacramento, CA; Dolores "Lorrie" Winter, California State University Fullerton, Buena Park, CA; Wendy Wish-Bogue, Valencia Community College, FL; Cissy Wong, Sacramento City College, CA; Sarah Worthington, Tucson, Arizona; Kimberly Yoder, Kent State University, ESL Center, OH.

ASIA

Nor Azni Abdullah, Universiti Teknologi Mara; Morgan Bapst, Seoul National University of Science and Technology; Herman Bartelen, Kanda Institute of Foreign Languages, Sano; Maiko Berger, Ritsumeikan Asia Pacific University; Thomas E. Bieri, Nagoya College; Paul Bournhonesque, Seoul National University of Technology; Joyce Cheah Kim Sim, Taylor's University, Selangor Darul Ehsan; Michael C. Cheng, National Chengchi University; Fu-Dong Chiou, National Taiwan University; Derek Currie, Korea University, Sejong Institute of Foreign Language Studies; Wendy Gough, St. Mary College/Nunoike Gaigo Senmon Gakko, Ichinomiya; Christoph A. Hafner, City University of Hong Kong; Monica Hamciuc, Ritsumeikan Asia-Pacific University, Kagoshima; Rob Higgens, Ritsumeikan University; Wenhua Hsu, I-Shou University; Helen Huntley, Hanoi University; Debra Jones, Tokyo Woman's Christian University, Tokyo; Shih Fan Kao, JinWen University of Science and Technology; Ikuko Kashiwabara, Osaka Electro-Communication University; Alyssa Kim, Hankuk University of Foreign Studies; Richard S. Lavin, Prefecturla University of Kumamoto; Mike Lay, American Institute Cambodia; Byoung-Kyo Lee, Yonsei University; Lin Li, Capital Normal University, Beijing; Bien Thi Thanh Mai, The International University – Vietnam National University, Ho Chi Minh City; Hudson Murrell, Baiko Gakuin University; Keiichi Narita, Niigata University; Orapin Nasawang, Udon Thani Rajabhat University; Huynh Thi Ai Nguyen, Vietnam USA Society; James Pham, IDP Phnom Penh; John Racine, Dokkyo University; Duncan Rose, British Council Singapore; Greg Rouault, Konan University, Hirao School of Management, Osaka; Simone Samuels, The Indonesia Australia Language Foundation, Jakarta; Yuko Shimizu, Ritsumeikan University; Wang Songmei, Beijing Institute of Education Faculty; Richmond Stroupe, Soka University; Peechaya Suriyawong, Udon Thani Rajabhat University; Teoh Swee Ai, Universiti Teknologi Mara; Chien-Wen Jenny Tseng, National Sun Yat-Sen University; Hajime Uematsu, Hirosaki University; Sy Vanna, Newton Thilay School, Phnom Penh; Matthew Watterson, Hongik University; Anthony Zak, English Language Center, Shantou University.

LATIN AMERICA AND THE CARIBBEAN

Ramon Aguilar, Universidad Tecnológica de Hermosillo, México; Lívia de Araújo Donnini Rodrigues, University of São Paolo, Brazil; Cecilia Avila, Universidad de Xapala, México; Beth Bartlett, Centro Cultural Colombo Americano, Cali, Colombia; Raúl Billini, Colegio Loyola, Dominican Republic; Nohora Edith Bryan, Universidad de La Sabana, Colombia; Raquel Hernández Cantú, Instituto Tecnológico de Monterrey, Mexico; Millie Commander, Inter American University of Puerto Rico, Puerto Rico; Alejandra Gamarra, ISTP Euroidiomas, Peru; José Alonso Gaxiola Soto, CEI Universidad Autonoma de Sinaloa, Mazatlán, Mexico; Raquel Hernandez, Tecnologico de Monterrey, Mexico; Edwin Marín-Arroyo, Instituto Tecnológico de Costa Rica; Rosario Mena, Instituto Cultural Dominico-Americano, Dominican Republic; Elizabeth Ortiz Lozada, COPEI-COPOL English Institute, Ecuador; Gilberto Rios Zamora, Sinaloa State Language Center, Mexico; Rosa E. Vásquez, John F. Kennedy Institute of Languages, Dominican Republic; Patricia Vecinos, El Instituto Cultural Argentino Norteamericano, Argentina; Isabela Villas Boas, Casa Thomas Jefferson, Brasília, Brazil; Roxana Viñes, Language Two School of English, Argentina.

EUROPE, MIDDLE EAST, AND NORTH AFRICA

Tom Farkas, American University of Cairo, Egypt; Ghada Hozayen, Arab Academy for Science, Technology and Maritime Transport, Egypt; Tamara Jones, ESL Instructor, SHAPE Language Center, Belgium; Jodi Lefort, Sultan Qaboos University, Muscat, Oman; Neil McBeath, Sultan Qaboos University, Oman; Barbara R. Reimer, CERTESL, UAE University, UAE; Nashwa Nashaat Sobhy, The American University in Cairo, Egypt; Virginia Van Hoot Bastaki, Kuwait University, Kuwait.

AUSTRALIA

Susan Austin, University of South Australia, Joanne Cummins, Swinburne College; Pamela Humphreys, Griffith University.

Special thanks to Vania da Rui, Kakani Katija, Christine Lee, Juan Martinez, Mireya Mayor, Katsufumi Sato, and Thomas Thwaites for their kind assistance during this book's development.

This series is dedicated to Kristin L. Johannsen, whose love for the world's cultures and concern for the world's environment were an inspiration to family, friends, students, and colleagues.

Credits

61: Cory Richards/National Geographic, **62-63:** Jose Azel/National Geographic, **65:** Christophe Launay/Aurora Photos/Corbis, **66:** Ambient Images Inc./SuperStock, **69:** Gari Wyn Williams / Alamy, **71:** Almega Projects, **72:** Almega Projects, **73:** Almega Projects, **73:** The Art Archive / Alamy, **81:** Paul Chesley/National Geographic, **82:** Jim Richardson/National Geographic, **83:** John Cancalosi/National Geographic, **83:** Bonnie Marsh/National Geographic My Shot, **83:** James L. Amos/National Geographic, **85:** Courtesy of Nick Ballon, **86:** Courtesy of Daniel Alexander, **86:** Courtesy of Thomas Thwaites, **88:** Courtesy of Daniel Alexander, **89:** Scott Goldsmith, ScottGoldsmith.com, **90-93:** Paul Chesley/National Geographic, **101:** Randy Olson/National Geographic, **102-103:** Max Aguilera-Hellweg/National Geographic, **105:** Paul Macleod/National Geographic, **106:** Max Aguilera-Hellweg/National Geographic, **108:** Yoshikazu Tsuno/AFP/Getty Images, **109:** Morrell, Stephen /National Geographic, **110:** NASA, J. Bell (Cornell U.) and M. Wolff (SSI)/NGIC, **112-113:** Morrell, Stephen /National Geographic, **116:** Max Aguilera-Hellweg/National Geographic, **121:** Wes C. Skiles/National Geographic, **122-123:** Stephen Alvarez/National Geographic, **122:** The Art Gallery Collection/Alamy, **123:** Everett Collection Inc/Alamy, **123:** Craig Barritt/Getty Images, **125:** Courtesy of Mireya Mayor, **126:** Courtesy of Mireya Mayor, **127:** Courtesy of Mireya Mayor, **128:** Burt Silverman/National Geographic Image Collection, **129:** Mark Thiessen/National Geographic, **130:** Mark Thiessen/National Geographic, **132-133:** Wes C. Skiles/National Geographic Image Collection, **132:** Wes. C. Skiles/National Geographic, **133:** Alejandro Tumas/National Geographic, **134:** Alejandro Tumas/National Geographic, **137:** David Doubilet/National Geographic, **139:** Randall J. Olson/National Geographic, **141:** William Albert Allard/National Geographic, **142-143:** Sam Abell/National Geographic, **143:** Alan Burles/Alamy, **145:** Courtesy of All City Media, **146:** Judith Burrows/Getty Image, **149:** John Kershaw/Alamy, **150:** Courtesy of All City Media, **152:** Charles Eshelman/Getty Images, **153:** AP Photo/Angela Rowlings, **153:** Courtesy of Glenn Minshal, Northfield Mount Hermon, **157:** ZUMA Wire Service/Alamy, **161:** Cheryl Molennor/National Geographic, **162-163:** Cyril Ruoso/Minden Pictures/National Geographic, **163:** Justin Guariglia/National Geographic, **165:** Mark Thiessen/National Geographic, **166:** Joel Sartore/National Geographic, **166:** Catherine Karnow/National Geographic, **169:** Ian Nichols/National Geographic, **172:** Roy Toft/National Geographic, **173:** Tim Laman/National Geographic, **176:** Andreas Gradin/Shutterstock.com, **176:** Marina Jay/Shutterstock.com, **181:** Dorthea Lange/[LC-DIG-fsa-8b29516]/Library of Congress Prints and Photographs Division, **182:** David Doubilet/National Geographic, **183:** Sisse Brimberg/National Geographic, **183:** James P. Blair/National Geographic, **185:** Michael Nichols/National Geographic, **186:** Jonas Bendiksen/National Geographic, **186:** Rubio, Elmar/National Geographic, **187:** Getty Images Inc/National Geographic, **187:** Brian J. Skerry/National Geographic, **188:** Randy Olson/National Geographic, **188:** Little Dancer, Aged Fourteen, c.1880-81 (bronze & fabric) (see also 419951-53), Degas, Edgar (1834-1917) / University of East Anglia, Norfolk, UK / Robert and Lisa, **189:** Rubio, Elmar/National Geographic, **189:** Jonas Bendiksen/National Geographic, **189:** Brian J. Skerry/National Geographic, **189:** Getty Images Inc/National Geographic, **189:** Randy Olson/National Geographic, **191:** John Stanmeyer LLC/National Geographic, **194 and 196:** Paul Nicklen/National Geographic, **195-196:** Paul Nicklen/National Geographic, **195-196:** Paul Nicklen/National Geographic, **199:** Peter Essick/National Geographic, **209:** Mark Thiessen/National Geographic, **223:** Vincent J. Musi/National Geographic

MAPS and GRAPHS

22: National Geographic Maps; **23:** National Geographic Maps; **46:** National Geographic Maps; **52-53:** National Geographic Maps; **73:** © 2012 National Geographic Society revised from National Geographic Magazine January 2008, "Recycling: the big picture" by Tom Zeller, Jr.; **82:** National Geographic Maps; **83:** National Geographic Maps; **126:** National Geographic Maps